CONFESSIONS OF A LABRADIVA

ANOTHER BLONDE LEADING THE BLIND

MARK CARLSON
and
SAFFRON

cover photo by
Joel De La Cruz Photography,
San Diego

CONFESSIONS OF A LABRADIVA
ANOTHER BLONDE LEADING THE BLIND

iUniverse books may be ordered through booksellers or by contacting:

iUniverse
1663 Liberty Drive
Bloomington, IN 47403
www.iuniverse.com
844-349-9409

Because of the dynamic nature of the Internet, any web addresses or links contained in this book may have changed since publication and may no longer be valid. The views expressed in this work are solely those of the author and do not necessarily reflect the views of the publisher, and the publisher hereby disclaims any responsibility for them.

Any people depicted in stock imagery provided by Getty Images are models, and such images are being used for illustrative purposes only.
Certain stock imagery © Getty Images.

ISBN: 978-1-6632-2596-2 (sc)
ISBN: 978-1-6632-2595-5 (e)

Library of Congress Control Number: 2021914165

Print information available on the last page.

iUniverse rev. date: 07/13/2021

DEDICATION

This work is dedicated to a wonderful young man who never had the chance to see his dreams and efforts come to fruition. He would have made a great difference. The world is a poorer place without him.

Matthew Troy O'Neill
November 16, 1980 to August 9, 2014

CONTENTS

ACKNOWLEDGEMENTS

"To err is human, to forgive, canine."
—Author Unknown

Where do I start? A full list of the people who made this book possible would be as long as the book itself. But I will begin with my wife, Jane. For twenty-five years Jane gave me what I needed to fulfill my destiny. I owe her everything. My success and accomplishments were only due to Jane providing the stable and strong foundation on which to build. I dedicated all my earlier books to Jane. But it is to my beloved Jane, who died in April of 2020 to whom I owe the deepest gratitude and devotion. At our church, Hope United Methodist in Rancho Bernardo, I had a bench dedicated to her memory. I left a lasting legacy to Jane, who was my wife, soul mate, best friend and supporter. We had our problems and I would not call her perfect, but she was my life and love. I could not have succeeded without her.

My closest friend Linda Stull was a great supporter of my work and writing. She has always been there when I was in doubt and struggling. It's not a stretch to say that without Linda's help with editing and encouragement this and many other books would not have been written. She is and has always been a true friend. A true dog lover, she was a big part of Musket and Saffron's lives.

Don Ramm, a retired USAF pilot is the owner of a computer service company. My friend Don as helped me out of scores of problems with my computer, and I could call him at any time. He kept my computers working. If not for his incredible generosity I would be writing this book like Fred Flintstone, using a slate and chisel.

Rob Wood lives not far from me and is as close to a brother as I have ever known. He and I have found many interests in common and he often drove me to some of my events, where I introduced him to the veterans. But what really sets Rob apart is how he took charge of the mass of legal and financial paperwork after Jane died and helped me find my way through the maze. He is a true friend and brother.

Barry Stemler, Molly Tosh, Keith Kirby, Alan Cutsinger, John Misoni, Vince Cramer, Dave Piontek, Dave Barnett, and many others have been fans of my writing and lectures. They were always there when I needed them. You will read more about them in the following pages.

Hope United Methodist Church and the residents of Madrid Manor have also contributed to my continued existence and ambition. Again, they are too numerous to name here, but fear not, you will meet them. They all play a role in the life of Saffron.

Introduction

BY MARK CARLSON

Just so you readers can get the mental momentum going, here are the last paragraphs of *Confessions of a Guide Dog - The Blonde Leading the Blind* published in 2011.

The people he loves and are loved by will always remember his kisses, his beautiful face, and playful spirit.

Jane and I will love him forever. He's our baby and the center of our lives. More than a working dog or even a pet, he's a friend, a comic, a beggar, a tease, a protector, a favored grandchild, a healer, a spoiled kid, a TV star, an ambassador, a friend to astronauts and veterans, a chick magnet, a heart-breaker and a scene stealer.

He's also my little buddy.

I had to go blind in order to get Musket.

It was well worth it.

It was a very good day when God gave Musket to the world.

Pretty corny, huh? But I meant every word. When I first began writing *Confessions of a Guide Dog*, Musket had been with me for eight years, long enough to amass a fair collection of stories, anecdotes, and memories. He was starting to slow down and as things worked out, was within two years of retirement. He was still alive when I went back to San Rafael in September of 2012, God it seems so long ago, and first met Saffron. Almost before we came back home

Mark and his Little Buddy

fans of Musket and our book were asking if I would be writing a book about Saffron. That was a good question. I first had to get to know my new Guide Dog and see how things turned out. But I needn't have worried. Saffron quickly came to capture my heart in her little paws and became a member of our family.

But it would take time, as with Musket, to accumulate enough stories and experiences to fill a book.

As it is now, in December 2020, I think it is time to finish telling the story. Everything in this book is post-2011, when *Confessions* was published. Since then almost a decade has passed. Along the way, the reader will follow a story that is chronological, but also relevant to certain events and people.

I first started writing down memories and ideas as early as 2013 when Saffron and I were traveling to promote my second book, *Flying on Film - A Century of Aviation in the Movies 1912 - 2012*. That was when we really began to work as a team. Meanwhile Musket was back at home enjoying his retirement and wondering how to get his Mommy to give him more treats.

Saffron is now ten years old and probably within a year or two of her own retirement. Many, many things have happened and changed. Musket died in July of 2014. But fortunately he wrote down his thoughts while he was alive.

My beloved Jane died in April of the terrible year of 2020. We live in a new home and life is very different. But all that will be covered in the following chapters.

Once I dived into finishing this book, many of my friends showed their support. They had been waiting for the book about Saffron. My friend Linda said she thought I was more enthusiastic about this manuscript than when I was working on Musket's book. I realized she was right. *Confessions of a Guide Dog* was going to be my very first published work. I had no idea if it would be popular or totally unnoticed. But now, having three published works under my belt — plus a few more pounds — I am confident. The readers of Musket's book will want to read this one, or at least I hope so. I arranged for the publisher to format this one exactly the same so my readers will feel right at home.

♡ Can we get on with it? Oh, by the way, I'm Saffron, Daddy's current Guide Dog! Hi! I'll be back. All yours, Daddy.

Sigh, here we go again. No wonder Jane called her a "Labradiva." I just knew it when she insisted that "Thou shalt have no other dogs before me."

♡ After all, I'm a very pretty southern California blonde! Giggle. Have you ever heard of one of those being modest?

Saffron and Musket will add their thoughts and comments.

♡ Musket? Hey, this is MY book. Why does he get to say anything? I didn't get to say anything in *his* stupid book, did I?

Because, my conceited little Labradiva, he is very much a part of your story. And remember, you weren't even born when we wrote *Confessions*. Don't worry, Musket won't try and steal the scene. Right, Little Buddy?

🐕 Zzzzzzzzzz...snort

That's my boy! In any event, I want this book to have the same flavor and emotion of Musket's book. I hope it will make the reader laugh and cry, shake their heads at the absurdities and smile at the victories.

So get into a comfortable chair, have a mug of hot cocoa ready and enjoy.

Chapter 1

THE STORY SO FAR

"Dogs are not our whole life but they make our lives whole."
— Roger Caras

"Dogs do speak, but only to those who know how to listen."
— Orhan Pamuk

On Being Blind

Well here we go again. Just to bring you all up to date, a lot has changed since the last book. I am a decade older, and I have a new career, a new Guide Dog, a lot more forehead and more nose hair. This brings me to one of those profound questions I am so famous for. Why is it that even though men lose their hair the cost of the haircut does not drop correspondingly? A few more years and my barber will be able to say, "Okay, here we go..." Bzzzzzzt! "That will be a buck fifty."

♡ He's getting into it right away. Sorry, folks.

I live in a different house and have a lot of new friends. But some things are the same. I'm still blind. In fact, even more than I was. The world is pretty much all shades of gray and black areas with no color or detail. I deal with it. I can't see pictures anymore, even on my computer. So I almost never turn on the monitor. My talking software JAWS speaks everything I do and look at. Keyboard hotkeys and shortcuts handle all the functions that a sighted user does with the mouse. When someone comes in my office they see me in a dark room facing a black monitor, typing away.

Well, as I said, I'm still blind. Some of my readers may recall that being blind is not my only disability. I have two others, one of which is being hearing impaired, or "half deaf" as I usually put it. That means half my hearing is gone, not that I only hear every other word. I have been wearing hearing aids since I was about eight years old. The last disability is being a guy. Yes, that is a disability, even if the Americans with Disabilities Act of 1990 has not recognized it. Being a guy is a major drawback. We are blamed for everything. World War Two, disco, Rubik's Cube, global warming and the sinking of the *Titanic*. Just ask any woman if guys are not fundamentally defective and you'll have your answer.

But I haven't lost my sense of humor. I guess you noticed.

Seeing With My Mind

I do occasionally get the upper hand with a sighted person. By that I mean sometimes I will find something they have lost and can't find with sight.

A few years ago Jane was in the car putting on her seatbelt when the shoulder strap knocked off her gold and pearl earring. She freaked out and looked everywhere for it, under the seat, on the ground, but with no luck. They were her favorites. I said I'd look for it.

"I couldn't find it. How will you?"

Oh ye of little faith. "No harm in trying," I replied and went out to the garage. Then I sat in the driver's seat and applied my analytical skills (why is it that analytical has "anal" in it?), what I call my "detective mode." After re-creating the crime by putting on the seat belt, I tried to figure out where the earring would have gone after being knocked off her left ear.

Then I reached down under the left side of the seat and traced my fingers along the metal seat rail. And there it was, right where I expected it to be.

I handed it to Jane. She was overjoyed and amazed. "How did you find it? Then she hugged me. "thank you, Honey."

"All in a day's work, Ma'am," I said in my best Jack Webb voice.

About a year later she misplaced her cell phone, not a small deal. She spent a full day tearing the house and car apart, looking in the laundry and under the furniture. Finally I asked her a few questions. "Where did you last see it?"

"I looked there! I can't find it, how will you?"

They never learn. "Humor me."

"I was going to take some books back to the library and I put it on the top of them."

"Okay," I said. "When was that exactly?"

"Um, Monday evening. I was going to drop them in the night box." Then she said "I thought of that. I put the books in one at a time. The phone did not end up at the library."

"Uh-huh," I said, still sounding like Jack Webb. "What were you doing just before you left to go to the library?"

She thought for a minute. "I was in my office and had some stuff to put in the recycle bin."

Bingo. "What did you do with that stuff?"

"I put it on top of the books so I could drop it in the bin before I went to the library."

"Your phone is gone, Honey. You put it in the recycle bin and they picked that up Tuesday morning."

For a long moment Jane said nothing. Then she let out a breath. "That's it. Yes, that's what happened. I feel so stupid."

All you hubbies out there, just a word of advice, when your wife admits to a big mistake, don't give her a hard time about it. Just be supportive. It's a good thing to have some "good guy" credit for the next time you do something stupid.

I said, "Well you wanted to get a new phone. Now you have a reason."

I've found things just by feeling my way around, instead of looking, and often it works. Jane had come home from a weekend trip with her friends, and that night we were getting ready for bed. "Honey where is the toothpaste?"

"It should be right there on the bathroom counter," I said.

"Well it's not. What did you do with it?" Jane had a way of inserting a very slight accusatory tone in her voice as if she suspected me of selling the Colgate on the black market.

"Okay," I said, going into the bathroom. I felt under the counters, in the closet and in the clothes hamper.

"I told you, it's not there." That had a very distinct smug tone to it. "I didn't touch it. You must have lost or moved it."

"Innocent until proven guilty, Honey," I said. Except in marriage, I thought to myself. Then it's the other way around. "Where is your travel bag?"

"Under the counter. Why? I told you I never touched it."

I opened the cabinet and pulled out the small cloth bag she kept her travel stuff in. Taking it out to the bedroom I unzipped it and reached in. "Never touched what? This?" In my hand was the Colgate.

"Oh." Her voice was very small. God I wish I could have seen her face. It must have been a lovely shade of red.

The moral is, never underestimate the blind.

The Carlson family in 2012

Blind Sight

I have noticed a difference in how I look at life. No, that is not a typo. I have always looked at life and human nature with an eye to trying to figure out how we managed to survive 3.5 million years. I'm still wondering. But what I mean is that, now being unable to see the world and humanity in all its bewildering and confusing chaos, I no longer "sweat the small stuff." It used to be that when Jane and I were in the car, I got irritated at the stupid antics of other drivers, or at some brain-dead advertisement on a building, or the way a parent allowed their kids to dress. Those things used to bug me.

But not anymore. "Out of sight, out of mind" is not just an aphorism.

It really works. I don't worry about such little things anymore. And when I listen to others griping, just as I used to do, I smile and let it roll off me. I'm pretty sure my blood pressure has dropped significantly since my sight faded entirely.

I am not suggesting going blind as a cure for hypertension, but it sure worked for me.

By Popular Request

More than once I have been asked to bring out some of my artwork. People who have only known me as a blind guy are astonished to see some of the artwork I did back in my sighted days. A few have suggested I put at least a few in this book. No, really! I will try and at least make them fit into the context of the narrative, but some things are going to have to stand alone. So here you go. While I am very proud of these, you should know I did not make any money in this venture. The only art that sells in San Diego are watercolors of the Hotel Del Coronado or velvet paintings of Elvis.

Two of Mark's Civil War portraits, circa 1998 of
Abraham Lincoln and General Robert E. Lee

Farewell to Nanny and Mom

Well, enough of that. Let's get into this book. I suppose it will be best to go back to the beginning of 2011. That was when we lost Jane's mother, Virginia Vogel. A gentle and loving woman, who was a mother to so many, began to decline while at Rancho Vista. She slowly grew weaker and just wanted to "go and dance with Dad in Heaven."

On January 17, Jane, Musket and I were there on her last day. I helped Musket up on Nanny's bed where she could pet him. He rested his head on her leg and stayed with her for hours. Nanny spoke to Musket in whispers. I told her I loved her.

She was at peace when the end came that evening.

Although we didn't know it until later, Nanny gave us a gift from Heaven.

That gift was born four days later.

In the fall of the same year my mother, Margit Carlson, who was in a nursing home in San Jose, died. She had been in declining physical and mental health for a year, so it was no surprise. I'd been very close to my mother, but the last time I saw her that summer, she didn't recognize me. I knew the woman who'd loved and raised me was long gone. We drove up to San Jose for the service, which was attended by over a hundred people. My older brother David asked me to do the eulogy. I spoke of Mom in loving terms, but did not allow my speech to become maudlin and somber. That wasn't her way. I related some funny stories and invited others to do the same. It was a very heartwarming service and I think Mom would have appreciated it. Her ashes were going to be spread in the garden of her childhood home in Sweden.

The only regret I had was that Mom had not lived to see my first book published. I know she would have been very proud.

Our mothers Margit Carlson and Virginia Vogel

Some of you may recall that I had pushed to get the book published while Musket was alive and healthy enough to help promote it and enjoy his celebrity. But no matter how hard my agent tried, she could not sell the book to any publishers. The reason was pure bad timing. This was the summer after *Marley and Me* came out. Sure it was a great book and told a wonderful story about a Yellow Lab. But it also made every dog owner think they could make millions on a book about their dog. Just like me.

Every publisher was being bombarded with dog books. Unfortunately I wrote one of them.

🐾 What was wrong with those publishers? It was like hearing about the bozos that turned down the Harry Potter books!

In the end I decided to self-publish. It worked out well since I had more control of the format and content. It finally happened in November 2011.

When a large box was delivered by FedEx I already knew what it was. After bringing it inside I called Jane downstairs and opened the box. Musket was right there, probably thinking it contained treats.

Inside were twenty paperback and five hardcover copies of *Confessions of a Guide Dog.* I slid one out of the stack and ran my hands over the smooth cover. There it was. My first book. I won't deny that I felt a great swelling in my...no, not my head! My heart. I had finally done it. I had written a book! Jane was very proud, but I think she was waiting for the huge royalty checks to start rolling in.

She showed the book to Musket and said "Look, Musket, there you are on the cover! My baby is going to be famous!"

"Ahem," I said.

"Oh, and you too, Honey."

Well I guess I'd have to get used to such adulation.

🐕 That was kind of neat. I did not really understand what Daddy was so excited about. After all, it was just a box of books. I have to admit that the dog on the cover was really good looking. Mommy gave me a hug and treat. Well that was the beginning of a new kind of life for us. But even as a world-famous author and future winner of the Nobel Prize for Literature, I was still a Guide Dog.

Last Tour

Jane and I decided to take a Holiday vacation up the coast on a motor coach. She was still coping with her mother's death and did not want to do Christmas at home.

AFC Tours had a trip that took us up to Pismo Beach, Morro Bay and San Luis Obispo. We knew this would probably be the last time Musket would take a trip with us, so we wanted it to be special.

We met the rest of the passengers in Encinitas near the coast and boarded.

The tour coordinator was a lovely and energetic lady named Leslie Winkel, who of course took to Musket right away. Most of the other riders also enjoyed having him along. He settled in under my seat and went to sleep. As we drove north, Leslie, who really took her job seriously and learned as much as possible about the attractions, culture and history of an area, told us some interesting facts. I liked her and so did Musket. He was always partial to pretty blondes.

Our hotel was in Pismo Beach, a place I'd never visited. Our room overlooked the rolling iron-blue waves of the wintry Pacific. But the weather was nice and we made friends on the tour, aided as usual by Musket's charm and personality.

On Christmas Eve we all went to the Madonna Inn in San Luis Obispo, a hotel famous for eclectic décor and fine dining. I brought Musket's Santa Claus hat and put it on him before boarding the bus. And as things turned out we were the last to board. And Musket, who was something of a celebrity because of the book, was instantly the center of attention.

"Oh, he's so cute! Let him come back here!"

"Hey, Musket, come back here and say hi!"

I let him go and he sauntered down the aisle in his Santa cap, being petted all the way to the back of the coach.

Then something funny happened. I called him to come forward, but with his harness on, he couldn't turn around. So he had to back up all the way.

All that was missing was "Beep, Beep, Beep," as he did the walk in reverse. That made everybody love him even more.

I wish we'd had a video camera because it would have been perfect on YouTube.

We had a delicious dinner at the Inn and passed Christmas Eve with some new friends. We particularly took to Leslie and promised to take another one of her tours in the future.

As suspected that was our last vacation trip with Musket.

Selling the Story

After returning home I went to work promoting the book. I had a good friend, Sharon McCabe, set up a website for Musket called

Musketmania.com. It had excerpts from the book, articles, photos and videos.

I took Musket back to Disneyland one more time, but this time we had a video camera so we could get some footage of him with Mickey Mouse. We went through Mickey's House in Toon Town and Musket met him. Later we found Pluto and filmed Pluto giving Musket treats. A ride on the paddle-wheeler *Mark Twain* and a few other attractions filled out the day. My best friend Monty took the raw footage and made a great short with sound effects and music. I posted it on YouTube along with several others which talked about the book. The title, if you want to look for it, is "Musket at Disneyland."

Within weeks of publication we were doing book signings in San Diego and appearing on local television shows and in the paper. Musket loved the attention he received, but he didn't have the pep and vigor of a few years before.

This was no surprise. By the time the book came out he was already eleven years old. Most of his classmates were retired by then, living in Fort Lauderdale and being driven around in golf carts.

🐕 But did I get any of that? Nope.

We didn't have room for the golf cart in the garage, Little Buddy. Sorry.

Toni Kraft owned Café Merlot, a nice bistro in the Rancho Bernardo Winery. As another Musketmaniac, Toni asked me if I'd like to do a book signing at the restaurant. She often hosted local authors and I was very pleased to accept. After ordering more copies of the book and agreeing on a date, we got the word out. It was a real success. At least three hundred people came and not all were the expected close friends and co-workers. Jane, Musket and I sat under an umbrella at a table covered with a dog paw print tablecloth Jane's sister Susan had made. She also made a few dozen Kleenex pack sleeves with the same print. Jane made some bookmarks with various Musket photos, and she put yellow tassels on them. Everyone who bought a book got one, and for two or more, they received a Kleenex pack.

Musket was his usual "meet 'n' greet" self, saying hello to his friends and making new ones. Toni had hors d'oeuvres and drinks, and a big bowl of iced water for the famous pooch. I was grinning all day long as the books sold. Some people had already bought them online and wanted my autograph. But we had another surprise for everyone. After I had signed a book Jane stamped a "Pawtograph" with Musket's name on the page.

The only thing was, it was kind of small. Like for a Chihuahua. But it was still cool.

🐾 I liked doing the book signings. But I kept telling people that I was the real author. Daddy just did the typing. Mommy stamped the books with my Pawtograph. Daddy originally wanted to try having me put my paw on an ink pad and stamp the book but even I knew that would have been a big mistake. We'd still be paying off the damage to carpets and clothing.

Altogether we sold about seventy books, a real good day. And Musket was the star of the show, as you might imagine.

Busy Blind Guy

Since 2009 I had been doing lectures for various adult education programs. OASIS in San Diego had me speak at various venues around the county about the book, but ONLY if I brought Musket. Duh. Of course I was going to bring him.

The talk, which I originally called "Tales from the Barkside" until I found that someone else had copyrighted it, just became "Confessions of a Guide Dog." For about an hour, with my trusty old dog snoring away on the floor I told stories from the book, accompanied by a Power Point slide show. Afterwards we autographed books. Musket's popularity never faded. He was a star every time, even if all he did most of the time was sleep.

🐾 I can't help it, Daddy. You just sort of put me to sleep.

Jane was great about driving us to these different events. She may not have been the celebrity, but she received plenty of attention as "Musket's Mommy." I never failed to sing her praises for her love and support, as I could tell she sometimes felt she was "only the driver." But we were a team. Musket, his Mommy, and me.

Another signing at an Escondido Italian restaurant named Vinz Wine Bar led to more sales and new friends, including a wonderful dog loving couple named Marsha and Steve Kahle. They owned a small craft winery in Ramona called Woof'n Rose, and their theme was dogs. They've won some prestigious awards and medals. I still buy wine from Woof'n Rose.

But that's not to say I don't drink other wines. After I'd written an article about a restored World War Two C-53 for a magazine, the plane's owner called me. It turned out he was also the owner of Bella Luna Estate Winery near Paso Robles, California. They have a signature wine called "Fighter Pilot Red," which was dedicated to holders of the Distinguished Flying Cross. Sherman Smoot told me I could buy the wine at a great price just for writing about the plane.

This job had some nice perks.

🐾 Hmph. I never got a drop. I liked Woof'n Rose better anyway.

I was still going to air shows, warbird fly-ins, museum events and parades. We went to meetings of the Distinguished Flying Cross Society, the Order of Daedelians, American Ex-POWs, and later, the Pearl Harbor Survivors Association. Linda was very well-known in these groups and very good at making connections. More on this later.

By this time I was writing for a dozen major aviation history magazines and getting a bit of a good reputation for my articles. Each month added more credits to my list and I felt I had at last found my niche. It helped to pay the bills. Musket went along for the interviews and seminars, and as usual was welcomed and petted. But I saw that he was definitely slowing down. He tended to lie down and go to sleep as soon as he was not needed to guide me. I was already thinking about his inevitable retirement.

Old Movies

In 2012 my next book, *Flying on Film - A Century of Aviation in the Movies 1912 - 2012* was published. Okay before you re-read it, yes that is true. Me, a blind guy, wrote a book about aviation on the silver screen. It was a work of four years, hundreds of phone and in-person interviews with actors, aviators, filmmakers, historians and veterans. I really loved working on that book. For most of my life I loved old movies, war films and airplanes.

🐾 Boy, when Daddy got involved in something he went all out! He collected hundreds of videos and DVDs, played them over and over, and made more phone calls than a telemarketer. It was kind of weird, since I knew he could not see the movie, but he was very good at figuring things out. He sometimes had a friend over to watch and help him with the details. I, of course, slept and begged.

It started when I was talking with John Finn, who at that time was the oldest living Medal of Honor recipient in the country. John, who I wrote about in *Confessions* was an old navy veteran who had shot down Japanese planes during the Pearl Harbor attack. One day, while a friend and I were visiting John in his home in Pine Valley, I asked him what he had thought about the motion picture *Tora! Tora! Tora!*

While sipping a sarsaparilla he said, "Well they did a good job on that movie. They had the kid playing me in just the right place." He went on to relate his thoughts on other war movies, and when I asked about the blockbuster *Pearl Harbor,* he said, "Well the less said about that film the better."

In a way that was the genesis of the book. It was a lot of work but I was amazed how supportive my friends were, and how lucky I was to always be in the right place at the right time. One of the people I got to know was William Wellman, Jr. His father was the director of the first film to win an Academy Award for Best Picture, *Wings*, in 1927. Bill Jr. was a gold mine of information on his father's films and contacts in Hollywood. He even wrote the Foreword. I talked to actors like Efrem Zimbalist, Jr., Cliff Robertson, Louis Gossett, Jr. and Jack Larson. I was (I am NOT name-dropping here, this really happened) talking by phone with David McCallum about a film he did in 1969 when I asked him if he would say hello to Jane, who was a BIG *NCIS* fan. I took the phone upstairs where Jane was at her desk. "Honey, I have someone on the phone who wants to say hello."

She took the phone and her face must have lit up like a Christmas tree. "Ducky!" she chatted with him and it made her day. She talked about that phone call for months.

I also got Cliff Robertson to wish Linda a happy birthday, as it turned out they shared the same birthday.

🐾 Well I never got a call from Lassie like Daddy promised. Snort.

I found a traditional publisher who jumped on the project. To make a long story much shorter, the book came out in late 2012. Its release coincided with my decision to retire Musket.

🐾 Yeah, by then even I noticed. All I wanted to do was sleep. When I guided Daddy, I noticed I was a half-step *behind* him. That was not right. He was kind and understanding, but I could tell that he was doing a lot of deep thinking.

Novel Writing 101

In order to improve my novel-writing I joined a writers' group. The Rancho Bernardo Writers' Group had been around for about sixteen years, run by a retired Academy Award winning Hollywood sound editor named Peter Berkos. Peter, who was 90 when I started, was a kind and easygoing widower. The group had between six and nine members. All had to be working on a novel or story for publication. We met every Friday at senior centers, and every member read five pages from their current work, and then we did a round robin critique.

When I joined just after the publication of *Confessions*, they made me feel very welcome. The old regular members, MJ Roe, Rosalie Kramer, Lillian Herzberg, Brae Wykoff and Terry Ambrose all took to Musket right away. There was no concern about my blindness at all.

🐾 They were really nice to me and Daddy. I felt right at home, and usually slept on the floor by Daddy's feet.

The only snag was how I would read my work. I tried a few ideas including recording myself reading from my computer at home, but what ultimately worked was when I used my laptop with the text-to-speech software. After I had my five pages I put them on a Flash Drive.

What made everyone laugh was when I was doing my part, Musket began snoring. "Oh, he's heard this before," I said over the droning noise under the table.

Over the next several months they were very supportive, coming to my book signings and other public appearances. They got to be very fond of Musket. When I started talking about retiring him, they wanted to know about the new dog.

I worked my way through three-quarters of my novel, *The Vengeance of the Last Legion*. Even though I was sure the book was pretty good, I knew it could be better. And the RBWG helped me do just that. One of the new members was Mo Kindle, a retired U.S. Navy helicopter pilot who had married a lovely Icelandic girl named Inga. He and I got to be friends over and above our time with the RBWG.

Confessions continued to sell and as the months went by, Musket and I were recognized around San Diego, in stores, on the bus and at parties. I was happy to introduce my own furry celebrity. As usual he generated the bulk of the attention.

🐾 Well what would you expect, Daddy? I was so Adoggable, as Pop-pop used to call me.

Taking a Stroll on Mars

Jane and I took a day coach tour of the Jet Propulsion Laboratory in Pasadena. JPL was a place I'd always wanted to see, since I was such a NASA nut. The facility oversaw all the unmanned probes and landers like the Voyager and Mariner series. We had to show our ID before we could enter and the tour guides kept us in a tight group. Musket took it right in stride as we went into the Mission Control Center where the various space projects were monitored. He went right to sleep and snored through the presentation. I was fascinated by the place, the domain of my heroes Carl Sagan and Jon von Neumann.

The best part was when we were shown the mockup of the Mars *Curiosity* rover launched in November 2011. We approached the mockup, which was set on a simulated Martian landscape. I was told I could move closer to touch it. But Musket, ever the Guide Dog, would not move any closer than about ten feet. At first I could not figure out what was stopping him. The tour guide said there was no barrier, but then I realized that the rover, about the size of a VW Beetle, represented a car to him and he would not let me get in front of it. I reached down and petted my wonderful dog. "It's okay, Little Buddy. It's not going to move. Not on Earth, at any rate."

The other visitors were amused and I was able to touch *Curiosity*. And *Voyager*, as well. And being a serious Trekkie, I had to trace the lettering on the name plate like William Shatner in *Star Trek: The Motion Picture*. "V...G...E-R. Vejer! V-O-Y-A-G-E-R. Voyager!"

🐕 You are such a nerd!

After JPL we went to Newport Beach to take a harbor cruise. The big boat was wide and comfortable and Musket didn't mind it at all. We were taken past the most magnificent mansions and estates, each with its own dock and a yacht or two. There was so much wealth in the air it was hard to breathe. Then we were shown the former home of George Burns and Gracie Allen, and just past that, the estate of novelist Dean Koontz. That had a profound effect on me. I leaned over to Jane and said, "See, Honey. It can be done. And I think I'm as good a writer as Dean Koontz."

The reason I brought that up was that I knew Jane had her doubts about my being able to make a living as a writer and novelist. In a way that day changed my life. I was determined to prove to her that I could not only make a living at it, I could be rich and famous.

Well I was off and running, But there would have to be a few changes first. For one thing, I had to get another Guide Dog.

CHAPTER 2

SAFFRON

"Have you ever notice how easily puppies make human friends? Yet all they do is wag their tails and fall over."
—Walter Anderson

Puppy Love

At the breeding kennels of Guide Dogs for the Blind in San Rafael on January 21, 2011, a Labrador named Darcy gave birth to a litter of puppies. While all were squirming, whimpering little balls of fur and energy, one of them stood out. She had rich yellow fur and big brown eyes that looked eagerly around the strange new world. But even with her insatiable curiosity, she went right for the teats and the warm, healthy milk within.

Soon she was asleep, but would not be for long. She had no name as yet.

♡ I don't remember very much about that first day, it was all so bright and exciting. But I knew just where to get my milk.

At about this time, in a home in Chula Vista south of San Diego, the phone rang. Mike O'Neill, a 32-year retired veteran of the San Diego Police Department and his wife Cheri, a retired director of their church pre-school, had already raised eight Guide dogs. The parents of three sons of high school and college age, Mike and Cheri were elated to learn that one of their former dogs, Darcy, had a litter of pups and they could have one to raise.

"Darcy had been chosen as a breeder before being trained as a working dog," Mike said.

At that time the O'Neill family had two adult Labradors, Autumn and Eve. As for the new dog's name, they were told that the pups of the January group were to be given names starting with "S."

"We were asked for suggestions," Cheri said. "Our oldest son Matthew, who was attending Whittier Law School, suggested the name of his favorite Thai restaurant on India Street in uptown San Diego. We added that to our list."

♡ Those first weeks of my life were filled with all kinds of new things to do. We played a lot, but I did notice that some of the play was not like fetching and running. The people got us to move up and down stairs, through doors, to walk on different surfaces and things like that. I know now why we did it, but at the time it was just fun. I was taken away from my Mommy Darcy after a while, but I was kept so busy with play and being taken to the vet for tests that I hardly noticed.

After eight weeks the new puppies were old enough to be given to puppy raisers. The O'Neills were told that a female yellow Lab was ready for puppy raising. "We were happy to have a puppy from Darcy," Cheri said. Then a special bus brought the prospective trainees to San Diego.

♡ It was a long trip in a crate with all those other dogs barking and whining. I had no idea where we were going.

The O'Neills were given this squirming little bundle of yellow fur with velvety ears, absurdly large feet, alert brown eyes and a furiously wagging tail. Her name was Saffron.

As things turned out, the name was perfect. Yellow, spicy, and very expensive.

By the time Saffron arrived in their home in the spring of 2011, the

O'Neills had already raised and owned eight dogs, having started with Guide Dogs in 2000. "Our first dog was Gaviota," Mike said," trying to remember all the names. "Darcy was our third, and that was Saffron's mom. Darcy had several litters for Guide Dogs."

There was a certain irony in that, since Jane's older brother, who died in 1993 was named Darcy.

♡ When I was led up to the house there were all these big people waiting. I was terribly excited at all the new smells and sights and sounds. They welcomed me in. I scampered around, sniffing and getting into everything. There were two other dogs there, grown-ups, but they only sniffed me. After I was fed and watered, I was shown where to sleep, and where I was to do my business. It was a lot for me to learn. They were so nice. Mike had a strong and deep voice, Cheri was gentle and loving. Matthew, who soon became my favorite, Craig and Kevin were going to teach me to be a good dog. I kept hearing them talk about me being a Guide Dog. I did not know what that meant. I was taken to all these strange and different places. My favorite was the park.

The job of the puppy raisers was not only to care for the puppy for the first year of its life, but to train it in basic obedience. This included teaching the dog to relieve itself outside the house, which as you might imagine, was a big issue.

They took the growing puppy, who would be wearing a cape declaring it to be a "Guide Dog in training," out to various public places to acclimate it to stores, shopping malls, sporting events, churches, offices and onto public transportation. Since most Guide Dog handlers would be using buses and trains, the puppy raisers taught their furry charges how to behave in such places. As the O'Neills were already experienced puppy raisers and dog owners, they knew how to handle the energetic little Saffron as she grew bigger and stronger.

The entire family was involved in the raising and training. Since playing was as much a part of the puppy's life as learning to behave in public, it was natural for the three sons to play with Saffron. Matthew, who at thirty was the oldest son, became an important part of young

Saffron's life. Even as a teenager in junior and senior high school he had developed a strong social conscience.

"The first day we had her," Mike said, "we went out to a restaurant. Matthew had Saffron and when we sat down she curled up on his lap and went to sleep. She always slept with her back against a person. I'm not sure if she was exhibiting some instinct to protect her rear or maybe she just wanted to make sure if you got up, she'd know it."

Cheri said, "Our two adult dogs, Autumn and Eve were generally quiet and conservative. When you have three dogs and one of them is a puppy, the energy level is unbelievable!"

Saffron's curiosity and playfulness was obvious from the start. "Eve, who was Autumn's mom, established herself as the alpha dog. She had to endure Saffron running at and nipping at her ears, trying to get a rise out of her." Mike recalled with a smile, "She watched her, and when Saffron got close enough, Eve clamped her mouth over her whole head! It was like she was saying, 'You know what I could do now, right kid?'"

♡ Okay I guess Eve kind of made me stop teasing her. She would not have hurt me...I hope.

Saffron the puppy with Autumn and Eve, spring 2011

Puppy raisers were given support from Guide Dogs for the Blind in the form of Puppy Raiser groups in their area. They met once a week and discussed the progress of their dogs under the tutelage of an experience raiser or trainer. Being in a room with a dozen active and playful puppies made every meeting a memorable experience. The O'Neills were no different, but having already raised several dogs, offered their own suggestions and ideas.

One of the things that characterize Guide dogs is how quiet they are. They almost never bark except when startled or playing. "We used one of the GDB techniques to train her to be quiet," Mike explained. "If she started barking, we put her in a room and closed the door and let her go at it until she grew tired. Then we let her out and rewarded her. After doing this two or three times she almost never barked again."

Saffron did resist her training in some cases. "One of the things Guide Dogs wanted us to teach the dogs was to walk on the grates at the curbs," Mike said. "But she refused, going around or over them. There was some talk about failing her, but she and I worked on that for a long time. As a reward I let her chase rabbits in the park near our house. She never caught one, and I don't think she would have known what to do if she did."

Saffron loved to play fetch. She always brought the toy back to whomever threw it.

"Saffron was the only dog I had that brought it back," Mike said. "All my other dogs dropped it and I had to go and get it."

Whenever Matthew was home from college, he helped his father with the training. "He walked with Saffron, making certain she stayed on the left side, teaching her to walk on grates and so on. He really helped to train her."

Matthew, as a student at law school, once took the rapidly growing Guide Dog in Training to use her as a prop in a class on Disability Law.

"Saffron lay on the floor at his feet," Cheri said. "She learned well to behave in public places."

Following his law degree, Matthew began as a Ph.D. candidate in Special Education and Disabilities studies at UC Santa Barbara. His passion was seeking ways for children and young adults to have access to better communicative experiences in public schools.

Saffron and the O'Neill family in the summer of 2011

By December Saffron was nearly full-grown and very strong. Her months with the O'Neills had taught her the basics of how to behave in public, how to obey verbal commands, and react appropriately to most situations. The time had come to send her back to Guide Dogs to learn the skills of being a working dog. While it was an emotional moment for the family, they regarded it the same way they would send one of their sons off to college.

Cheri said, "When Saffron went back to Guide Dogs, the energy level in the house went way down."

Intelligent Disobedience

After more than seventy years of raising and training over ten thousand Guide Dogs, the school developed a careful curriculum for new dogs.

Once Saffron was back at GDB, she was put in what was called a "string" of sixteen dogs under four trainers. They were encouraged to play and get used to one another. Then their general health, eyes, hips and hearing were checked. In some cases female dogs were chosen to be breeders. But Saffron didn't make the cut.

♡ Did you mean to use the word "cut," Daddy? Because that is what they did to me.

Sorry, Saffron. Melanie Harris was one of the four trainers for the string. The first part of training involved teaching the dogs to recognize the collar as a means of controlling their movement, adding the voice commands for each movement. Later they were acclimated to the harness, whereupon they were put on a treadmill. This trained the dog to walk with the harness when one of the trainers held the handle, making the dog pull forward.

♡ Melanie stood in front of me holding a treat, but I could not reach it no matter how fast I went! How mean can you get?

Working on the sidewalks was the first outdoor training in public. The dogs were taught to recognize different kinds of curbs and obstacles and stop for them. An important part of the training in traffic situations was known as "intelligent disobedience." If the handler gave the command of "forward," but the dog saw a car or other obstacle, it would not move.

♡ Daddy says I'm really good at intelligent disobedience. I *think* that is supposed to be a compliment.

The maturing trainees were taught to respond to verbal commands and react to changing situations. Commands such as "forward," "halt," "left," "right," "steady," "hop up," "stay" and several others soon became part of their daily routine. They learned to stop before ascending or descending stairs, look for doors, follow sighted guides, cross streets from corner to corner, and stop for obstacles or dangers like moving cars. The dogs not only had to learn to spontaneously obey commands but to recognize hazards before they became a threat. This is where the excellent training and the intelligence of the Labrador breed worked its greatest magic.

♡ Aw, Daddy. You're making me blush. But that training was hard work! Every single day we went out and worked in stores and on the streets, shopping malls, up and down stairs, in elevators and on escalators. Some things I did easily and others I had to work on to get right. I did react to sudden noises, but in time I learned to understand what might be a potential danger and what was not worth worrying about. One thing I picked up real quick was to never let a moving car get too close. That was where my good hearing helped. My trainers said I was going to be a good Guide Dog.

Guide work training could last anywhere from three to four months, depending on the dog. Saffron rated "Excellent" on every aspect of her training. She had the right posture, pace, and response to commands. The trainers continued to keep the string of dogs up to par even after they had been accepted as qualified Guide Dogs. Saffron made the cut in August of 2012, a month before I went back to San Rafael. For her it was a period of work, play and waiting.

Meanwhile, back in San Diego...

CHAPTER 3

BACK TO SCHOOL

"Choosing a dog may be the only chance you get to pick a relative."
— Mordecai Wyatt Johnson

The Big Decision

As the spring of 2012 approached, I was certain I would have to retire Musket. Musket no longer had that creamy yellow fur. He was almost white. I did not know that could happen to dogs. One man even asked if he was a new breed of white Labrador. But most only asked his age.

🐕 Daddy said "Oh, he's over eleven now." And then people would say "Wow, I didn't know Labradors lived that long." I don't know about you, but hearing things like that sort of scared me.

When Daddy and I walked together he sometimes slowed his pace to match mine. I guess age was creeping up on me. I still thought like a puppy, but my body and legs were not paying attention any more.

I called Keith Tomlinson, my field services representative at Guide Dogs. Keith told me what signs to look for. A slowing down, a reluctance to work, a general lack of energy. All those signs were becoming obvious.

The reality was unavoidable. I'd had him by my side for over a decade. How could I go out into the world without my loving, loyal and protective little buddy by my side? It would be like trying to take a walk and suddenly noticing I had one leg too few.

It wasn't fair to make Musket work any more. He'd long since earned a rest. After leading me from one end of the country to the other and protecting me from moving cars and open construction pits, he was ready to put on the Hawaiian aloha shirt and sandals over black socks while playing golf.

🐾 Oh, give me a break, Daddy. I have better taste than that! I'd wear Dockers and an Izod polo shirt!

My point being it was time to let him rest on his well-earned laurels. And to be honest, I wasn't sure how long he'd live. He'd had some more health problems. A persistent skin problem caused several warts and oozing pustules on his belly and legs, and he was starting to limp. We later learned he had developed arthritis in his right shoulder, which made it hard for him to walk up and down the stairs. Remember this is the same dog who charged up the stairs like Teddy Roosevelt on San Juan Hill when we came home, and down the stairs like a truckload of bowling balls when it was time to eat.

🐾 Yeah, those were the days. Sigh. Okay I'm going back to sleep now.

I called the Admissions office at Guide Dogs in San Rafael and asked them for an application. To my surprise, they sent me one. Even though some of the instructors remembered me, and many of them had read *Confessions,* they were still willing to give me another dog! After all, I, along with Jane and her parents had pretty much ruined Musket by overindulging and spoiling him. And let's not forget the food we weren't supposed to give him.

🐾 You mean there was more?

I thought you were asleep, Musket. A few weeks later they said I could be in class #747 starting on September 2, 2012.

And that was that. No more denial, no more lying to myself.

In a way it was the end of an era. The Golden Age of Musket. For ten years he and I went everywhere and did everything, met people all over the country and helped to change lives. In my work at the Independent Living Center he filled the dual roles of Blind and Low Vision Mobility Specialist and Stress Relief Counselor. He gave comfort to the sick and sad, made children and seniors laugh and gave unconditional love to everyone he met. Jane's parents were devoted to him to their last hours. He guided and kept me safe. With Musket by my side I was able to travel and work with confidence and safety. At air shows and museums, on trains, planes and automobiles he was there, doing his job.

Not a bad legacy for an old dog.

🐕 I noticed Daddy was being very easy on me. He didn't make me work as much, instead using his cane. And for the first time I didn't mind. He said "Hey I'm going to the bank, be back in an hour," and grabbed his cane. I just felt a bit of relief. And guilt. It was not easy to let him go out alone. Daddy could trip on a painted line. I was his Guide Dog. He needed me. I guess it was partly habit, partially a sense of duty, but I still stood by the newel post where my harness was hung. But Daddy bent down and kissed my head and said "Hey, Old Timer, you can stay home and rest. I'll be okay."

That was okay, I guess, but being called "Old Timer" was a little disconcerting.

All good things must come to an end, but sometimes they are only the closing of one era and the beginning of another.

And that's the story of this book. The changing of the guide.

Hanging Up the Harness

Musket and I had our birthdays at the end of August. I was turning, and I'm finally going to admit the truth, fifty-two years old, and Musket was twelve.

🐾 Will wonders never cease? He finally admitted his age. Notify the news media, this is big!

Sheesh. I had my plane tickets and we'd made the arrangements. I was packed and ready for being at Guide Dogs for two weeks. It was going to be the first time in over ten years that I was traveling alone.

On September 1, 2012 I put the harness on Musket for the last time. I slipped it over his head and clipped the belly strap. I had a small lump in my throat I could not swallow as I talked to him. "Well little buddy, this is it. Let's take a walk and talk." He led me outside and turned left at the driveway to the road. I let him set the pace and began to talk to him. "Musket, tomorrow I'm going back to San Rafael. I'll be gone for two weeks. Mommy will take care of you, and you'll be fine. When I come back I'll have a new younger brother or sister for you. I know you don't understand, but this is the way it has to be. You're not able to do the job anymore and it's just not fair to make you work. You have earned your rest." I had tiny tears in my eyes as we walked slowly up the sidewalk. It was harder than I thought it would be. I was saying goodbye to my stalwart friend and constant companion. Musket plodded along, stopping occasionally to sniff the grass. He didn't seem to have a care in the world. Of course I knew he'd be fine while I was gone, and probably miss me. But it was that first meeting in two weeks that had me worried. How would he take it? Would he feel betrayed? Abandoned? Jilted? Relieved?

With Musket anything was possible. We finally reached the end of the road and turned around. He showed no reluctance to go back home. He was already panting. Compared to the walks we'd taken for years, this was hardly worth mentioning. He still did a great job as a Guide Dog. But it was his last time.

🐾 I remember that. At first it was just like a thousand other times. I put my head into the harness and he clipped it on. Then we went out. He let me walk at my own pace. It was sort of like a normal walk, not working. He let me sniff and pee. He talked to me about going away for a while, but I really didn't catch on. I thought he meant for a day or so.

When he talked about a "new brother or sister," it just didn't sink in. But he seemed very sad about something.

When we stepped back into the house I unclipped the harness. Then I bent over and wrapped my arms around his neck. "Thank you, Little Buddy. Thanks for taking such good care of me all these years. I love you. You'll always be the best dog I ever had."

He panted and licked the tears off my face. Then I held out a treat for him. Just like old times.

🐾 Daddy took the harness off me and instead of hanging it back on the newel post he put it in the closet. Just then I felt a tiny twinge of worry. What was going on? He bent over and hugged me. I was panting because I was kind of tired. I licked Daddy's face. He was crying. I've always been nice to someone who was sad and crying, but Daddy almost never acted that way.

Musket ate the treat and then went to lie down. I stood there for a long time, listening to his breathing slow down. My own heartbeat felt like it was going to bust my ribcage. Jane came downstairs and asked how it went. I told her and she hugged me. Then Musket awoke and begged for a treat. Well, old or not, he was still the same dog.

🐾 Mommy still treated me the same. Even if Daddy was going to can me I could work for her. She'd find a job for her baby. I ate the treat and wondered if I'd at least get a gold watch for my ten years of devoted service. Then I'd be a watch dog. Yuk, yuk.

Ow. That was an awful pun. One day about that time I was looking through a drawer and found some old papers I couldn't identify. I put them on my scanner and converted them to text for the computer to read to me. They were from Musket's puppy raiser. She wrote an evaluation of his behavior and obedience. It basically said he was a strong, intelligent and loving dog. He learned fast and rarely made a mistake, after being acclimated to every kind of public environment from stores to restaurants to offices and transportation Musket had done well in all of them.

This was no surprise to me in retrospect but it was nice to know that he had been a star long before he even started Guidework training.

The final line in the evaluation was the most interesting. "Musket is a dog with a sense of humor."

I started to laugh and in moments, was convulsed in hysterics. Musket was lying on the rug by my desk and came over.

🐾 Oh, he's okay. He's laughing at something he read. Must have been funny.

Still chuckling, I sat on the floor with him. I hugged my wonderful Guide Dog and kissed him on the head. He licked my face. To this day, whenever I remember those words, I smile. Yes, Musket was a dog with a sense of humor.

Thank Dog.

On The Way

Readers of the last book might recall I had speculated about what it would be like to go back to San Rafael and Guide Dogs. I had it pretty clear in my mind and even knew what I'd say at graduation. But you know how you can plan out a vacation in your mind and when it happens, it comes out totally different? Look at Custer. He planned a nice little jaunt in Montana and had a rotten time.

Boy was it ever different. I felt just like a newbie again, even with a decade as a seasoned dog handler behind me.

On the morning of September 2, I said goodbye to Musket and loaded my bag into the car. Jane drove me to the airport. It felt weird not having Musket in the car. Jane, as usual was telling me about hanging up my clothes when I got into my room...blah, blah...as if I couldn't take care of myself. She warned me about washing the colors with the whites, yada, yada. What was the big deal? I'd be able to buy new underwear in San Rafael. And most of the people there were blind, for crying out loud!

We arrived at the airport and I got out, pulling my big carry-on bag from the back. Then I hugged and kissed Jane. She of course called for a skycap to help me find the ticket counter. Sigh. But after our goodbyes I went into the terminal. Ticket counter, then to security. I smiled to myself, remembering the times I'd had Musket at the TSA lines. I was probably the only person smiling, now I come to think about it.

Finally I was at the gate and sat down to wait. I called a couple of friends to let them know I was on my way. They wanted to know about the new dog ASAP. They wanted pictures and details. Funny thing was they didn't seem to be very concerned about me. If I just sent the new dog home and disappeared...oh, well.

Just kidding, but the new dog, whoever he or she was, was going to be the center of attention without any effort.

Arriving at San Francisco International I picked up my bag, working my way up the ramp to the terminal. I was met by a GDB instructor named Kevin who took me to meet the other students. There were about ten of us from all over the country. Jenny Wood was a Texas mom who had recently retired her first dog. Susan McNeish was a former counselor from Erie, Pennsylvania who likewise would be getting a second dog. Travis Taylor was an ultra-walker who did thousand-mile walks across the country, paid by sponsors. I was already thinking that his dog was in for a BIG surprise.

We climbed into the GDB bus and drove across the Golden Gate Bridge to San Rafael, but not to the campus. The dorm I remembered so well had been demolished, and a new two-story one was under construction. The students of Class #747 would be staying in a Sheraton Four Points. We'd each have our own room and everything we needed. Even our laundry was washed for us. I lucked out there.

A crate for the dog was provided with bowls, plenty of food and a grooming kit. They even gave us a new bottle of Palmolive dishwashing soap to wash the dog food bowls. I was not kidding when I said GDB has its stuff together.

Life at the Sheraton wasn't bad, but the food was far below what we'd known in the old dining hall. Just adequate. But we did not complain.

After all, we weren't paying for it. There was a relieving area for the dogs outside the rooms and we could use the pool and gym.

The training would only take two weeks. A pair of students worked with a single instructor who took us both out and gave us personalized instruction, based on what each student needed, i.e. urban or suburban environments, rural or country roads, busy traffic, quiet small town roads, whatever.

It had both advantages and shortcomings, but I was eager to meet and work with my new dog.

For the first day, a Sunday, we met with our instructors. Jenny and I would be working with Heather Foster, a vivacious lady in her twenties. She was high-spirited and fun, and she knew all about Musket and the book. I actually thought that would be a liability but she was glad to be working with me.

That Special Feeling

On Monday we gathered in a small meeting room. I think there were about ten of us with the instructors. They explained that our dogs would be brought into each of our rooms where we would be able to sit down and get to know them. I remembered my first meeting with Musket, when he acted is if he couldn't care less if I was there or not. Well at least I knew better this time.

After three other students were told what dog they would receive, Heather turned to me.

On my application and review I had asked for another yellow Labrador. I was rather fond of the breed. But as with Musket, I wanted a strong and loving dog. It was not important that it be playful or active. Keith had suggested I request a female. Musket, as the alpha male would feel less threatened by a new dog if it were a submissive male or better yet, a female.

"Mark," Heather began, "you'll be receiving Saffron, a female Yellow Labrador. She was born on January 21, 2011 and weighs fifty-six pounds."

A girl! I was going to have a little daughter. That was a new feeling. Saffron. What a sweet name.

Then...the weirdest feeling started to come over me. Some of you may remember those awful song parodies I wrote for Musket? No, don't worry, I'm not going to sing them. But one of Musket's songs was the 1966 soft rock hit "Mellow Yellow" by Donovan.

That was a perfect song for him. Musket was easygoing and nothing ever fazed him. Mellow Yellow Labrador.

That song suddenly began playing in my head for some reason. And you know that feeling like a mild warm electric shock winding up your spine? It hit me. The first line of that song was "I'm just mad about Saffron, and Saffron's mad about me..."

This was a *Twilight Zone* moment. All that was missing was the theme music.

Back in my room I called Jane to give her the news. In contrast to her negative reaction to Musket's name, she loved Saffron. But she still had some misgivings. Musket was her baby. They had developed a very close and tight bond over the years. She wasn't sure how she'd feel about the new dog. She admitted she would probably like and care about the new dog, but she didn't want to make Musket feel abandoned. I understood this. I was sure it would work out.

A short time later there was a knock on my door. I went to answer it. Heather was there. "I have Saffron with me. Why don't you go and sit down on the floor by the bed and I'll bring her to you."

Feeling just as nervous as I'd been in 2002, I sat down by the bed. Then this scampering, active little ball of energy came right up to me and began licking my face and ears. No ambiguity there. She was a lover girl. She was licking at my ears so eagerly I was afraid she'd short out my hearing aid. Since then I've learned, although I have no earthly idea why, Saffron loves the taste of ears.

She was certainly happy to meet me. I was petting and rubbing her ears and back and talking to her. I got her to lie down on my lap, no easy task with such a hyperactive dog, and she let me rub her belly. Heather told me to look up while she used her phone to take a picture of the new Daddy and Daughter. She asked me for Jane's e-mail address and sent it to her.

Saffron seemed very comfortable with me. Heather gave me a couple of toys and suggested I play with her until lunchtime.

That sure showed me what Saffron was like. Musket had always been a "run and fetch three times" dog. But Saffron had more energy than a runaway nuclear reactor. I tossed the kong down the hallway to the room door and she ran off to get it like a Tomcat being fired off a carrier's catapult. Zoom! And again. Zoom! Zoom! I got tired just hearing her. Thank God we weren't on the second floor. The people below would have screamed bloody murder at all the noise.

In time she settled down and I called Jane. She'd gotten the picture and said Saffron was a very beautiful dog. I told her about how active and loving she was. I didn't realize it then, but I'd again been given the perfect dog. Saffron was as loving and playful as Musket had ever been. She was also very quiet. She never barked, just like Musket.

The only sound she made was when she yawned. You remember the sound Snoopy made when he yawned in the old Charlie Brown animated cartoons? That's what Saffron sounded like when she yawned. It was really cute. I had no trouble falling in love with Saffron.

♡ Hey, even supersonic jets have to slow down sometimes. Well that was a wonderful day for me. Ever since I was brought back to Guide dogs, I was Miss Busy Bee. Veterinary tests, training, more tests and more training; what happened to those wonderful fun days with Mike, Cheri, Matthew, Craig, and Kevin? But after months of hard work and more testing all over San Rafael, they decided I was ready.

Then came that day when I was taken, along with a lot of other dogs in crates to this big building. One by one we were taken to a door. Heather knocked on the door. Inside was this big man. I did not know who he was, but Heather told him to sit down on the floor. I liked it when people did that. It made meeting them a lot easier. He was very nice and had a nice deep voice, just like my Daddy Mike. I licked his face and he hugged me. After a while I laid on his lap and he gave me this really goooooooood belly rub. He found my "magic spot" right away and I kicked like crazy.

Heather left and this man began to talk to me and told me about Musket, a woman named Jane who would be my new Mommy and where I would be living. It slowly dawned on me that this was my new Daddy! We played and cuddled and he kept talking to me. That was a wonderful day. I had a new family and home.

A whole New Kind of Dog

We began to work together the next day. It wasn't always outside. Every day I took her out to the relieving area, to the dining room, and around the hotel. Just basic stuff, it helped us to learn to work as a team. We had to trust one another.

Every day the bus took us to the Guide Dog Lounge on 4th Street in downtown San Rafael. The town was a small, quiet residential community of about 22 square miles and a year-round population of less than 60,000 people. The town's history was rich with artists and writers and most of the homes in the older parts were the beautiful "painted ladies" so famous in San Francisco. Thank you, Wikipedia.

San Rafael was a peaceful place well-suited for new Guide Dog teams to learn the ropes.

One way I like to describe how a Guide Dog and Handler work together is to use the illustration of a computer. Saffron was already loaded with all the software. It was my job to learn to use what she had "programmed" into her by the training. The human handler has the ability to make reasoned decisions based on experience. It was a synergy of cooperation between human and canine; the dog learning from the handler, the handler from the dog.

♡ I don't like the idea of being "programmed." Let's just say I was a very smart dog.

We got comfortable walking on residential streets and around the shops in downtown. Saffron didn't get as easily distracted by food smells as Musket did, but she was a bit skittish with sudden noises. If a car horn honked or a door slammed, her head snapped around like a whip. I learned to get her focused right away and move on.

37

Working with Saffron was a whole new experience. For the past few years I'd gotten used to Musket's slow, plodding pace. For the last year it was a bit like having a push mower. I did a lot of the work.

But along came Saffron, who was like a power mower with only one speed setting: Mach 1!

But that's not to say she was always at full tilt. Some days she needed a bit of encouragement. Heather, who was right behind us, sometimes told me to give Saffron a nudge. I said "Saffy, hop up."

"Mark," said the voice from behind, "She doesn't know that name. Use her full name for now."

"Okay. Saffron, hop up."

Sometime she did, sometimes not. In the latter cases, I was to give the harness handle a little nudge and say "Saffron, hop up," more firmly. If that didn't work, I was to take the leash from my left hand and give it a gentle jerk straight ahead of Saffron's head. This was a clear, physical indicator to move faster. That most often did it.

♡ Sometimes Daddy didn't pull the leash straight ahead, but off to the right a little. This confused me until Heather...uh, straightened him out. Maybe he needed a leash too.

Don't give them any ideas. One thing we had to perfect was crossing controlled and uncontrolled intersections. For some reason Saffron and I were not making it right across, but hitting the opposite curb either to the right or left, even missing it entirely. In 2002 I still had enough sight left to be able to tell when Musket did this, but in 2012 it was a different story. It was both frustrating and a little scary, finding myself out on the street and not knowing where the curb was. Heather was there to help. She reasoned the problem was that Saffron and I were not starting out from the curb perpendicular to the street we were crossing. So we worked that one several times until I was more confident. In a few days it was no longer a problem.

♡ I felt very good working with Daddy. He had a good strong voice and praised me when I did something right. He carried a small pack of kibble on a belt around on his waist. Sometimes when he was very pleased with my work, he gave me a few bits. But Heather, who was so mean, told Daddy not to give me treats every time I did something right. "She should not learn to expect the treats," she said. How mean can you get? They're supposed to be nice to their dogs!

To Bee or Not to Bee?

The Yeoman Warders that guard the Tower of London who wear those blue and red Elizabethan uniforms are called "Beefeaters." Saffron is a Bee-eater. I learned this on one of our early walks on a residential street.

I felt Saffron moving her head around very quickly. "Saffron, what is it, girl?" I asked.

"There's a bee buzzing around her head," said Heather.

Then everything happened at once. Saffron lunged forward and I heard a distinct "snap!"

Heather said "Oh, she ate it!"

"What?" I said, completely in the dark, not to make a pun.

She said, "Let's get back to the Lounge. Follow me." She took the leash while I held the handle. Fortunately the Lounge was about two blocks away and Heather was already on her phone to the vet office.

Saffron had taken the bee as a flying treat and snatched it in mid-air. She was certainly having some issues with the bee. I guess it never occurred to her to let it go, and the poor bee, just doing its thing, had suddenly found itself in the position of Pinocchio in Monstro's mouth.

We reached the Lounge and Heather went into the room where the medical supplies were. Saffron was shaking her head as if trying to assemble a jigsaw puzzle by shaking the box.

"Here," Heather said, giving Saffron a Benadryl and making her swallow it. After drinking a bowl of water, Saffron settled down.

Heather said that dogs can be allergic to bee stings so they had to be sure she was okay.

I sat on the floor with her and rubbed her belly, where presumably a very pissed-off bee was buzzing around.

But she seemed to be fine. There were no ill effects. The only casualty was the bee.

"Did we learn anything, Saffron?" I asked her in that slightly condescending tone grown-ups use with kids.

♡ Okay I guess I shouldn't' have eaten the bee. But it was buzzing around my face, really being a nuisance. I just reacted instinctively. At first there was no problem. That bee was not going to "be" a problem anymore. Then it stung me on the tongue! That really hurt, and I tried to get it out of my mouth. No good. It was down my throat. Daddy and Heather were worried but I felt fine. My tongue hurt for a few hours, though. But you know, I still try to eat flying bugs! Butterflies are good. Sort of like eating a flying potato chip. But NO MORE BEES!

Since then I've learned that Saffron has zero memory for any lesson that involves her impulsive eating. She will eat ANYTHING on the floor/ground/patio/grass. She's like a shark. Eat first and identify later. But to be fair to sharks they stop eating when they're full. Not my Saffron. A wood chipper is a more discerning gourmet. And a lot quieter.

♡ I think Daddy's making fun of me. So I eat? Is that a crime?

By the end of the first week we were doing well together. Saffron's sweet and loving personality was very infectious. She made me happy because she was always so happy.

I fed her in the morning and then relieved her, and went up to breakfast. The other students were there with their dogs. We soon formed about three groups. Susan McNeish had learned about my book and wanted a copy. Fortunately I had a few in my bag. There were classes in dog health care, the new GDB veterinary care policies and so on. Again I was impressed with the efficiency of the GDB organization. We could go shopping in a local store if we wanted any snack foods or sundries, and our instructors were as helpful as could be. Heather was a sweetie.

♡ Even if she was stingy with the treats. I did like her, but I was going to have to work on Daddy when we were on our own.

Road Work

Overall, the training was on a smaller scale than it had been in 2002. Heather drove Jenny and me to various locations in the San Francisco Bay area where we worked with our dogs. We went into the city to work at crossing busy city streets and into Berkeley for a try at the campus. We went to restaurants and sidewalk cafes, residential neighborhoods with old, cracked sidewalks and others with no sidewalks at all. That last one took some getting used to. There was a specific way to do it. Let's say you're walking on the left side of a street with no sidewalk. There are cars parked here and there. Every car is an obstacle. When you reach one, the dog will stop. Then you do a 'hard' right turn and face the street. If it is quiet and safe, you move forward, then do a moving left turn, saying "left, left, left," until you reach the back of the car, then turn to the curb again. Easy enough. But most areas without sidewalks don't have clearly defined corners. They're wide and gradual. So the dog has no specific spot to use as the stepping off point. GDB taught its students to follow the curve of the corner until it was straight again, then halt. Do a hard right and aim for the opposite side. When it is clear, give the "forward" command and walk across. When on the other side, stop, do another hard right again and continue until you reach and follow the curve around the corner. Then you're back on the same road you were before.

It was a tricky thing to learn, and at that time I did not take it too seriously. All the streets in Carmel Mountain Ranch had sidewalks.

One day was a real treat. The entire class was taken up to the Muir Woods National Monument. The vans dropped us off at the entrance parking area where we gathered together. I remembered going there as a kid with my parents and the smells of tall redwoods and fresh sea-laden air was intoxicating. Since it was morning, the persistent fog that was so much part of the north San Francisco Bay climate hung in the trees like laundry on a line. We broke up into small groups and walked along the boardwalk trails and paths. Saffron was very excited. She was curious about everything, especially when we went into a redwood that had been burned out by a lightning strike. It was like a tall black chimney.

♡ Trees! Big ones, little ones, tall ones, short ones. There were trees lying on the ground and trees in big bunches. All I could think was Oh, no, if I have to pee, where do I start?

After the walk I went into the gift shop and bought Jane some cards and a few souvenirs. She was a serious scramper (Scrapbooker/Stamper) and loves sets of postcards to use in her creations. Walking with Saffron in the Muir Woods was a nice treat and diversion.

A phone call from Harry Potter

One evening I was writing on my laptop when my cell phone rang. "Hello?"

"Is this Mark Carlson," a strangely familiar male voice asked.

"Yes it is," I replied.

"This is Eric Sandvold. I am going to be doing the audio recording of your book for the National Library Service."

I almost fell out of my chair. Eric Sandvold was one of the best readers for NLS audio books in the country. I had submitted *Confessions* for the NLS in the spring and asked if Eric could do it. I was a fan of his reading ever since I read the entire *Harry Potter* series. He had a great voice. Now he was calling me!

"That is great," I said. "How can I help you?"

"Well," he began in that voice I knew so well," I wanted to ask you about some of the voices and words in your book. I want to do it correctly."

We had a terrific talk where I told him about Musket and his "voice," and personality. He took some notes and said he was looking forward to reading the book.

In a few months my book would be available for the blind and disabled. I felt great.

♡ Daddy was all excited about this book. But I did not even know Musket yet. He was like this big important celebrity. How was anyone going to notice little me?

But you learned better since, haven't you? Musket never upstaged my little Labradiva, did he?

The training period was almost over. Guide Dogs then took us each in turn to meet the veterinarians who had cared for our dogs. They gave the dogs a full screening and explained their medical history. Saffron, like all the other dogs had been chipped, and they explained how that worked. I'd assumed it was like Lo-Jack, that stolen car recovery system. I learned if Saffron ever got found by someone, they could take her to a vet that could scan the chip in her skin and know who she was. She wore a tag that showed she was chipped.

♡ Isn't that totally cool? I'm like, hooked up to Satellites!

As it turned out, it came in REAL handy. But more on that later.

No Loss for Words

Graduation Day approached. Jane would not be coming up this time, but my brother David, his wife Carol, and David's son and daughter-in-law were also going to be there with their baby, Caleb.

Since the old Graduation Patio was gone along with the dorm, it would be on the grass lawn where most of the big ceremonies were held.

Saffron's puppy raisers were from San Diego! Mike and Cheri O'Neill lived in Chula Vista in South Bay. They were coming to the graduation and Saffron would get to see her original Mommy and Daddy.

♡ I was so excited when Daddy told me that my puppy raisers were coming. But I should probably have told Daddy about "Big Mike."

Yeah, you should have. On Graduation Day I was taken out to one of the patio areas where the O'Neill family met me. Mike was a retired police officer, big and burly. I'd never want to have him on my case. But in temperament, he was a wonderful and warm man. Cheri was a retired school director, and they had three sons, Matthew, Craig, and Kevin, all of whom were intelligent, ambitious and socially conscious.

They were happy to see Saffron, who was nearly berserk with joy. I was still trying to learn her personality and to get her under control. But Mike simply gave her a firm command and she sat down like a Marine recruit. The only thing I didn't hear was "Sir, yes, Sir!"

The O'Neills had heard of Musket and the book, and when they realized their little girl was being given to me, they were very happy. I gave them an autographed copy. But to be honest, I was a little nervous. As readers of *Confessions* well know, I had not done an exemplary job with Musket's food and discipline. Of course the majority of that could be traced to Jane and her family, but I didn't enforce the GDB laws much.

In any case, we had a nice talk before graduation.

The students met up with their families and friends. I met a woman who had been in the puppy raising group that had known Musket and was so glad to meet me at last.

The ceremony was short and simple, with the GDB Director making a speech, then turning the microphone over to the head instructor.

Then it was my turn. As some of you remember, I never forgave myself for my poor performance at my first graduation. I had choked and was unable to say anything.

Not this time. After being led to the podium by Heather, I waited as she announced, "Our next graduate is Mark Carlson of San Diego, who is being given Saffron, a female Yellow Labrador raised by the O'Neill family of Chula Vista. This is Mark's second dog. His first was Musket, and Mark is the author of *Confessions of a Guide Dog, the Blonde Leading the Blind*." This earned some laughter and applause from the audience, and I think I heard David cheering.

Then the O'Neills brought a tail-wagging Saffron to me and handed me the leash. Mike made a nice speech about how much he had loved raising Saffron and that they were happy she was going to be my Guide Dog.

When he handed the microphone to me, this time I was able to talk and thanked the wonderful people at Guide Dogs, the O'Neills and everyone who contributed to the raising and training of these magnificent animals. Then I mentioned that Musket was now retired and he would have to get used to a new dog doing his job. I leaned over and said to Saffron, "Saffron, you're going to be a perfect Guide Dog, but I have to give you one word of advice. When we get home, don't listen to a word Musket says!"

The audience laughed. I ended with the comment that if the U.S. Government was run as efficiently as Guide Dogs, we would rule this planet.

Mark, Saffron and the O'Neills at GDB Graduation in September 2012

♡ That was a big day for me. I knew that they were all there to see me, of course. But Daddy and my former family were happy too. I met Uncle David and his dog Winchester. He was nice, but I was a lot more interested in this famous Musket.

Saffron led me back to my chair and we listened as the other graduates were given their dogs.

Then it was over. Saffron was mine. We sat down with David and the family, chatting about Guide Dogs and family matters. All in all, a wonderful and full day.

The New Celebrity

But it wasn't over by a long shot. At the airport I was waiting by the gate for the flight to San Diego to be called. This would be my first time on a plane with Saffron. She was curious about all the new smells and sounds and sights. Her head was constantly craning around like a periscope.

♡ I was very excited. My new Daddy was taking me someplace. He kept telling me about my new Mommy and our house and everything.

The gate agent came by and told me the plane was delayed but she'd tell me when it was time to board. Meanwhile I called Jane and a couple of my friends.

An hour later the jet had arrived and was disgorging passengers. The agent led me to the gate. Saffron took me down the jetway to the flight attendant at the plane's door. When we reached the first row of seats on the starboard side, I took off Saffron's harness and put it in the overhead bin. Then something amazing happened. Just as I was settling in and talking to Saffron, a woman behind me said, "Excuse me, is that Musket?"

For a second, I was nearly speechless.

♡ That never happens, according to Mommy.

Ahem. I turned to the lady behind me and said, "Ah no, it's not."

"Oh," she said, obviously disappointed.

"Actually it is Musket's new little sister. We just graduated from Guide Dogs today."

Her reaction was totally unexpected. "Oh my god! I'm reading your book!"

"Really?" I said, flabbergasted but very pleased. What are the odds?

"Yes, I love it. You're Mark Carlson!" I heard her talking to her seat mate. "That's the book I was telling you about. The one Marcia loaned me. The one about that wonderful Guide Dog, Musket. This is Mark Carlson. I can't believe it."

Neither could I. Poor Saffron, she was already in her predecessor's tall shadow.

♡ Give me time, Daddy. I'll be in the spotlight soon enough.

Then this lady said "Can I come up and meet her?"

"Sure." She came up and I introduced Saffron to her. The lady's name was Kathy Tinsley, who had borrowed the book from a woman who'd bought one at Gillespie Field a couple of months before. It turned out we had a few mutual friends. She had known John Finn. Saffron was happy to make a new friend, but Kathy began talking about a "famous author" being on the plane. I'm still wondering if she meant me.

Some passengers came by and took pictures of Saffron and me. The lady sitting to my left asked about the book and my new publicist, Kathy, told her about it. "Okay," the passenger said. "I'll order it on Kindle right now." And she did.

♡ All these people wanted to meet me. But I'm not sure if it was me or because I had a famous Daddy and older brother. Well, fame is as fame does, I guess. I milked it for everything I could get!

What a way to return home. I exchanged phone numbers with Kathy and we promised to get together in San Diego so she could meet Musket and Jane.

For the rest of the flight I was thinking about the remarkable coincidence of meeting a fan on the plane. But it would not be the last time. It was evening when the plane carrying the "famous author" and his excited Guide Dog landed in San Diego. Once we were in the terminal I asked a gate agent if someone could lead me out to the curb. I called Jane, who was waiting in the Cell Phone Lot. She said she'd be by in about ten minutes.

After a fast-paced trot out of the terminal we arrived at the busy curb. Dozens of cars were pulling over and dropping off passengers and their luggage while others were picking up. I tried to make sure I was visible by standing on an open part of the curb but that was like taking apart a brick wall from the bottom. Every time you pull one brick out another one falls into its place. (I don't understand this analogy at all. Are you referring to the other travelers or to Saffron blocking your movement?)

Then I heard a horn honk nearby and Jane calling me. She pulled over and got out.

Well, this was it! We hugged and kissed while Saffron watched. Then Jane bent down. "Hi Saffron, you're my new little girl. I'm your Mommy."

Saffron didn't need to hear that. She already knew.

♡ I saw Daddy hugging this lady and I knew he loved her. I loved him so I would love her. I gave her a lot of kisses. She was wonderful. Daddy asked if Musket was in the car, but my new mommy said no, he was still back home.

Jane had decided to leave Musket at home because it was so late. "They'll meet at home."

Keith told me that Musket and Saffron should meet on neutral ground so there would not be any advantage on either side. I'd just have to make the best of it.

All the way home, Saffron curled up on the sheepskin cover on the back seat while Jane and I caught up on local news.

We were all pretty tired when she stopped the car outside the garage and pushed the door control button. "Okay, Honey," she said. "Let Saffron out."

The Big Moment had arrived

CHAPTER 4

CHANGING OF THE GUIDE

"The gift which I am sending you is called a dog, and is in fact
the most precious and valuable possession of mankind."
— Theodorus Gaza

Meeting of the Noses

♡ Daddy stood there with me and we waited.
Then Mommy said "Okay, Musket, here's your new little sister."
Musket came sauntering out and saw me. He stopped and stared.

🐕 There was my Daddy. I'd missed him while he was gone. But...
there was another dog with him. A dog wearing MY harness. Doing MY
job! Guiding MY Daddy! What was this all about? I looked at the dog.
It was like me, a yellow Labrador, and its tail was wagging furiously.
It didn't seem to be threatening or hostile. Just excited. I could smell
that. And something else...huh? It was a girl! A girl dog! In my house?
What did this mean? Mommy nudged me over to the stranger. Daddy
got down on his knees and pulled me to him. "Hey, little buddy. I missed
you. I want you to meet Saffron. Saffron, this is Musket."

♡ So this was the famous Musket. He was big, much bigger than I.
He was also really old. He looked like some big old lion with his broad

head. But he didn't seem to be dangerous. Only sort of bewildered. I can't blame him. Here I was, a young and pretty girl with his daddy. But then our noses met. He sniffed me and I sniffed him. No threat there. I didn't want him to feel like I was a threat to him either. But then he sort of gave Daddy a look like "Okay, whatever. So did you bring me any treats?" Right then I knew we'd get along fine.

Musket and Saffron met but there was none of the butt-sniffing I would have expected. I guess Musket was way past that stage in his life. He stood there looking at Saffron, who did the same. For a full minute nothing happened. Then he went to the yard to do his business. Hmm, talk about anti-climactic.

Jane had already bought some dishes and a bed for Saffron. It was on the floor on the other side of the television armoire. She took to it just fine. I was told that she was very comfortable in a crate, but I never liked that idea. In any case, she was good about staying in her bed, unlike Musket, who still had squatters' rights to the floor by Jane's side of the bed.

The first few days I took Saffron for walks so she could get to know the neighborhood. She caught on fast, even the specific landmarks I used for navigation.

I recently came up with a good analogy for what Saffron really did. As with the crew of an airliner, I played the role of the navigator while Saffron was the pilot. I had to know where to go and how to get there. She flew the plane and got us there safely. In other words, if I knew there was a huge mountain on our route she made sure we avoided hitting it.

We went to the bank, store, library and on the bus. Every time I lifted her harness off the newel post, Musket began to get up. "No, Musket," I said gently. "Stay there. You can have the day off."

It usually worked. But it was kind of hard to realize he still felt the pull of his former job. When we were ready to leave, I tossed some kibble on the floor by him and left.

🐾 Daddy thought he was tricking me by doing that. But I was on to him. And I got treats out of it.

Some Big Paws to Fill

The next few months had a learning curve that was as steep as a brick wall. Everything I learned and put to use about Musket and Guide Dogs in general were put to the test with Saffron. She did her job, as we will discuss later, and she was a fairly obedient dog, but she was as different from Musket as Grape Nuts are from road gravel. Oh, sorry. There is no difference.

Yet on one subject they were in complete accord. Food. I don't know if it was a Labrador trait, but Musket and Saffron could have eaten us out of house and home. As you might guess the monthly dog food consumption doubled.

And that stuff ain't cheap. Musket needed a low-fat formula for older dogs, while Saffron ate the normal kibble. And from the start I had to learn a whole new way of feeding two ravenous dogs.

Musket ate pretty fast, but he was still at it when Saffron was done and went over to help him. Boy did the red flags go up at that! But Musket, ever the mellow one, just moved so she could not get her muzzle into the bowl.

Soon I figured out how to make sure they did not interfere with each other. I filled both bowls, then put Musket's down under the kitchen desk and held Saffron's bowl over her while I walked very slowly to where her place was under the kitchen window.

She watched like a hawk as I lowered it to the floor and buried her face in it with a sound like a Hoover Wet-Dry vacuum. If I timed it right, Musket was able to finish his food before she did.

Musket was Saffron's mentor and sensei. He showed her all his tricks, as if to assure his legacy would live on. And boy did she learn fast!

Eating a meal was like having two avid spectators, both of whom watched every move Jane and I made. From plate to mouth, every bit of food was observed by those two. I swear they never blinked.

But they were two totally different personalities even if they were both Yellow Labrador Retrievers. And the funny thing was, Jane and I did everything the same way with both dogs.

Wolves in the Fold

Having two big and hungry dogs in the house was a bit disconcerting. Just one more and I'd have a pack, suitable for roaming the tundra and attacking herds of elk and reindeer. I've always admired how organized and cooperative wolf packs are in the wild, but I never would have thought that faint traces of instinctual behavior would turn up in my own kitchen.

Let me give you an example of cooperative pack behavior. A typical evening at Casa Carlson had Jane watching television upstairs, and both dogs sleeping by her chair. Both were essentially comatose. More on this later.

Musket's hearing was not what it used to be, but he could still see. Saffron had better hearing than Jane, who could hear an ant fart in the next county.

Let's say I decided to have a snack. Down to the kitchen I went, opening the cabinet for the potato chips. We kept them in Tupperware so they stayed fresh, but also had the advantage of being opened quietly. Wrong!

"Poof," went the lid.

"Zoom!" came the dogs.

Saffron was suddenly there, and so was Musket! She heard me opening the container and raced down the stairs. Musket saw her zipping past and joined her. No matter how old and slow he got, he could move plenty fast when food was the goal.

And there they were, tails wagging while they watched me try to ignore them.

Remember what I said about cooperative pack behavior? If I had the temerity to pretend I didn't see them, one would nudge my leg or hand while the other circled around to head off my retreat. Eventually I gave in. I gave them each a piece of kibble from the dish on the counter. I had learned to hold them out with my arms wide apart so one dog could not get both.

Another part of this pack behavior was how they played Jane and I against one another. You know how kids sometimes go to their father and say "Dad, can I go to the movies with my friends?" and Dad says "If Mom says it is okay, then you can go." The kid goes to Mom and says "Mom, Daddy said I can go to the movies."

Kids are just as smart as wolves, and even more dangerous.

Back to the two dogs eating from my hands. Then Jane came downstairs. This was like hitting the "Reset" button. A different parent.

The begging began anew. "Honey," I said, "I just gave them treats."

♡ Hope springs eternal in the dog's breast.

"You heard what Daddy said, " Jane told them. "You got treats.

♡ But that was Daddy, Now you have to give us one. It's only fair.

🐾 I like the way you think, little sister!

Jane had zero willpower when faced with four sad brown eyes. "Okay, Here you go."

♡ Works for the wolves, big brother.

What's In a Name?

Most dog owners give their furry kids a few names beyond the proper one. We certainly did that with Musket. He was used to being addressed as "little buddy," as in "Okay, little buddy, forward."

Saffron's name evoked images and thoughts of the color yellow, of the aroma of fresh-baked bread and fragrant flowers. The most common name was "Saffy," an obvious diminutive of her name. This led to using semi-alliterative words like "Saffy Daffy." Jane added "Saffronalia," "Saffodil," "Buttercup" and "Sunshine," as in the song she often sang when they snuggled, "You are my Sunshine."

As with Lord Musket Carlson, PhDog, Saffron was soon known as Princess Saffron Carlson.

Musket liked being retired. In fact he loved it!

🐾 Why didn't I do this years ago? Daddy kept me working and missing out on all this sleeping and eating!

I had been sheltering a future monarch, like Miles Hendon in *The Prince and the Pauper.*

Lord Musket Carlson, PhDog received the ultimate peerage. He became Musket I, His Furry Majesty, who thought I was his personal servant. His Furry Majesty has taken to lying pretty much anywhere he liked. In doorways, in front of the kitchen sink, at the foot of the stairs, in short, he was like the Visa card. "He was EVERYWHERE I wanted to be!"

Walking through the house was like driving down a road where the speed bumps moved at random. Coming down the stairs had a whole new dimension when the last step was replaced by a big Labrador retriever.

I called it "Running the Doggauntlet."

One day Jane told me she had washed all the linen and bedding. This included the cover of Musket's bed. While it was all in the dryer, she saw Musket come upstairs. He went over to his bed and stopped cold. It was gone! He looked right at her and let out a distinct "Snort!"

🐾 So first you take my job away from me and now you've given away my bed?

Jane hustled to the dryer and pulled out the cover. She zipped it around the foam pillow and placed it on the floor. Musket watched her every move.

"There you go, Musket," Jane said, poofing the bed for him.

His Furry Majesty planted all four Royal Paws on the bed, laid down and gave her a loud, Regal "Harumph!"

I'd really like to continue on this subject, but I just heard His Furry Majesty ringing the bell cord.

"Coming, Your Furriness!"

Male, Female, or Other?

You may recall that Musket in his heyday was a very beautiful dog. He had a lovely, even pretty face with eyes most women would die for. When we were out and about, people often said "She's beautiful. What's her name?"

I always said, "*His* name is Musket."

🐕 I had some issues with that. Didn't anyone ever bend over to check out the plumbing?

The reason I bring this up is that with Saffron the reverse happened. "Hey, nice dog. What's his name?"

Beautiful Saffron just seemed to look male to the public. A male dog that looked female and a female that looked male. Weird, huh?

♡ I have some gender identification issues now. Maybe I need therapy. Or a treat.

On a sort of related note, I had been concerned about their relieving area. At our condo in Carmel Mountain we had a dirt area with bushes near the front door. Musket did his thing there and either I or Jane picked it up. With Saffron I was not certain if the same arrangement would work. Would the two dogs interfere with one another or would they feel inhibited? I was considering having a short wall put up and those blue signs with the words "Setter" and "Pointers."

♡ Boy, Musket was not kidding when he warned me about Daddy's sense of humor. There was no problem at all. Musket did his thing and I did mine. Case closed. But he did pee kind of weird, come to think of it.

As the months turned into a year, Musket's advanced age led to some new and unexpected problems. He really had difficulty getting up. Early on, I assumed his butt had just fallen asleep and he needed a little help. "Hey, Old Timer, Daddy will help you."

Then I'd help him stand and gave his butt and hind legs a brisk massage to get the circulation going again.

As it happened more and more, I realized he just didn't have the strength to stand on a slick wooden floor. He could do better on carpet. Those were the early signs that Musket was really having trouble as he got older.

One thing that always got him going was the promise of a treat. All I had to do was open the treat jar and Musket managed to rise to his feet and sauntered (no more scampering) over to get his treat. But occasionally he didn't notice the jar being opened. Or he might have been asleep upstairs and I brought one to him. A few times he gave me a real scare. I held the treat in front of his nose and...nothing happened. He didn't flinch or awaken. A tiny cold chill went through me and I knelt down to rub his face. "Hey, pal, you want a treat?"

Then his eyes opened.

🐕 Huh? Oh, thanks Daddy. Sorry, I guess I was sleeping like the dead.

Yeah, that's what worried me. It happened to Jane too, and she admitted it was a scary moment. I knew in my heart that sooner or later it would be for real. I only hoped it would happen in his sleep, when he was comfortable and happy.

🐕 Boy, this has taken a morbid turn, huh?

Teaching a New Dog Old Tricks

Let's talk about something else. Saffron adored her big brother. She liked to be close to him and snuggle. A few times we found them spooning on the big pillow in the living room, most often with Musket on the outside and Saffron tucked in against his belly.

"Aw, isn't that wonderful," Jane said. "She really loves him."

♡ Yeah, on cold days his belly is like a big soft heating pad.

When Musket was sound asleep and Saffron was close by, she often licked his face. Jane said it was so wonderful to watch her patiently licking him from nose to ears. "Saffron, you're taking care of your big brother?"

Musket didn't seem to mind. He laid there and pretended to sleep. But I think he secretly liked the attention.

🐾 Okay I admit it. It felt nice. And she worshipped me, so who was I to deride her adoration?

He sometimes kissed Saffron too, giving her a kiss on the face. I'd give a lot to have a photo of that to put in this book but sorry, no go.

Saffron and her big brother snuggling. Saffron always took the top.

I recently recalled one of the funnier things about Musket and Saffron. They both hogged the back seat of the car. While our Hyundai Santa Fe had plenty of room for both dogs, you could not prove it by them. On long or short trips, they each tried to get on top. When I felt behind me, I usually found Musket lying flat while Saffron was lying half on top of him. But he never griped.

♡ Yeah, he was pretty cool about it. Besides, he didn't have to wear a harness.

Tumbleweeds

All straight-haired dogs shed. No argument there. Over the years we got used to Musket's shedding. He'd shed in the late spring to early summer and again as winter set in. That was to be expected and Saffron was no different. But for some reason, the year 2013 was worth mentioning, if for no other reason than it was like the difference between drought and flood. Musket had a heavy coat and very thick skin. Hugging him was like hugging a Grizzly Bear but without the mauling. When summer approached, he began to shed his thick winter coat and grow in his light summer coat. Saffron did the same. So for a few weeks there was plenty of stray dog fur around the house; in the carpet, in corners, under the bed and furniture (FUR-niture, get it?) Sorry, and everywhere else. Then it would stop and life resumed its normal fur-free pace.

But that year Musket seemed to outdo himself. He was shedding his winter coat and growing in the summer fur, but the winter coat, like relatives that arrived for a weekend and stayed for months showed no signs of leaving. He kept shedding fur. Jane expressed shock at seeing big yellow tufts of fur rolling across the wooden floor in the breeze. I sang a song like Jack Palance in *City Slickers*."

"I'm a roaming blind guy stumbling all day long,
Fur tumbleweeds around me sing their lonely song.
See them tumbling down
Pledging their love to the ground

Lonely but free I'll be found
Stumbling along with the tumbling fur tumbleweeds..."

♡ I heard Musket tell me about Daddy's songs but I never believed him. Now I do.

🐕 I warned you, little sister.

For some reason Jane didn't seem to like my singing so I slunk off and started grooming him with the Furminator. At first it was about once a week. "He'll stop soon," I said, unconcerned. But he kept shedding copious amounts of blonde hair. So I groomed him twice, then three times a week. And even when I'd spent half an hour on him, I could still run my fingers through his coat and come away with a handful of fur. He had more hair than Robin Williams.

It was like he was importing fur from other dogs. We used up three—count 'em— THREE vacuum cleaner bags in one month. I even asked his vet, Dr. Grey if this was something to be concerned about.

She asked me if he was showing any bald or thinning spots.

"Nope," I replied. "Not a bit."

"Well," she said, "he'll stop eventually."

That was a big help. Jane used the Swiffer on the floors downstairs every day and still he blasted fur all over the house like shrapnel from a plush toy grenade.

I began checking the browsing history on my computer to see if Musket was importing fur. That might have explained the $1,100 charge for Peruvian Llama fur on my Visa. Okay that's a joke. But we never figured it out.

Saffron, whose own coat was much thinner than his, went through her shedding period in less time. About ten minutes. But she did learn from him. In time her own shedding cycle grew longer and longer. "Hello, Wal-Mart? Can you send me another case of Hoover vacuum cleaner bags?"

Fast and S-L-O-W

Their personalities were different, he was mellow and malleable while she was energetic and headstrong.

But one day something happened that made me think that I had to get used to a new way of things. When I let Musket outside to do his business at night, I stayed by the open door until he came back in. sometimes he slipped past me without me noticing. After a minute he nudged my hand with his nose to let me know he was there. "Oh, there you are, little buddy. Okay, let's go upstairs."

Musket knew I could not see him and touched me so I'd know he was there.

But with Saffron, it was a different matter. Being smaller and much quicker, she was able to zip past without me noticing. But then she just stood there. Even when I called for her, "Come on, Saffy." She never let on that she was right there next to me. I'd have to bend over and feel around until I found her.

In short, she did not understand the need to alert me. My Guide Dog didn't know I was blind. How's that for irony?

Saffron could make a greyhound insecure. And if I had the front door open for even a second...Zip! And of course I didn't notice, and closed the door.

One day I was working in my office and the phone rang. "Hello?"

"Is this Mark Carlson?"

"Yes, it is."

"This is the AVID (What is AVID?) call center. Do you know where your Guide Dog Saffron is?"

For just a second I remembered that old public service announcement, "Do you know where your children are?"

"Uh, sure, she's upstairs with my wife," I said, suddenly not sure.

"Well we received a call from someone who says they have your dog."

"What?" Then thoughts of dognapping, ransom and the FBI Hostage Rescue Team entered my mind. "What do you mean? Who called you?"

"I can have her call you."

"Okay please. I'll look for my dog. She's got to be in the house."

Then I ran into the kitchen and to the stairs, calling for Saffron.

Jane poked her head over the railing "What is it, Honey?"

"Have you seen Saffron?"

"No, I haven't seen her in a long time. Are you sure she's in the house?"

"Well I just got a call from AVID. They said someone called and they have Saffron. They called AVID and AVID called me."

"What?"

"That's what I said." Then the phone in my hand rang. "Hello?"

"Mr. Carlson, I have the number of the person who called."

"Okay, what is it?"

They gave me a number in the 619 Area Code. "619? That's way down in the city! How in hell did she get down there?" I was thinking that Saffron had just started to run, and with an hour or so, she could be in downtown San Diego by now.

I asked Jane to call the number while I went outside to call for Saffron. We weren't in a panic, but close to it.

A minute later Jane said, "She's at 11973, number 4, Honey."

A light went on in my head. "That's Crystal and Jameson's house."

Then we started to laugh. Our neighbors Crystal and Jameson Rienick were out of town and his mother was watching their place.

"Saffron went over to see Pickle!" I laughed. "Okay I'll go get her."

Pickle was their Chihuahua, and Saffron was crazy about him. They had a little thing going. I supposed that Saffron had been left outside and went over there, and Jameson's mom saw her at the screen door. Not knowing Saffron yet, she checked her collar and found the AVID tag and called the number. I wish she'd just called us, since Saffron had two tags with our names and number.

♡ Hi Daddy! I was wondering when you were going to notice I was gone.

I thanked Mrs. Rienick and Saffron followed me home. All the while I was thinking, This kid is going to be a handful.

From that point on, I was very careful to keep her at bay when the door was open. I bought her a small bell to wear around her neck so I could hear if she tried to run past me. Eventually she learned to stay put and didn't run out the door.

Only occasionally she got left outside but obediently remained at the door until someone noticed and let her in.

But just so you know that for every systole there is a diastole. When she wanted to be lazy, Saffron could pose for statues. One day I was making the bed with fresh linen. Saffron was lying asleep on the mattress. I told her to move but she snored on, oblivious. So I pulled the fitted sheet over her and began to fit the corners. Then Jane came in and, fully understanding what I was doing, said, "Where's my Saffron?"

The lump under the sheet stirred. "Saffron?" Jane asked again. Nothing.

I lifted one edge of the sheet and said, "Saffron? Mommy wants you."

But she merely shifted and went right on sleeping.

I reckon I could have put on the upper sheet, blanket and bedspread without her making the slightest effort to move. At last I took up one corner and said, "Saffron! Off the bed!"

She actually grumbled as if I was making the most unreasonable request in the world. She condescended to comply, but very slowly. Then she slid out and jumped to the floor.

I thought Musket had a patent on lazy slowness, but apparently Saffron pays him royalties.

Musket's fame continued, and sometimes it came out of nowhere. I received an e-mail from the *Chicken Soup for the Soul* book publishers. Seems a story I'd sent in about Musket and Jane's dad was chosen to be in the next book, called *The Dog Did What?* I was astonished, since I'd sent that story to them three years before and never heard from them. I assumed they didn't want it. The book was released in August 2014. I received a nice check and ten copies. And without so much as lifting a paw, Musket scored another P.R. bullseye.

🐾 Well, what would you expect? Even Sean Connery, as old as he was, still had sex appeal.

♡ Yeah, but he didn't poop on the sidewalk. At least I don't think so.

Mommy's Little Girl

It didn't take long for Saffron to work her way into Jane's heart. There was always plenty of room, and Musket didn't lose his "most favored baby" status. When Jane said "Saffron, Mommy loves you," she always added "Musket, you're still Mommy's baby."

🐕 I don't mind admitting I was jealous for a while. Saffron seemed to want to take all of Mommy's attention and love. But Mommy showed me she still loved me just as much as ever.

Musket had been a gift from Jane's brother Darcy. But we soon realized that Saffron had also been a gift from Heaven. Jane's mother had died four days before Saffron was born. Jane truly believed that Mom had given Saffron to us, and as time went by, I felt the same way. Saffron had just as much love and spirit as Musket, whom Mom had loved so much. And I think Mom knew that someday Musket would be coming up to Heaven to be with her and Pop-pop, so she sent Saffron to carry the torch.

"Nanny and Pop-pop would have loved you, Saffron," Jane often said.

♡ I never knew them but if Mommy said so, it must be true.

As the year 2013 waned and the holidays came closer, we began to decorate the house. When I say "we," I mean that Jane supervised and I did the work. Stop grinning, ladies.

I got the ladder, climbed up into the attic, brought down the tree, wreath, and the sixteen boxes and cases of decorations, hauled them downstairs to the living room, set up the tree, untangled the lights and garlands, then waited for Jane to say "Honey, I think we should try a minimalist theme this year. Take all those boxes and the tree back up. We'll just do lights and a wreath."

Stop laughing! The life of a hubby.

♡ Oh, stop complaining, Daddy. You needed the exercise.

Tell me females don't stick together.

Saffron and Musket's Christmas photo, 2013nb

CHAPTER 5

IN PRAISE OF THE RESCUERS

"If you pick up a starving dog and make him prosperous he will not
bite you. This is the principal difference between a dog and man."
— Mark Twain

I started writing for a local magazine called *San
Diego Pets* in 2012. The owner and editor, Casey Dean, who was a
wonderful and enthusiastic dog lover, and I worked out a deal where
I would write a monthly column called "The Tale Wagging the Dog."
I originally wanted it to be called "Tales from the Barkside" but that
was taken. The deal was I'd write the stories and Casey put an ad for
Confessions in every issue. Worked out nicely. And of course I wrote
a lot about Musket, using excerpts from the book and some original
stories. When Saffron came along, she too became the subject of my
column. It was very popular. I also wrote some serious articles about
pet shelters and service dogs for veterans.

Dogs, for those of us who love them, are truly wonderful. They're
furry miracles, angels on four paws and the closest thing to unconditional
love anyone can find on Earth.

That being said, there are plenty of them around. In fact, even
though this sounds contrary to what I just said, there are too many. If
you want proof, just go to any county animal shelter and walk among
the cages. If you can pass by those big brown eyes pleading with you to

give him a home without any emotional reaction, I suggest you go find the nearest funeral parlor and check in. Your heart has stopped.

Every shelter has dozens of unwanted and abandoned dogs, cats and other animals. Some never had a home, while others were left behind by callous owners who didn't know what to do with them. Still more were abused and taken away by compassionate neighbors or the ASPCA. I applaud the remarkable love and selfless effort the staff at shelters all over the country put into caring for these helpless and lonely animals. Caught in a world they cannot understand, where cars honk at them and they have to dig in garbage to eat, an abandoned dog or cat has little chance to survive.

Fortunately there are many wonderful and generous rescue organizations to help. Thousands of good, healthy dogs and cats who want only a home and someone to love them are rescued and cared for. To all those who work with rescues and have found homes for our furry friends, thank you for what you do.

♡ Sniff. I wish I could have them all here with us. Poor things.

🐕 I feel the same way, little sister. But read on, Daddy will make you smile.

Plenty of people want dogs or cats with a pedigree or are "show quality." They would never consider going to a shelter to find a loving and devoted pet that will give years of joy and comfort to a home. They only want papers that show their pet is special and expensive. Too bad. I want to tell you two stories about friends of ours who have found something priceless on four paws, and they did it not for bragging rights, but because they cared.

Saffron, like Musket before her has melted some hearts. With her at my side I've made friends. One of these was Alan Cutsinger, who I met at the Gillespie Field Air Show in 2011. In addition to being just as plane crazy as me, Alan was also a true dog lover. He fell in love with Saffron on their first meeting, and for a time I was actually concerned he was considering dognapping her. Seriously though, he'd never do that but I always had to make sure I came home with the same dog I started out with.

♡ Alan's my big boyfriend! He's so wonderful and handsome and just loves me! He had three dogs at his home, all rescues. And how he and his wife Kate got one of them is a wonderful story.

Yeah, I don't just write whimsical anecdotes about my crazy Guide Dogs. Sometimes I find a story that touches my heart. So I'm passing it on to you animal lovers.

Alan and Kate hadn't planned on changing a dog's life, but that's exactly what happened. Alan tells the story.

"In October 2009 Kate and I were headed up to the desert for our monthly dirt bike weekend," said Alan, who is retired from the San Diego Sherriff's Department. "Kate, her son Ben and I had our camper and the bikes hitched to my truck. But on that long grade up Cajon Pass on the way to Victorville, my truck started having some trouble and I pulled into a gas station. It was late, so the mechanic wouldn't be able to work on it until Saturday morning."

They learned of a nearby trailer park where they could spend the night. "We set up the camper."

While there, they saw a medium-sized female dog running around and visiting all the other campers in the park. Although the dog was friendly, she would not enter anyone's camper or tent. "She had the most beautiful expressive brown eyes," said Kate.

"We thought she belonged to the folks next door," said Alan. "I complemented them on their nice dog, but they said she was a stray. She was almost feral, thin, but not starving."

Alan saw that their own dog, a large mixed breed named Paddington got along with the stray, and asked the trailer park manager about her. "He said her name was Brownie and she sort of belonged to everybody who came to the park. He told me about a family with a little girl who stayed there for a few days. The girl had fallen in love with Brownie. But when they moved on, Brownie spent hours every day afterwards waiting for her little friend to come back. But she never did."

Kate's heart melted when she heard this. "It was obvious she wanted a family so badly. The manager suggested we take Brownie with us. But since we were not going directly home after the truck had been repaired, we would stop by on the way back."

Alan, Kate and Ben drove off on Saturday and continued their vacation. But Kate's mind was on Brownie. "All that day and Sunday I prayed Brownie would be there when we came back. I really wanted to bring this sweet dog home with us."

On Sunday afternoon Alan pulled back into the trailer park driveway. "We got out and looked for Brownie, but she was nowhere to be seen. We asked if anyone had seen her, but no one had."

"My heart was sinking," Kate said.

Then, just as they had given up, Brownie came trotting around a corner and saw them. "She was very happy to see us again," said Alan. "I scooped her up and put her in the truck. Then we drove home."

Arriving at their home in North County, they brought the excited dog into the house. "I took her into the shower and got to work," Alan continued. "It took half a bottle of shampoo before the water started coming out clean."

Brownie had spent her life sleeping on the dirt or under trailers in the winter. But now she had her own bed in Alan and Kate's room. "That first night she whimpered and cried. I sat down and comforted her."

Brownie had been living off food scraps and handouts for who knew how long. She soon learned she could expect two healthy meals a day. "For the first few days, when I put the food before her, she wolfed it down like she didn't expect to be fed again."

Their house, which had two stories, proved to have an obstacle Brownie had never encountered before. "She didn't know how to climb stairs," Alan laughed. "We had to teach her."

Kate fell in love with Brownie, calling her Angel and Sugar.

Alan made an appointment with their veterinarian to give their new dog a complete health exam. "On Thursday I put her in the truck and drove to my vet. All the way there Brownie was leaning against me and trembling. She was pretty upset. I talked to her but it was obvious she must have thought her new dream was coming to an end."

The vet examined Brownie and pronounced her healthy but undernourished. "She was completely cooperative. He gave her all her shots, and chipped her. She'd already been spayed. Then I took her back out to the truck."

Brownie jumped in and Alan drove back to the house. When he called her down from the truck she looked around and saw where she was. "Brownie just took off, yanking the leash from my hand and ran to the front gate. She couldn't get it open, so I did it for her. Then she ran to the front door and scratched at it until I opened it. She tore through the house, sniffing and wagging her tail like crazy."

The dog whose life once consisted of hard concrete and old food now had a real home and good care. Brownie had been abandoned many times, but now had a loving family. "She is just the sweetest and most loyal dog we have ever had," Alan said with a smile. Kate said, "All our three dogs are rescues, but Brownie is the one we feel the best about bringing home. When we go to bed, the first thing Brownie does is jump on the bed to make sure we're all tucked in for the night, and then goes to her own bed. I think she still needs to know her family is still there."

Linda Stull, who is as crazy about dogs as she is about airplanes, was often asked to dog-sit for the furry trio. She truly loved them and they loved her. Big, gentle Paddington passed away in 2019. We'll miss him.

Some readers may remember the old 1970s phrase "If you love something set it free; if it comes back it's yours, if not it was never yours to begin with."

Sometimes without any forethought or planning on our part, things have a way of working out for the better. And all it takes is to do the right thing.

This story is about a neighbor of ours, Crystal Rienick, a high school literature teacher who works in Valley Center. Crystal and her husband

Jameson have a perky, active 8-year old Miniature Pinscher named Pippin. Crystal, a lovely, ebullient and free-spirited woman who loves all animals considered getting a second dog as a companion for Pippin.

About two weeks before Christmas, she was driving home from work, passing through Escondido, when she saw a Chihuahua running loose on the street. Being a dog lover, she acted immediately to rescue the frightened dog.

"So, of course," she said, "I flipped a U-turn and spent fifteen minutes trying to coax him over to grab him. He had no tags, and when I took him to our vet, they found no chip. I took him home and he immediately began to sniff and pee on everything I owned. I could overlook this, however, due to the amazing fact that he and Pippin hit it off instantly."

Crystal brought the Chihuahua over to meet us, that is, Jane, myself, Musket and Saffron. She said in a grave voice, "We have a problem." She put the dog in my hands. "Okay," I replied, knowing of Crystal's sense of humor, "but what's this 'we' stuff?"

She explained about finding the dog on the street and intended to try and find its owner, but it was obvious she was already smitten with the little canine.

For the next few days, while on Christmas break she fell under the new dog's charm. "I posted 'Found Chihuahua' signs the next morning in the area where I'd found him, but when I heard nothing after two days I decided to take him to the Escondido Humane Society. If I didn't take him right away I was going to keep him forever. I had already fallen in love with him and had named him Pickle. I learned I could pay the adoption fee up front and if the owners didn't claim him, he would be ours. I would have him neutered, micro chipped and vaccinated."

Then fate intervened. "Pickle was with me on the way to the shelter. As I was crossing Citrus Avenue my phone rang. It was a little girl who said she saw my signs and believed I had her dog, whose name was Spikey." The girl described him in perfect detail. When Crystal said the name Spikey he responded and she felt a little chill in her heart. "'Where do you live?' I asked her. 'Citrus Avenue,' she told me."

Almost within sight of the shelter, Crystal turned around and drove to Citrus where she found Spikey's owner waiting with open arms. The little dog was ecstatic to see her.

"She thanked me and I made my retreat before the tears started."

That might have been the end of it, but Crystal had been bitten hard by the little dog's tiny beating heart. "I began my quest for a second dog. Pippin and Pickle had gotten along so well. He was so damned snuggly and affectionate. I wanted that, too. I began obsessing on Petfinder and the local shelter sites until I knew all the dogs by sight. I gravitated to Min Pins and Chihuahua mixes, trying to recreate the compatibility with Pippin combined with the snuggliness for me."

Christmas was approaching and she knew time was short. Once she and Jameson were back at work acclimating a new dog to the house would be almost impossible. She wanted to be home to help smooth the way.

Three possible dogs were at that same Escondido Humane Society shelter. "On Christmas Eve I broke out my laptop to show my family the pictures."

Not one to leave any stone unturned, she scrolled down the page to see if there had been any postings since she'd last looked.

"And what to my wandering eye did appear, than Pickle himself! It was him, I knew it instantly. Same markings, same colors. The shelter was closed on Christmas Day so I had to wait until the 26th."

Unable to sleep, Crystal hoped the little Chihuahua would still be there when the shelter re-opened.

"We packed up Pippin and off we went. The place was packed, and as we waited we told our story to other hopeful pet adopters. People were supportive for us. Finally we went out to the interaction yard. And there he was. It was my Pickle, without a doubt! He knew me right away. The shelter staff told me he had been left there just three days after I had returned him to his family." That was it. Pickle was going to have a new home.

It didn't take long for the new pooch to feel at home. Crystal told me a few days later, "He has peed twenty-three times, only once in the house, eaten too much, and has been sleeping wrapped in blankets on my lap for hours."

The happy Chihuahua Pickle, home at last
Photo courtesy Crystal Rienick

Crystal did the right thing and the miracle came back home to live with her.

Those are only two of countless other stories about people who gave and received love from a dog that had no papers, no pedigree, had never been on the Westminster Dog Show, or even had much of a chance to survive.

Yet now Pickle and Brownie are both happy. They have homes and families that love them. That love is returned a thousand fold.

I urge my readers and their friends to do the same. If you want a dog or cat, find a rescue or shelter. Look not with your eyes, but with your heart and feelings. Somewhere there is a heart that is beating in the same rhythm as yours. You will know it when it happens.

Give a heart a home and give your home a heart.
That's all. Thanks for listening.

CHAPTER 6

THEY'RE JUST MAD ABOUT SAFFRON

"The reason a dog has so many friends is that
he wags his tail instead of his tongue."
— Anonymous

In Musket's book I had a chapter called
"Musketmaniacs." And some of them are now Saffronalians. Sorry but
that was the best name I could come up with. In any case, Saffron did
inherit some of Musket's friends and fans. Here you will meet some of
them. they run the gamut of retired police officers, teachers, nurses,
bank vice-presidents, former Department of Defense contractors,
business executives, and of course, veterans. Here are just a few of the
ones whose stories really stand out.

The staff at OASIS in Mission Valley where I started doing lectures
in 2009 were the nicest and most enthusiastic fans of my work. I did
about one or two presentations a month there. Even after Musket retired
and technically did not have the same access to public places, they
still insisted that we bring him along. Since we did not like to leave
him alone for very long, we did. Led by Saffron, I went up to the
stage, while behind me was Jane with the plodding Musket. Sarah
Cushman, Roxanne Prine, Brandon Harding, and the other people at
OASIS welcomed us as if we were special. But I knew it was the dogs
that really made the difference.

♡ The first time I went with Daddy he brought me to the ramp at the side of the stage. But it was very slick, and I could not get any traction on it. I kept slipping until Daddy realized what was happening and gave me a little help. Now I think back, it was kind of funny, but very disconcerting. They eventually put some non-skid strips on it for me.

While I set up my laptop and plugged in the projector, they got water for the dogs (and me, sometimes) and made sure everything I needed was covered.

As the audience started filing in, many of whom were regulars and fans of Musket and Saffron, they came over to say hello. During my talk, which usually lasted from one to two hours, the dogs slept on the floor behind me. When the Q/A session started, I often got questions about the dogs. One woman, who was so fond of Musket, gave me a donation to send to GDB in his name.

One of the women we met through OASIS was Lois Novitz, who was the events coordinator for the local City of Hope. She had seen me talk at one of the OASIS lectures. She got my number and one day left a message for me. Now bear in mind that Lois was then in her eighties, widowed and the image of the sweet but slightly crotchety little old lady. "I want you," the voice said on the phone. "I want you and I will have you. I can't stop thinking about you."

"Huh?" what was this all about? No name, no return number, nothing. I played the message for Jane, who said, "It's just another of your little old lady groupies." She laughed and walked away.

It turned out she was right.

Lois was determined to have me speak for city of Hope. And so I did. She really made us feel like celebrities. Jane joined the club and soon was involved in raising money and planning events.

♡ What can I say about Miss Lois? Crazy, sweet,..,

and totally in love with my Daddy. She called him "my love" or something like that. But Mommy always said "He's yours if you want him."

One of my regular venues was Cypress Court, a retirement community in Escondido. One day after I did my talk, this nice couple came and introduced themselves as Anita and John Campbell. John had worked for the navy as a contractor while Anita was involved with foreign exchange students. They were big fans of my lectures and sort of adopted Jane and me. For the next few years we all met for dinner, holidays and social events. They loved Jane and my dogs, but as it turned out, were crazy about me! The sweetest and most generous of people, they were always offering to help if we ever needed it. As it turned out, we did. They often drove me to my lectures, no matter how far away it was.

On one early visit to their home, while Musket was still alive, they introduced us to their two tortoises. Musket just stared at the two reptiles, which were about the size of dinner plates, but Saffron did not know what to make of them. She kept trying to get one of the tortoises to poke his head out and she stuck her nose in the shell. You can guess what happened. She did not try that again!

♡ I did not expect that thing to bite! Nipped me right on the nose! How mean can you get?

The Campbells had two small dogs, Bailey and Bradley. I had a standing request that pet owners should pick up any food dishes so Saffron could not get at them. One day saffron ran in and found the food still in bowls. Before I could do anything she had wolfed down both bowls. Just like that!

And then she threw up. On the carpet. In the hallway. On the front walk, where I was trying to get her outside. I swear she only ate about two cups of food but she ralphed up at least three quarts, or so it seemed. It was very embarrassing. Jane was mortified. I was very angry.

Saffron was a nice shade of green.

But John and Anita brushed it off and wiped up the mess. I never let that happen again.

The Campbells were so kind and generous. In March of 2017 our Hyundai Santa Fe van (or was it an SUV? I get them mixed up) broke down with an engine fire. On the I-15 North freeway in the rain. The car was a dead loss. We did not have a prayer of buying a new car at that time.

Yet then the Campbells were coming. They bought us a used Hyundai Sonata sedan. Just like that with no strings attached, our adopted parents bought us a car. It was the most wonderful gesture of friendship I have ever known in my life.

John and Anita are now living in a retirement home and since Covid has cut us off, rarely get to see us. But we talk often. I cherish their friendship and am forever grateful for their generosity and forgiveness for my puking pup.

♡ Okay, let me get my side of the story in. They had been warned not to leave food on the floor. They were asking for it. If their dogs can't finish the food, then it is fair game. Survival of the fastest. The puking was a bit gross, but it was probably just something I ate.

Uh-huh. Let's move on. As a board member of the Distinguished Flying Cross Society, Linda often invited me to some events, including parades. Riding in one of the orange Old Town Trolleys, the veterans waved at the spectators at the Fourth of July and Veteran's Day Parade. Even though I was not a veteran, I was often invited by the DFCS chapter. This was a great honor for me to be with my friends and our nation's heroes. Some rode in open convertibles or restored Jeeps. Saffron, of course was happy to see all her fans.

Saffron in the 2014 Veterans Day Parade

♡ Daddy tied an American flag scarf around my neck. I wish I could have waved but all I could do was pant. While Daddy waved a flag, I waved my tongue.

We met a lot of new people at the parades but the most memorable was at Coronado for the Veterans' Day Parade when Linda spotted a man wearing a *USS John Finn* ball cap. It was the standard navy blue with gold lettering and the ship's number, DDG-113. She almost jumped the poor guy, asking where he had gotten the cap. Since she and I had known John, it was very important. It turned out the cap had been bought from a man named Barry Stemler, who ran a small online business called "Ordie-Mart." Ordies are the Navy's Aviation ordnancemen, who handle and load weapons on fighters and bombers. John Finn had been an Aviation chief Ordnanceman of Patrol Squadron 14 at Kaneohe Bay on Oahu when the Japanese attacked. The Navy named a new frigate after John. So Linda, in the manner she is best known for, found Barry Stemler. A retired navy chief, he lived, of all places, about ten minutes from my house in Carmel Mountain Ranch! Talk about a small world.

That was the start of a wonderful friendship. Barry was an avid fan of the Pearl Harbor Survivors and often came to some of the events. Of course I got one of the hats.

As time went on, Barry became fascinated with my writing. An easygoing and kind man, Barry read all my articles and became my second biggest fan. He helped me a lot on my book about VMF-422. When the book was published, I gave him one of the first signed copies.

Now, as to his relationship with Saffron, once I realized that Barry was not strictly speaking a "dog lover," I tried to keep Saffron from doing her usual "I am adorable and you *will* adore me!" bit.

Barry was glad to take me to some of my speaking gigs in his big, immaculate King Cab truck. But I did my best to keep Saffron from shedding all over the pristine black upholstery. She shed like mad in there. But Barry never complained. He was my friend and knew that Saffron was an important part of my life.

♡ Barry was always very nice and respectful to me, even though I could tell he didn't really like dogs. But I was working on him. Sooner or later, Barry, you will succumb...

Old Planes

We spent time with the Commemorative (formerly Confederate in the pre-P.C. era) Air Force, a nationwide organization that collects, restores and flies vintage military aircraft. In a way they are the worlds' largest privately owned air force. Air Group One was the San Diego chapter. We had a lot of fun with them at local air shows. Musket was always there and welcomed by the pilots and members. If I got a ride in a B-17, B-24, B-25, C-53, SNJ, ford Tri-motor, or some other antique aircraft, Musket stayed on the ground.

When Saffron came along, she took center stage. And like her older brother, she remained on *Terra Firma* while her looney daddy went for a ride in an airplane that was old enough to qualify for Social Security.

♡ My Daddy is wonderful but totally nuts. How can he want to fly in a plane that does not serve meals? But he seemed to enjoy them. Linda kept me company while I wondered about Daddy's life insurance.

Two people we met through the CAF were Vicki Moen and Mike Dralle. Vicki's dad was a photographer in B-24s in the Pacific. Mike worked for General Atomics on the Predator UAV program. We found a lot of mutual interests and often went to events and air shows together. One recurring event was the re-enactment of the 1942 Great Los Angeles Air Raid. Held at Fort MacArthur near San Pedro, the annual event re-created the night Los Angeles thought it was being attacked by Japanese aircraft. With the guns and cannon firing, and white bursts of simulated anti-aircraft strobing over the city, it was not a place for a Guide Dog. I wore an army officer's uniform. It was kind of funny, if you think about it, a United States Army Air Corps officer with a white cane.

Musket stayed home for those events. Mike was a collector of military and Disney memorabilia, in which I also found an avid interest. We could rant on and on about *war movies, airplanes, battleships, Mel Brooks, Twilight Zone, Star Trek, Disney* and a bunch of other useless pop-culture Americana.

What really set them apart from other people was how considerate and helpful they are. Mike was like a big brother to me and Vicki was one of the sweetest and kindest people I ever knew.

♡ I liked them both very much. And Mike was the neatest guy to hang out with. He and daddy were just like big kids.

Jane and I banked at a credit union in Carmel Mountain Ranch and later, in San Marcos. The branch manager and later vice president, Molly Tosh, adopted Musket early on, and we never passed her office on a visit to the bank without stopping in to say hello. In fact, Musket refused to head to the tellers until he had poked his big head into Molly's office. She was a big fan of my writing and bought all my books.

Well, when Saffron came along Molly welcomed her too. A lovely and compassionate lady, Molly was the epitome of customer service.

She took very good care of the credit union's members, Jane and I being no exception.

♡ Good golly Miss Molly! Sorry, I had to do it. She was so sweet and always made me feel special. I am glad she handles Daddy's money. He needs a keeper.

Jane and I had been looking for a new church since First Presbyterian in downtown San Diego was too far to go. We first tried a Rancho Bernardo church, which was considered the nicest and (to the congregation) most prestigious church in the area. We had gone there on occasion for various events and concerts, but when we started attending Sunday worship services, an odd thing happened. As you know, Musket was a major magnet. He drew people toward us and made friends easily. After one Sunday service, the congregation milled around the patio, drinking coffee and chatting. It was a nice way to relax and get to know one another. Jane went to use the restroom while Musket and I enjoyed the warm late-morning sunshine. From what I could hear, there were at least fifty people around us. And not one came over to say hello. They acted, and I admit this is only my personal impression, as if we were not even there. I actually felt like a leper. "Unclean, beware, unclean." All this chatting and laughing but we were invisible. Ironic, huh?

Jane rejoined us and we wandered around, looking for an opportunity to meet someone.

🐕 Nope. Daddy is right. It was really strange. I had all my charm turned on full blast, but they passed us as if I had poop in my fur.

After an hour we left, and Jane said she felt that those people were very cliquish. I agreed. Musket didn't even garner a "What a nice dog" from anyone. We tried a few more times with the same result.

So that was it for that church. We were pretty discouraged.

But then I remembered going to the funeral of a veteran friend at Hope United Methodist Church in Rancho Bernardo. I told Jane it was very nice, not too large and did not seem to go for the huge Jumbo-Tron and mega-speakers multi-media sound and light show that many of the modern churches used.

One Sunday in early 2016 we went there. Saffron was now our Ambassadog. Just as we stepped from the parking lot onto the courtyard we were welcomed with handshakes and warm greetings. It wasn't a mob, but several individuals and small knots of people wanted to meet us. What a difference. Saffron was in her element and even before we reached the Sanctuary we had met at least fifty people who were genuinely happy to see us there.

They made us feel like part of a big family, exactly what we were looking for.

Every Sunday was the same and we made many new friends. The three Carlsons joined the Hope UMC flock. I will write more about these people, many of whom I consider Earthbound Angels, in a later chapter.

♡ They were so nice! Once a month they had tables out for some groups to recruit people to join. Mommy joined a women's Bible study, and Daddy joined a men's group called The Thursday Knights.

I felt very happy there. The Thursday Knights were my buddies and spiritual supporters. I grew closer to God, but still did not see His hand guiding me. I thought that if God had a plan for me, He would make it known. In other words, I was waiting for the light to come on.

♡ When we went to services, we sat in the same pew, right side of the main aisle, second from the back. Daddy slid in first with me, then Mommy sat at the end. I lay down and went to sleep. Until the "Passing the Peace," as they called it. Then everybody stood and shook hands and said, "Peace be with you." That was when I got involved. People wanted to meet me and I stood with my front paws on the seat so I could say hello. We made more new friends that way.

But here is the funny part. Once a month at Communion we went down the main aisle to the front, where our Pastor, a very kind and funny man named Brian Kent waited. Mommy got her bread and grape juice and then Daddy opened his mouth to get his from Mommy. But did I get any? Nope! A few times I puzzled over this, and Daddy always gave me a bit of kibble when we returned to the pew. But then I wised up. At next Communion I started checking out the floor. And there it was! Some people had dropped their bread. I took care of that!

Pastor Brian saw what Saffron was doing, and after Communion was over said, "Well, Saffron is performing a valuable service to the church. She is now the Ecumenical Vacuum." That earned a lot of laughs and applause. We had found a home.

While working on this book I learned of a curious coincidence regarding our pastor. Mike and Cheri O'Neill, Saffron's puppy raisers, attended First United Methodist Church in Chula Vista. Brian Kent was the Associate Pastor. He had known the family who raise the Ecumenical Vacuum. What a small world.

I will end this chapter with a very special lady, Samantha "Sammie" Shipman.

A sweet and very devout Christian who has been blind since birth from Retinopathy of Prematurity (ROP) and later, Glaucoma, Sammie has a black Labrador named Mozart, or Mozie. She called me after being inspired by Musket's book. We shared stories and experiences.

In 2013 she came down by train from Los Angeles to attend the CSUN Assistive Technology Expo at the Convention Center. It was interesting to meet and talk while Mozart and Saffron got to know one another. She needed a guide to help her find her way from the Santa Fe depot to the center. I did not do a great job guiding her. In fact I almost got her run over by a trolley. Fortunately she forgave me.

♡ Of course she did. Mozie and I were the ones who kept you alive.

Sammie and Mozart

Sammie has always had an ambition to work in a field where she could help people and has been going to college for her degree in Psychology and Mental Health Counseling. Despite never having had any sight, Sammie has a beautiful view of the world. You can find her original song "You Save Me," on the Sound Cloud at:

https://soundcloud.com/ssmusick/you-save-me

Being much younger than me, she has a lot to give the world. I am honored to be her friend.

To paraphrase Samuel Morse, "What hath Dog wrought?"

CHAPTER 7

OUT AND ABOUT, BLIND-STYLE

"Dogs have given us their absolute all. We are the center
of their universe. We are the focus of their love and
faith and trust. They serve us in return for scraps. It is
without a doubt the best deal man has ever made."
— Roger Caras

This chapter will try to address some of the
questions readers of *Confessions* asked me and ones I did not cover in
the original book. To start with, let's outline what a Guide Dog actually
does. For those of you who read the previous book, just jump ahead a
couple of paragraphs. This is old stuff to you.

Put simply, a Guide or Seeing Eye Dog's job is to be the eyes of
their owner/handler. They are trained to see and react to anything that
might be a danger or obstacle to the team, such as moving cars, open
manholes, staircases, closed doors and so on. It's the handler's job to
know the route and where they are going. It's the dog's job to get them
there safely by either stopping at or moving around a barrier. They are
also trained to go up and down stairs, find and use elevators, find doors
or exits, follow a sighted guide, stop at curbs, use crosswalks, ride on
buses, trains and airlines and many other duties.

♡ Boy, I am impressed! Maybe I should ask for a raise. No, seriously,
we were all trained to do the same basic things, but as we got more

experience, we learned a lot of new stuff. I was really good in the city but not so good on open land and big lots where I got confused.

If they encounter an unusual situation that the dog is not specifically trained to handle, it is up to the handler to assess the matter, identify the obstacle and decide how to get past it safely.

For instance, if a team is walking along a sidewalk past some houses and the dog sees a parked car blocking the sidewalk, it is trained to stop. The handler then reaches out to identify the obstruction. Then, after listening to the traffic, they make a hard turn to go past the car's bumper, and immediately begin saying "Left, left, left," in order to keep the dog following the contour of the bumper until they are past it and back on the sidewalk. Then after they are back on the route, "Forward" puts them on their way. This is how a team works together to get to and from their destination. What I call the "Three T's" of Training, Trust and Teamwork.

♡ You forgot Treats.

No, I did not, Saffron. Try to keep focused. Together these elements help the team to deal with many unexpected hazards and situations. But not all.

Hearing Too Well

Since they do play a role in this and future chapters, let me tell you about my hearing aids. With my hearing growing worse, by 2014 it was necessary to get new and stronger ones. Unlike the devices I have been wearing for nearly half a century, these did not have the vinyl tubing to the earpiece, but wires that led to a tiny speaker in the earpiece. They were programmable and synchronize, meaning each one received the sound picked up by the others. The left one received and equalized what the right one picked up and vice versa. That feature turned out to be bad for me. I very much depended on my hearing, especially when crossing the street. The first day Saffron and I went on errands with the new aids

I was confronted with too much traffic noise. Not in volume but from all directions at once. It was like being in the "sweet spot" at a concert. I could not tell whether a car was on my left or right since both hearing aids equalized the sound. It scared the heck out of me. I went back home and called my audiologist.

♡ I remember that day. We were doing fine until we got to the first lighted intersection. Then Daddy stopped at the corner and waited. And waited. He kept turning his head back and forth like he was lost. When he was about to step off, I stopped him. There was a car coming he had not heard.

Margie Houston at the House of Hearing in Escondido took my concerns to heart. "I never thought of that before," she said. "Having the aids connected is fine if you can see."

"Right," I said. "but it makes me even more blind."

Long story short, she disconnected the automatic synchronization. I wrote to the American Council for the Blind and the Helen Keller National Center to alert them to this potential risk to deaf-blind people. I hope it helped. It was a good example of two-edged technology. Like electric cars. Good for the environment, but dangerous to blind people who can't hear them.

♡ It got better after that. Daddy heard the cars and I guided him. My hearing is very good, but there was no way I could tell him from what direction a car was coming. Thank you, Margie.

In *Confessions* I wrote about some of the bozos Musket and I encountered in our travels. In fact, it was one of the most asked-about chapters. I also told stories about the good people, but sometimes it just seemed to me that while the amount of intelligence in the world is a finite, fixed quantity, the population continues to increase. The Millennials are a good example.

♡ You can say that again, Daddy.

They're out there, lurking, waiting to strike. The species known as the Common American twit.

I'll use my favorite example from Musket's book. This really happened. In a line at Costco a man turned to me and said, "So, what's this? You're supposed to be blind or something?" His tone was as if I were wearing a Halloween costume he didn't quite understand.

I shrugged. "No, I'm not supposed to be but it seemed like a good idea. I really enjoy taking advantage of all the wonderful opportunities and chances for advancement I can get from being disabled."

I don't think he got it. A woman behind us was laughing. She got it just fine.

Anyone with a visible disability has had to deal with them. I'm not going to pretend speaking for all persons with disabilities but enough of my fellows have expressed the same opinions. We don't expect preferential treatment, but don't want life to be harder either. We don't like to be ignored as if we were invisible. That's worse than pointing at us. We don't want pity, just respect. After all, we're human beings first. I for one never wanted pity. I have been relatively able and independent. I knew my limitations and asked for help when I needed it.

A lot of people aren't sure whether to assist a person with a disability.

Actually it's a bit of a minefield. Some don't want any help, and some expect it. Best course is to let the person know assistance is available if they wish.

Go online and look for 'The Ten Commandments of Communicating with Someone with a Disability.' Great stuff.

Hey! We're walkin' here!

Most of the time I was out on my own, walking to the bank, stores, library, or dozens of other places. I liked walking, the freedom. I never have to deal with traffic congestion at Rush Hour or Road Rage. My biggest obstacles were things lying on the sidewalks, rainy weather, and bad, unconscious drivers. Today, the modern automobile is an insulated cocoon of comfort and luxury. Drivers are so surrounded in climate-controlled, sound-proofed, and option-loaded seclusion it is very easy to forget there is a real world out there beyond the windshield and the back window. Most drivers pay attention, but four different times I was almost hit by people who honestly never realized that there are others who are full-time pedestrians.

Carmel Mountain Ranch was a nice quiet suburban community in North County. We were walking down the sidewalk along a row of houses on my left. Every fifty feet or so was a driveway. Saffron led on my left side. All was quiet, very little traffic. Then suddenly two things happened in quick order. I heard the sound of a car engine ahead to my left and Saffron came to an abrupt stop. The car backed up as if I was not there. I waited for a moment, and then spoke in a strong voice, "Are you looking where you're going?"

The car stopped directly on the sidewalk. For nearly ten seconds nothing happened. Then the driver's window came down and the driver, a woman, said, "Oh. Sorry, I didn't see you. That's a nice dog."

♡ Don't change the subject, lady.

You know when someone says something really lame, you can't help but respond? "Do you realize," I said to her, "how close you came to running me and my dog down? If she hadn't stopped me, I'd have been right behind you."

Again her response was lame. "Oh. Well, have a great rest of the day." And then she pulled out, turned down the street and drove away.

I remained there for a minute, praising Saffron for doing a good job. But I really could not believe what just happened. If Saffron hadn't stopped me at just that moment, I don't know if I'd have recognized the danger in time and the car would have backed right over us. Scary.

♡ Not as long as you're with me, Daddy.

We, that is, folks who don't drive, (children, elderly or disabled) have the same rights to freedom of travel as the guy in the Lexus or the girl in the Prius. We are out there, moving around. You'll see us walking through parking lots, along sidewalks, and past driveways. Believe it or not, the PEDESTRIAN has the right of way.

And some of us have dogs. Musket and Saffron have been my eyes. And when I'm out there I have to keep my other senses on high alert. I never know when someone will back out of their parking space or attempt to run the red light because they're in a hurry. A two-ton automobile will turn Saffron and me into very expensive road kill.

So please, when you're driving and sipping the Starbucks triple iced mocha latte and listening to your favorite band on the iPod, take a look out the window. Give us a break. And then you can stop, roll down the window and say "Hey, that's a nice dog!"

"Thank you," I'll say. "And thank you for being a good driver."

Just needed to get that off my chest.

♡ Yeah, Daddy can get a little windy sometimes. But he means well.

Remember how the Boy Scouts used to help little old ladies across the street? That used to happen a lot in Middle America in my youth. I don't know if they still do, but if they do, they probably have the troop lawyer along to mediate any legal disputes if the little old lady wants to sue.

Those scouts grew up and either became environmentalists, Fortune 500 tycoons, politicians or military offices. But a few still roam the sidewalks and streets looking for someone on whom to bestow a good deed, whether they want it or not.

Saffron and I were out on some errands and we reached an uncontrolled intersection. No signals, just stop signs. In that case all I had to do was wait at the curb until I was sure that there were no cars approaching, and give Saffron the "Forward" command.

But then the overgrown boy scout happened by. Now, to be fair, I am sure this guy had his heart in the right place. I'm sure he just wanted to be helpful. We need more people like that in the world.

But this is what he did. "Hey, it's clear, I'll take you across the street." He came out of the blue and took my right arm. Even before I could react, he was off the curb and literally pulling me into the street. Saffron didn't move, so suddenly I was a human wishbone being pulled in two directions.

♡ That was scary. I didn't know why this strange man was taking my Daddy, and since Daddy didn't tell me "Forward," I was not going to move.

"Hey, " I said, "I don't need any help, Thanks. I am fine."

The guy let go of my arm, and while I stepped back on the curb, said "Okay, no problem. Have a nice day."

I was about to reply when I heard the screech of car brakes and the guy yelled "Hey! Watch it!"

The car he apparently hadn't seen or paid any attention to honked at him and moved on. Boy I wish I could have seen the look on his face.

♡ It was pretty red, Daddy.

The scout, for some reason, did not seem to be in a talkative mood anymore. He slinked off before I could offer him any assistance in crossing the street. How sweet that would have been.

My Little Home on the Corner

Bad timing hits all of us sooner or later. One day a while ago I was out with Saffron, headed to the bank to deposit some checks.

♡ This is a good one. Check it out.

We reached a controlled intersection. We were on the near left corner, with cross traffic moving to the right, and parallel traffic coming down along our right. The traffic was crossing in front of us, so we stopped and waited. Then the light changed and we prepared to step off.

But...there was a car in our way. The driver was going to turn right and was looking at the oncoming traffic before moving out.

The problem was, the car was blocking our way. A sighted pedestrian would just go around the car and move on. That was not an option in the case of a person with a disability. Saffron would not move with the car there. I could not tell if the driver even knew we were there, so I did not dare move out in front of the car. That might be the moment when the traffic opened up and...well, you know what that would mean.

Going around the car's rear was not an option since that would take us out of the crosswalk corridor, which we'd have to find and orientate on.

♡ It was my job to get Daddy to the other side safely and I never saw a moment when I could do that.

The light changed and I hit the button again while the driver finally found his opening and turned the corner. I still don't know if they saw me.

We waited out another light and then prepare to step off again. But guess what?

Yep, another vehicle did the same thing. Our way was blocked again. "Oh, Saffron, Lady Luck is just not looking our way today."

Again the driver was there until it was too late to cross safely. Again I hit the button. Again we waited for the cross traffic and this time we would make it.

Wrong.

"I don't believe it," I said to the traffic gods. "What do you want out of me?"

No reply, of course. There never is. But this time, feeling just a bit persecuted, I said loudly "Hey, do you see me here?"

The driver apparently had his window open and said. "Oh, sorry, I didn't see you there. Can't you go around me?"

Even though I'm blind I can still roll my eyes. Of course he didn't pull away until it was too late.

I was getting ready to have some rental furniture moved in, since I was apparently going to be staying for a while.

♡ My bed would look nice near that bush, Daddy. And you can put my bowls over there by that tree.

On the fourth try the gods finally left the way clear for me. No cars blocked my way. "Okay Saffron, forward."

But she'd gone to sleep. Just kidding

Now these people didn't really do anything wrong. They had every right to use the road as I did, and they were being responsible, defensive drivers. It wasn't their fault I was trying to cross just then. But each of them could have done one thing differently. They could have LOOKED TO THEIR RIGHT! If any of them had seen me and Saffron standing there they might have stopped clear of the crosswalk so we could move out. But nope, none did. A person in a wheelchair or using a walker or cane would have just as much, or even more difficulty getting off the curb and around a car as a blind person.

So, next time you're out and about looking for the nearest Starbuck's, glance to your right. You might see Saffron and me, waiting for the light. Saffron will be the sleeping one.

♡ *Zzzzzzzz...*

Not all our misadventures happened on the road. I was at the supermarket doing some grocery shopping. I was in the mood for chili dogs and needed the vital ingredients. Hot dogs, buns, Stagg's Classic Chili, and American cheese. Simple, basic, tasty and UN-nutritious as hell.

Most of the local stores knew Saffron and me, so when we came in the clerks came over and said, "Hi, Mark, can I help you with anything?"

"Yeah," I said. "I'd like to make some chili dogs. Can someone help me?"

"No problem. Wait here."

Well on this particular day, this young guy comes over and says, "What can I help you find, Sir?"

I told him and he led me off to the cold meats department. "Saffron, follow."

Then he disappeared. Oops. Saffron had lost him and so had I.

♡ I was staying with him but he kept making turns and I got confused.

I knew the store pretty well and found my way to the cold cuts and hot dogs. He was there, and asked, "What did you need?"

"A pack of Ball Park® Beef Franks and some Kraft® American Cheese," I said.

"Okay." He handed me a pack of Zacky Farms® Chicken Wieners. I know because I recognized the packaging. "No, I said Ball Park Franks. They come in an eight-pack, not ten."

Again he gave me the wrong item. I was starting to wonder about this guy. If he had a learning disability, then no problem, we'd work it out together. But what I was starting to think was that he just didn't listen. Finally I started touching the hot dog packages until I found one that seemed to be right and asked him what the label said.

"Ball Park," he said. "Is that what you wanted?"

"Yes."

"Okay, we got that. Now what?"

♡ What do you mean, "we?"

The cheese was another trial. He seemed to have no idea what sliced American cheese was. I again found it by feel while he was handing me packets of shredded cheddar. Finally I said, "Hey, I think I'll be fine on my own. Thanks for your help."

"Okay," he said, and walked off. Then the manager, a nice guy named Dennis came over. "Hey Mark, how're you doing?"

"Okay," I replied. "You know that guy who was helping me?"

He turned and said, "Oh, yeah, did he find what you wanted?"

I explained what happened. Dennis let out a breath. "He's the nephew of the franchise owner. Not much motivation."

I nodded. "Ah, I see. Well, not much in the way of brains either." I considered asking Dennis for a job, and I bet he'd have hired me on the spot.

He helped me find the buns and chili with no problem. But that other guy was worse than no help at all. I guess he assumed I would not recognize the difference in the products. Wrong! Just to make the point, if I had a dietary restriction, he might have handed me something that could cause a severe reaction. Thank God I have no restrictions except jalapenos, pickles, liver, sauerkraut and all cabbages, peanuts, limburger cheese, avocados, and artichokes, (which are not bad for me but I hate them).

When we were done, I told Saffron, "Take me to the front, Saffron." She led the way and we checked out. I knew I could depend on her.

Sometimes a bad attitude is a disability

♡ But the ADA doesn't deal with that. If they did, they'd need a lot bigger budget.

While at the library to pick up an audio book, I was waiting in line at the desk. I heard a man behind me say "Nice dog."

I turned. "Thank you," I said. "Her name is Saffron." Saffron, hearing her name wagged her tail.

"What does she do?"

"She's my Guide Dog," I replied, wondering how the man missed seeing the big "Guide Dogs for the Blind" on the harness handle.

"Oh. That's okay."

I'm glad you approve, I thought.

Then he said "You do know you're in a library, right?"

"Yeah..." I was not sure why he was asking.

"So what are you doing in here?"

What? "What do you mean?"

"Well, you're blind, right? You don't read books or anything. Why are you in here?"

For a few seconds I didn't say anything, scarcely able to believe this bonehead. "Just because I'm blind does not mean I don't read books," I said in an even, remarkably tolerant voice. "I read audio books and even scan printed books into my computer and it reads to me."

"Oh, that's okay, I guess," he said, apparently not recognizing how insulting he was being.

♡ I wanted to pee on his foot, but Daddy doesn't think that's nice. That was something Musket taught me.

Just then Carla, the library manager came over. "Hi Mr. Carlson, I have your book here. How are you today?"

"Fine," I said, turning away from the clueless man.

"By the way," Carla said as she ran my card through the scanner, "we had a request for your new book. I checked the database and we have two copies of it. But they're both on a waiting list."

"Hey that's nice to hear." I could have kissed her. "Has *Confessions of a Guide Dog* been requested?"

"Yep," she said. "It's checked out often. Here's your card, Mr. Carlson. Thank you for coming in."

"Thank you, Carla," I said, feeling very good. When I was putting the book in my backpack I heard the bozo say to her, "He wrote a book?"

"Mr. Carlson? Yes. Two, in fact. And he writes for several magazines. About airplanes, I think."

I was definitely going to kiss her next chance I got. Or at least shake her hand.

But wait, it gets better. One day Jane and I went to the bank. Since she was having difficulty getting in and out of the car, I did the errands. So I opened the passenger door just a bit too fast and bumped the car next to my side. I pulled it back just as an angry male voice said, "Hey dumbass! Why don't you be careful?"

"I'm sorry," I said sincerely. "I did not see you." I climbed out and went to the back door to let Saffron out. Then, with her in the lead, I moved carefully between the cars to the curb. But I bumped his mirror.

"Sure, just go charging around and bang into my car," he barked at me. "Why the hell don't you look where you're going?"

That was too much. I had apologized but this jerk wanted to be confrontational. So in a very smooth voice I held Saffron's harness handle and said, "I don't know. Why *don't* I look where I'm going?"

At that point I heard a hushed female voice and the guy shut up. I can only assume his wife/girlfriend/slave told him I was blind. But naturally he did not apologize, like most other people would do. I went into the bank and took care of business, said hello to Molly and went back outside.

Jane was on the phone when I climbed back in. That other car was gone. She was telling the story about the bozo in the next car and laughing. "Mark really shut him up!"

I admit I could have been a bit more careful opening the door, and to this day I make a point of doing so, but did apologize. He was a jerk, plain and simple as that.

I hope I don't come across as a whining malcontent who does nothing but complain about other people. But you have to admit some of the ones I just mentioned are beyond belief. I admit I don't suffer fools gladly. It's just that there seem to be a lot more of them than there used to be. And I'm sure that texting and twitter play a role in the "duh" mode a lot of people are in these days. I'm a keen observer of the human condition (even if I can't see it) and recognize the good, the bad and the clueless in humanity. It's one of the better things about being a writer.

♡ One of the things I love about my job is how Daddy takes these little things and makes them into fun stories. I love hearing him tell them to other people. I feel kind of special to be a part of great literature.

How nice of you to say that, Saffron. Thank you.

♡ Well, he's not John Steinbeck or F. Scott Fitzgerald, but I still love him.

Ah-huh. One thing that some sighted folks don't think about, and this is in no way a criticism, since they simply might never have been taught otherwise, is how a blind person needs to use their other senses, like hearing.

As an example, even when I was single and dating, I never liked going into bars and nightclubs with live music. They invariably had the volume up to where it caused bleeding of the eardrums. Conversation was nearly impossible for someone with hearing aids, which amplified EVERYTHING! How was anyone supposed to have a nice intimate conversation with the walls vibrating and the floor heaving from the seismic tremors? So that was probably why I met Jane at a bus stop.

♡ Daddy is right. I went to one of those places with him and a couple of friends. I hated it. Noise, noise, noise! I felt like the Grinch complaining about the Whos in Whoville.

Noise pollution came up a lot when we were outside. We had to listen to know which way the traffic was going and when a car was approaching. I learned most of the tricks of the trade while at the Davidson Program for Independence back in 2001. I learned to discern between "all quiet" and "all clear." The latter was the safe time to cross a street. If I heard a car coming I waited. But I needed to be able to hear.

A while back I was going on some errands with Saffron. At the end of our street was an uncontrolled "T" intersection. No lights or Stop signs. I wanted to cross the top of the T to the sidewalk on the other side. The traffic moved in both directions. Normally I would stop on the corner and listen, and when I was sure it was clear, told Saffron "Forward" and off we went.

But on this day there was a guy with the most horrible and cruel machines ever devised by the evil mind of man. No, not the Atom Bomb. I'm talking about something much worse. A leaf blower.

He was doing his thing, blowing away leaves that anyone (even me) could have swept up with a broom and dustpan. I heard this guy when I first left the house ten minutes before and he was still roaring away when we reached the corner. I could not hear the traffic. Saffron would have stopped me if a car was coming but it was never a good idea to step onto a street in front of a moving car.

I tried to listen but it was no use. Waving towards the guy I tried to get his attention, but he kept on, oblivious to the world. Finally I walked in his direction and got his attention. He slowed the blower and yelled "What?"

"Can you cut that off until I get across the street please? I can't hear the traffic."

"Go ahead, there are no cars coming." Then he resumed blowing as loud as before. Again I used the sign of cutting across my throat to get him to stop. At last he did and I said "Thank you, I appreciate it."

I turned and went to the corner. It sounded clear, then just as I stepped off, he turned that infernal machine on again! I was in a quandary. For the moment it was clear, but that could change in a second. And it did. A car came down the street to turn at the same corner and I didn't hear it. Saffron stayed firm and I felt the car pass by. Now I was really steamed. The bozo never stopped. Again I made the cutting motion, which was more an indication of what I wanted to do to him, and he shut it off. As soon as I was sure it was clear, we scurried across the street. By the time my foot touched the sidewalk, Mr. Oblivious was back on the job.

All that took about ten minutes. I had tried to tell him what I needed, but he just didn't think that sound was that important for safety.

To be fair, it was not just other people who were bozos. I qualify for the title too. While I am supposed to be alert as we work together, I have sometimes buried my head in the clouds. Fortunately Saffron tended to be on the ball. Recently we were walking up the street near home. Our normal route took us up past twelve driveways, whereupon we'd find a streetlight power junction box. Both Musket and Saffron have been trained to stop at this box, at which point we turned 90 degrees to the left and crossed the street and intersected the sidewalk on the other side which took us right home.

On this particular day I wasn't paying attention and didn't sense Saffron's push to the right at the junction box. I kept on walking while I tried to mentally solve the riddles of the universe.

I gradually noticed some strange action on her part. She kept turning her head to the left. I assumed she was looking at another dog across the street. But when she did this twice more, it finally got through my befuddled brain that Saffron was trying to tell me something. "Did we pass our turn?"

♡ Well, duh.

We made a turn and crossed the street. And sure enough, we were about a hundred yards past the intersection. Oops.

"Good girl, Saffron," I said sheepishly. "You knew we'd passed it and were telling me to pay attention." I gave her a few kibbles. What a remarkable dog. Now all I had to do was make sure she didn't spill the beans to Jane.

♡ Mommy, guess what a boner Daddy pulled today!

Another time at nearly the same spot I was crossing what I thought was an empty street when there was this terrifying "HONNNNK!" and screeching of tires. I felt Saffron twisting and pulling back as a huge roaring mass of truck swept past us. It all happened in less than five seconds. I lunged for the curb and hugged Saffron. I never heard that truck coming. It might have been going very fast, but I was certain the road was clear. Saffron got a lot of treats and love for that. Good girl. That was April 20, 2017. The day Saffron saved my life.

♡ Just doing my job, Daddy.

Now that I have vented about the bad and ugly, here are a couple of the good. Different day, same place. And the leaf blower was howling away like tortured demons having a proctology exam by Edward Scissorhands. But this time as we approached the intersection, the blower stopped and went silent. Just like that. I waved towards the man, who may or may not have been the same guy, and said "Thank you!" When it was clear we crossed the street.

Whoever that was, he got it. He seemed to know I needed to hear the traffic. And I was grateful, even if I hate leaf blowers.

When Saffron and I went to one of our veterans' meetings, she was an instant hit. One Friday at Bagels and Baloney I arrived with Alan, and as we found seats, Denny Schafer the leader called out. "Hey we have some special guests with us today. Saffron and Mark are here!"

There was applause from the members and several of them said hello to Saffron.

After the meeting was over, I was chatting with Colonel Steve Pisanos, a World War Two fighter ace, when another member came over and got my attention. "Hello," he said. "Can I ask you something?"

"Sure," I said. "What's up?"

"Were you ever a pilot?"

I laughed. "No, never. Believe me, you don't want me at the controls of a plane, or even a car, for that matter."

Steve laughed. The man then said, "Well it's just that you know so much about military aviation, I figured you had to have been a pilot."

"I'm flattered," I said, meaning it. "Not many people would think a blind guy could have been a pilot, especially a military one."

"Hey you could have lost your sight in an accident or something. You just don't, you know, act like you're blind."

Again I laughed. "It's an acquired skill. But I'm grateful for the compliment. I wish I had been a pilot. I revere you guys."

"Well, if you ever set your mind to it, I bet you could be one."

Steve agreed. "Marco could do anything he doggone wanted to," he said with his booming voice.

It felt good to have someone give me the benefit of the doubt instead of assuming I was helpless.

CHAPTER 8

LABRADORLAND

"If you think dogs can't count, try putting three dog biscuits
in your pocket and then give him only two of them."
— Phil Pastoret

An Easy Choice

"In my next life I want to come back as a..." How
many times have we heard that or spoken it ourselves?

Whether or not you believe in reincarnation, we all have experienced
those moments when we wish we could do parts of our lives over
again. I'm certainly no different, but reality can't be overcome. We can't
change the past or go back in time.

Yet some of us hope for another crack at the great roulette wheel of
life. Some want to come back as rich, healthy, good-looking and famous
people. Like Hugh Jackman, Tiger Woods or Angelina Jolie.

Others would be happy to be themselves again. In my case, rather
than come back as a human, which I have long come to believe is more
trouble than it's worth, I want to come back as a dog, specifically a
yellow Labrador Retriever. Yep, you heard me right. A dog.

This may sound like a demotion. Why would I want to give up my
status as a member of the dominant intelligent carbon-based life form
on Earth? Why would I want to be a lower life form, unable to speak,

drive a car or appreciate the subtle nuances of "Here Comes Honey Boo-Boo?" What more could we want?

You have to ask? Let's examine just a few of the pros and cons of being a member of the species *H. Sapiens* in the early Twenty-first century.

It's not easy being a human today. Work, money, taxes, home and car payments, relationships, health care and a hundred other matters constantly add to our daily problems and stress. No wonder so many people need expensive and extensive therapy, anti-depressants, and a constant desperate drive to find out what life is all about.

Now go and find a Labrador Retriever. Chances are the dog is doing what its best at: Sleeping. Look at its face. Contented, happy. Totally at peace. If you have a mirror handy, look at your own face. Then compare the two. Need I say more?

A dog's life is exactly what Henry David Thoreau wrote about in *Walden*. Simplify, simplify. They haven't a care in the world. They are fed and watered, walked, petted, loved and cared for. You won't catch a dog worrying about rising gas prices, politics, global warming or who to vote for on "Dancing With the Stars."

The biggest, most daunting decision a dog has to face is what side they will sleep on.

Getting back to the matter of reincarnation, consider this: if we could listen to what dogs say to one another when they hang out, I'm reasonably sure they are not saying "In my next life I want to come back as a human. I want to spend all my time worrying about money and whether the Padres will ever take the Pennant."

Labs are supposed to be smart. There's your proof. They don't care about the Padres, just the peanuts on the floor.

Sounds like a no-brainer to me. With their smiles, expressive brown eyes, soft fur, wagging tails and sweet personalities, Labs are arguably the most perfect dogs on Earth.

Now, you Corgi and Beagle lovers, Doberman and Collie owners, don't start foaming at the mouth. You'll be suspected of having rabies.

I love most dog breeds, but have long had a special place in my heart for the lovable Labs.

Musket and Saffron are both sweet and beautiful. Everywhere they go heads turn. Little girls run up to hug them and people want to give them treats. Grown men like to sit down with Musket and Saffron and rub their bellies or throw their favorite toys again and again.

On sunny days they lie down on the pavement and sleep, absorbing the warm yellow rays. Total, uncomplicated bliss. Great work if you can get it.

If that's a dog's life, I only have one question: Where do I sign up?

But it may be a moot point. Even if reincarnation can happen, I'm not sure I have a shot at coming back as a Labrador. That would be something of a reward for a life well spent.

Whoever makes those decisions would look at my application, laugh, and cut my name from the list. I'll be slotted into the Duck-billed Platypus department. By the way, they are the perfect example of an animal designed by committee.

Even if I can't come back as my favorite dog, that's okay. For one thing, despite all the slings and arrows of outrageous fortune we have to cope within this mortal coil, there are plenty of dogs around. They make life a lot more bearable and fun. I don't know if they are reincarnated people, but even if not, they are a blessing we can all enjoy. Just sit down with a lovable puppy sometime and let it lick your face. Dogs have a way of making us feel as if we are the most important thing in their lives.

I guess being a human does have its perks.

Sandy and Taffy, or was it Saffy and Tandy?

My cousin Katarina, whom we have always called Chick, lived in San Pedro near Los Angeles. A devoted dog lover, she had several Dobermans. Her last Dobie was Cassius, whom readers of *Confessions* may remember was Musket's big buddy. They played like there was no tomorrow. And after they tore around the house there was no unbroken furniture. Just kidding. Chick was living in an apartment and met a Guide Dog owner named Charlie. His dog was a female Yellow Lab named Tandy, who was five years old.

Well, Charlie was not in the best of health and he occasionally asked Chick to walk Tandy, which she was only too happy to do. She missed having a dog of her own. As things turned out, she began walking and playing with Tandy more and more as the weeks passed. Charlie almost never left his apartment.

In early 2014, he took a turn for the worse and was taken to the hospital. He asked Chick to take care of Tandy for him.

In a week, Charlie had died, and Tandy had lost her owner.

Chick had been keeping Jane and me informed on developments and asked what she should do. I called my old GDB Field Services rep, Keith Tomlinson and asked his advice. He called Chick and since Tandy was too old for retraining, she could be adopted. Talk about relieved joy. Chick could not believe she suddenly found herself the owner of a loving, happy and healthy retired Guide Dog.

I was very happy about how it turned out. The new Mommy and Doggy were bonding fast, and Tandy seemed to be okay with not being with Charlie anymore.

His family was glad Tandy would be adopted by Chick and she helped them to take care of his apartment. That's the kind of person she was. Generous and compassionate.

So without adding any new blind people to the family we suddenly had a new Guide Dog. Tandy was just like Saffron, according to Chick, but we had no idea how much until the day came for them to meet. That happened in mid July 2014.

Chick drove down to visit. I was at a lunch date with some friends when she arrived.

When Saffron and I returned home, she was suddenly confronted with a strange dog in her house. She didn't seem to know how to react. Tandy was eager to play but Saffron was wary of the new dog.

♡ Let's get this straight. I went in to the house, planning on getting some water and finding a good toy to mangle. Then I stopped. What was that scent? Another dog? In MY house? Then I saw her. She looked just like me! I sensed no hostility. Daddy and Mommy kept talking to me in soothing voices. I sniffed her and she sniffed me. It was cool.

I pulled out a few toys, the only ones Saffron hadn't shredded and tossed them on the floor. And just like that their playful instinct took over.

Pandemonium!

Those two tore around the house like it was the Indianapolis Speedway. Up and down the stairs, through the halls and doors, in and out of rooms. Saffron was running and playing, chasing and being chased.

One favorite toy was a long, stuffed Snoopy, shaped like a hotdog with a squeaker in it. And when those two dogs got ahold of it they tore at it in a tug-of-war like it was one of those Christmas crackers the English love so much. Bang! Snoopy was torn to bits as a cloud of Fiberfill floated to the floor. "That was Musket's last toy," I said, astonished. It lasted all of ten seconds.

Saffron had a new best friend. Musket, on the other hand, just slept and occasionally grumbled at all the ruckus.

🐕 Why can't they make less noise? I want to sleep.

Three Guide Dog Night

At seventy thousand dollars each, we had nearly a quarter of a million bucks worth of mutts in the house. Jane and Chick took them to an enclosed dog park in Rancho Bernardo and from what I heard later, they covered every inch of the play area at a full run.

There was no doubt that Tandy was a hit with Saffron and vice versa. She was a happy and loving addition to the family. As Jane told me, Tandy's fur was just a bit more golden than Saffron's but of the same texture. They were both the same size.

They even had the same kind of collar. So I could not tell them apart.

It was like having twins that liked to switch clothes and identities to fool their parents.

The only way I could tell was by their tags. Saffron's ID tag was in the shape of a heart, and Tandy's was shaped like a bone.

So every time I had to take Saffron out or feed her, I had to check the collar to feel for the heart. "Okay, this is Saffy," I said.

The next surprise was when I was lying on the bed reading an audio book and Saffron jumped up to lie next to me.

Then Tandy did the same thing! She made herself right at home, snuggling against Jane's pillow like she'd been living there for years.

Chick came in from the guest bedroom to find she'd been abandoned. But she took a picture with her phone of the cute scene.

Saffron and her Bestie, Tandy. Note they are identical.

Tandy stayed for two days. And when it was time for them to leave on Thursday night, Saffron didn't want her new Bestie to leave.

I promised her Tandy would be back soon.

She was bummed and moped around the house for a couple of days.

♡ Just when I was getting her trained. I had so much fun with her! Two girls just playing.

Sin Twisters

The next time Tandy came to visit was in November. Chick was traveling back east and asked us to dogsit her. No problem. Both dogs needed a bath, so one sunny day I pulled the towels from the cabinet and went at it. I took both their collars off and turned on the water. Tandy was first, only because Saffron was too fast for me to catch. Tandy went in with a minimum of coaxing. Wet down, shampoo, rinse, dry. Simple.

Tandy did the "shake and bake" thing and soon she was out on the balcony drying off. Then it was Saffron's turn. She tried to run but I cornered her and pushed her into the shower. She dug in her claws as if I were trying to throw her into a pool of sharks.

Again the same routine. She shook off and after I was sure it was safe to let her go, she tore out of there like Seabiscuit at the Triple Crown.

♡ Just in case you don't get it yet, I HATE BEING WET!

Jane said she had to go run some errands. When she returned we'd take the dogs out front and let them run and play. So far this was fine.

Then I found the Achilles Heel of my strategy. Remember I had taken off their collars?

Both were the same size, weight, and female. Oops.

♡ Daddy, which dog is which?

I had a pair of sin twisters, and That is not a spoonerism. I mean Sin Twisters!

I could not tell them apart. I felt all over, but with them both damp there was no difference in the texture of their fur. This was kind of important. What if I put the wrong dog on the harness? Then I had an idea. "Saffron," I said in my command voice, "Come here."

♡ Tandy, let's have some fun with Daddy. Just do what I do.

To my horror both dogs came and nuzzled my hand. Oh-kayyy. "Saffron, sit."

Both obediently sat down. "Crap. No, that wasn't a command!"

My last hope was Saffron's rapacious appetite. Taking both collars I went downstairs to where we kept the treat jar.

Guess what? It didn't work. Both dogs had the same appetite.

In a flash of genius, I held out the harness. "Come, Saffron," I said.

One dog calmly and properly put her head in the harness. "Gotcha!"

I reached for the other dog, who hadn't moved. Saffron never willingly put her head in the harness.

♡ Tandy! You're such a brown-noser!

Which way did she go?

When Chick had some surgery in August 2016 she asked Jane and me to take care of Tandy for her. We drove up to Orange County and met her. By that time Tandy and Chick had bonded pretty well. When we found them at a pre-arranged location Tandy and Saffy were obviously happy to see one another. Chick gave us Tandy's food, bowls, toys and a favorite blanket. She would be with us for at least two months

We wanted Tandy to feel welcome so we did give her a lot of extra attention. Jane had washed Musket's old bed and I got Tandy to lie down in it. She accepted that, as it did not have his scent in it.

Well, for the first couple of days I took them both for walks. This way Tandy would feel used to the area and Saffron would not be left out.

Jane was able to let her out the front door to do her business, but when I tried it one night, she bolted. I yelled for Jane to come down and she went outside. No Tandy.

This was just great. "Gee, Chick, you know that dog you were so fond of? Well, here's the deal..."

Jane took the car while I continued to call for Tandy. About ten minutes later Jane came back with the wayward pooch. She had been just down the street, sniffing and doing her thing. But I never took the chance again. She remained on the leash.

That was a heart-stopping 15 minutes we didn't need.

Anyone who knows me will not be surprise that I always hold myself accountable for my actions. Well, almost always. There was that one time...umm, maybe it was two or three times....Ahem. Well, I am going to admit to a really dumb thing I did. And it concerns Tandy. Chick was still recovering from surgery. Jane and I drove down to Mission Valley where I did a lecture for OASIS. Sandy and Taffy...er, oh you know who I mean, came with us. Tandy was welcome at OASIS just as Saffron and Musket were before her.

Afterwards, we went out to the car. I opened the right side back door and Saffron jumped in. Then I called for Tandy to get in. I climbed in the passenger seat and we drove off, headed for the CVS in the next shopping center. While Jane went in, I reached back to pet the dogs. I found Saffron, but not Tandy. I called for her, and thought she might be on the back deck. I got out and felt around. No Tandy. I began to panic. Where was she?

♡ She never got in the car, but Daddy did not see that. I was wondering why they left her behind.

When Jane came out I told her we had to go back to Mission Valley. She was, to say the least, very upset. Actually she was royally pissed at me. Now I might have said, "Hey, you might have looked to make sure both dogs were in the car," but I was too worried to put up a defense. Keep that in mind next time you're on the witness stand.

We drove like hell back to the parking lot. Just then Jane's phone rang. It was Chick, telling us that Tandy was with the mall security office after she had been found wandering in the parking lot. They had called her number.

We arrived a minute later and saw a guard holding Tandy's leash. With more relief than I could express I thanked him and got Tandy into the car, making absolutely certain she was in. Then I gave her a big treat. She licked my hand. I guess she forgave me.

Chick did too, glad it had worked out.

As for Jane, it took a little longer. About a year, give or take a decade.

That was one blunder I never forgot nor repeated.

♡ Tandy and I joked about it all the way home. She told me that she was bewildered but then this nice man found her and gave her some water. It only took about fifteen minutes. But Daddy was really hard on himself.

Tandy was very affectionate and playful, and just a bit more assertive than Saffron. When I had them both out front to let them play with the rope toy, it was like watching some primeval beasts fighting for dominance. There was some serious growling and that poor rope was in danger of being shredded to a thread. I didn't even try to get close to them. I like my hands with all ten fingers attached. I could imagine a pair of wolves tearing apart a caribou on the tundra. All that was missing was the cracking of bones.

I finally got the rope back from the dueling mastiffs and went inside. My sweet little Labrador Guide Dog actually had a very strong hunting instinct in her.

You know how some parents with more than one child will get their names mixed up? I was called David, Honey, our dog Puff, and even names she probably made up before my Mom got around to Mark. Well, it happened to me with the two dogs. Saffron and Tandy soon became Saffy and Tandy, and more and more often, Sandy and Taffy!

♡ It was so funny to watch Daddy get all tongue-tied over our names! But it did not matter. Taffy and I knew who we were.

Tandy came to stay with us a few more times from 2017 to 2018. Then Chick began showing signs of poor health. Like Charlie before her, she began asking a neighbor, Steve, to walk Tandy and play with her. Steve was a Godsend and did so willingly. But the end came on October 3, 2018 when Chick died. Her son Tony, with whom I have always been close, took care of the details. Steve took care of Tandy, who we realized had now lost two owners. I called Guide Dogs and had them contact

Tandy's original puppy raiser, who lived on a large farm in Oregon. It only took a few days to work it out for Tandy to be taken there.

Saffron did not know that she would never see Tandy again. I had lost my favorite relative. Jane and Chick had been as close as sisters, so she too was grieving.

We went to a memorial service at a small Swedish church in San Pedro. Tony had done a remarkable job of seeing to it that his Mom's remains and wishes were well taken care of. But anyone who knew Chick would expect no less from her son.

I'll miss her deeply. Another loss to the world. Tandy is now up in Oregon, with a huge yard and lots of other dogs to play with. At last she has security and happiness. I wish her the best.

♡ I miss Tandy. Daddy explained I would not see her again but I should be glad she is happy now. I guess I am, but gee, we had so much fun!

CHAPTER 9

GOOD NIGHT, SWEET PRINCE

"Once you have had a wonderful dog, a life
without one is a life diminished."
— Dean Koontz

"Dogs come into our lives to teach us about love,
they depart to teach us about loss. A new dog never
replaces an old dog. It merely expands the heart."
— Author Unknown

This chapter is going to be the hardest to write. In fact, I am writing even as the tears are drying on my cheeks.

All good things must come to an end. There has to be a last day. Some are expected, like the last day of the Olympics, the last day of the county fair, or the last day of spring. But others are unpredictable. And those tend to be the ones we most fear. What was the last day of Musket's life going to be like? Like any pet owner, I worried about that inevitable day. I knew it was coming. I knew Musket, even with his boundless love and life, would not live forever. Someday he would die.

As it was, he had already outlived all his classmates. Most Labradors live about ten or eleven years, while some live to be thirteen or fourteen. His working life was much longer than expected. He had had a great life and traveled all over the country, loved and been loved by people from coast to coast and around the world. Even those who never met him knew Musket's story.

So I had nothing to regret. Yet I worried. I was scared that his last days would be painful and bewildering, that he would not understand why he could not work anymore, why he was unable to climb the stairs or jump into his Mommy's lap.

I worried that he would know fear and pain.

So I watched my little buddy closely. Yet somehow he always rallied. His tail wagged when it was dinnertime, he snapped up treats like always, and he had an endless supply of kisses for us.

So it was easy to convince myself he was basically healthy. Just a lot slower. He slept more than before, but since he always managed to make Rip Van Winkle's twenty years look like a catnap, that wasn't a concern. After all, at more than thirteen, Musket was the equivalent of 91 in dog years.

His friends still came to see him, which elicited a wagging tail and slurpy kisses. We took him along when we went to the dentist, Dr. Melinda Marino. She and her technician, Janet, had been in love with him from the start. They said I was not allowed in their office without him.

We took him along when I did lectures and public appearances. He still knew how to charm the public.

When I started this book Musket was doing okay, but in July 2014 he started having trouble breathing. Even allowing for the heat, he was panting like a racehorse after the Kentucky Derby. He needed to be helped up and down the stairs, but I didn't know what was really happening inside him.

On the evening of July 27, I helped Musket upstairs to the bedroom so he could be near Jane as she read in her chair. Then I lay back on the bed and began to read a novel, *The Map of Time* by Felix Palma. A very good Sci-Fi novel, so I was totally engrossed in it when I heard some wheezing and gasping from Musket. I pulled off the headset and got on the floor with him to see what was happening.

Musket was lying on his belly and gasping as if he were choking. This reminded me of the seizure he'd had in 2007, but he wasn't shaking.

I patted him and said in a loud but calming voice, "Hey little buddy, Daddy's here. What's wrong?"

He soon stopped gasping and panted rapidly, then calmed down. I waited, but nothing else happened. I kissed his head. Jane, who was watching, said "He's been having trouble breathing for a few days now."

"Yeah," I replied, feeling a cold stab of worry. What was going on?

After going back to my book, I kept one ear cocked. And in a few minutes, it happened again. The same sudden gasp, like an asthmatic desperately trying to get air into their lungs. I went back to Musket and tried to get him to lie on his side. I was thinking he might have some sort of nasal blockage and could not breathe through his nose. And if he was on his side, he could breathe through his open mouth. But he rolled back on his stomach.

This happened several times over the next hour and I was stumped. Naturally it was late on Sunday night.

"I'm going to take him down and give him some water and let him out," I told Jane. "I may sleep on the couch to stay near him."

"Okay," she said, equally worried. "Mommy loves you, Musket."

♡ I could tell Daddy was worried about Musket. The poor thing was trying so hard to breathe. I went over to lick his face, which he usually liked, but he didn't even seem to notice.

He was still panting as I walked backward down the stairs while holding him. Then I opened the front door and let him out. He went, but did not do anything.

Then I tried to give him some water on the hope that he was just experiencing some irritation to his throat. Nothing. I tossed a few kibble into the water, which worked. He ate them and got some water down.

Then I took him into the living room and got him to lie near the couch so I could hear what he was doing.

I settled in for a long, restless night.

The gasping and wheezing continued, every ten minutes or so. It was silent in the dark, then the gasps, wheezes, several minutes of panting, rapid breathing and then he'd settle down.

After a couple of hours I went over to him and spoke into his ear.

"Musket, Daddy loves you. It's okay. I want to help you. But I don't know what to do."

There was an emergency vet clinic in Poway but they were often not open. Go figure.

With a weight on my heart, I leaned over and said, "Musket, if you are ready, it's okay. You can go. You don't have to suffer any more. I want you to be okay but if you want to leave us, it's okay."

There were tears streaming down my face as I said it, hoping he heard and understood. I didn't want him to suffer anymore.

Dawn came at last and I called our vet and asked for an appointment that morning. Musket was finally asleep, perhaps the worst was over. But deep down, I knew better.

I filled his bowl and waited, but he made no move to go to it. Then I helped him up and moved the bowl to him. Again, he made no effort to eat. This was serious, as all of you who knew Musket would know.

But Saffron took up the slack.

♡ I ate Musket's food for him. I'm sure he'd have done the same for me.

After taking a shower and dressing, Jane and I took Musket out to the car and put him in the back seat with Saffron. He was like a sack of potatoes.

At the vet we brought him inside and were taken to an examination room. The vet came in and examined him after we told him what had been happening. Of course, since we were talking about the gasping, he didn't do it.

"Well, his lungs and heart sound fine," the vet said. "But let's do a chest X-ray and take some blood. We might be able to see what is bothering him."

♡ Musket was very sick. Mommy and Daddy were very worried. When we left him behind, I started feeling that something bad was going to happen.

We left my little buddy there with heavy hearts. At home I called Guide Dogs and updated them. The counselor, a very compassionate and helpful guy named Tripp told me they would approve any tests needed to determine what was going on with Musket.

The hours dragged by as we waited. I called Linda, who was very close to Musket and told her that she might want to come and see him, just in case. She grew very emotional and said she'd come by the next day, Tuesday, to see him.

After a few more calls I had some lunch. I was drained from the long, exhausting night.

In my heart, I was already thinking that this might be it. The final days of Musket's life. He'd lived a long and happy life and had long since earned his rest. But like any other dog owner, I was selfish. I didn't want it to end. But how could I keep him, if he was literally unable to breathe?

The vet called and said they found some fluid in Musket's chest cavity and that was why he was having so much trouble. He could not expand his lungs fully. They could tap and drain the fluid, which I approved. He also had a very high white blood cell count which was a sign that he was fighting off an infection.

We could pick him up later in the afternoon and he'd be groggy and need to sleep.

That was certainly the case when we put my groggy doggy into the back seat. I had to carry him into the house through the front door and put him on his bed in the living room. Then we had dinner. It was strange not having Musket begging, as he'd done only the night before. That night I stayed on the couch and listened.

♡ When I had my dinner, Musket was sound asleep. I lay down next to him. I hope he knew I was there for him. Once again I licked his face, and again he didn't move. I didn't want to lose my big brother.

During the evening Musket was breathing almost normally, but rapidly.

The night again passed slowly with my dread hardly mollified. In the morning we were going to have a cardiac ultrasound done to find out where the fluid was coming from. Musket was a dead weight when

I got him to the door in the morning but he refused to go out. He did eat a little but drank a lot. I felt a little relief.

Then we took him back to the vet while Jane went to breakfast with a friend. I tried to catch up on sleep but the phone kept ringing, our friends calling to find out about Musket.

♡ The whole morning Daddy talked to me about Musket, and told me he was very sick. I knew this, and gave Daddy lots of kisses to make him feel better. I tasted the tears on his face.

Then at about 10:30 Jane called and told me the vet had called her and said that Musket had a big tumor—that dreaded word—on his heart.

That was the moment I had both dreaded and knew was coming.

"It's time to let him go. Come and get me and we'll go to see him."

The decision was hard, but I never hesitated. Musket was going to die and he was going to die with dignity and in peace.

He was old and tired. Even though GDB was open to the idea of surgery, it would only postpone the inevitable. Musket deserved better.

When Jane got home, I was showered and dressed, waiting. Saffron jumped in back and we left.

I called Linda and told her to be at the vet at 11:30 if she wanted to say goodbye to Musket. She said that it was really a time for family but I insisted that she see him one last time.

When we parked, I got out and Saffron led me in, followed by Jane, and a minute later, Linda.

She was in tears but tried to be strong and supportive. We were led into a private room where I paced like a tiger in a cage.

Linda and Jane talked about Musket. A short time later Brittney came in and led us to another room where my little buddy was lying on a mat on the floor. We sat in chairs around him and he saw us, but made no attempt to stand. We were all crying. I sat on the floor with him and patted his big head. He was not panting or even breathing hard. I sensed nothing but calmness from him. Jane spoke to her baby while Saffron licked his face just as she'd always done.

I held a few kibble by his mouth and he ate it right down, which made us all smile.

♡ We went into this room I'd never seen before. On the floor was my big brother. He was awake but didn't seem to see us. My heart was pounding. I knew this was a bad thing, and lay down next to him. I started licking his face and this time he gave me a little lick too. That made me happy. When Daddy gave him a few treats, I didn't try to get some for me. This was all about Musket.

Linda bent close and patted him, saying she loved him and would never forget her Musket. Then, after giving me a hug, she left in tears.

I knelt close to him and said into his ear, "Musket you were the best Guide Dog I ever knew. Thank you for taking care of me, for guiding me, for protecting me. Thank you for being my little buddy and loving me. I'll never forget you and will always love you. Go in peace, Little Buddy." My face was streaming in tears when I went to sit next to Jane.

Vanessa came in with Dr. Grey, our favorite vet, who asked us if we were sure we wanted to do this. She did not think there was any alternative, but wanted to be sure.

We both nodded. Then, while she explained the procedure, Vanessa shaved Musket's forearm for the injection. Saffron became upset and crawled forward to lie over his arm. That was when Jane really lost it. She sobbed and began to pray. She asked God to take Musket into the Kingdom of Heaven. I held her while she spoke, and felt a warm trickle of fresh tears. Musket, the most loving and unselfish of dogs would soon be soaring with the angels where he belonged.

♡ I saw these people working on Musket. They shaved his leg. I didn't know what it meant, but since Mommy and Daddy and everyone were so sad I knew it was a bad thing. I tried to stop them. You can't take my big brother away! I love him. I'll take care of him. But Daddy helped me up and pulled me into his lap. He was really crying and I licked his face. Then I kissed Mommy too.

Saffron didn't want to move as Dr. Grey bent down and began to work. She spoke soothingly to Musket, saying she loved him and would miss him. "It's going to be okay, Musket," she said. "You're a good boy and we'll never forget you."

We waited. I bent down and placed my hand on his side. He was breathing slowly.

Then it stopped. I kept my hand on him, hoping I was wrong, but also hoping I was right. I felt no rising and falling of his great deep chest, no gentle thump of his ever-loving heart. He was still.

It was very peaceful and he did not suffer. He left the world in a gentle and quiet way, just as he lived in it. And that, I suppose is the best way to go.

Musket was dead. For a long moment I listened, but could only hear Jane's quiet sobs and Saffron's panting. I don't know what I expected or hoped to hear, maybe the sound of "Taps" on a bugle, or something from *Les Miserables*.

But there was only silence from the Heavens. I closed his beautiful brown eyes that had guided me for so long.

♡ I was watching Musket. He was breathing real slow. And then... he stopped. At first, I didn't know what it meant, but then when Daddy leaned over and closed Musket's eyes I knew he was gone.

After a last touch on his soft fur, we stood up and left the room. I knew I'd never see Musket again. There was an empty hole in my heart, a feeling like a cold void.

"He was looking at me," Jane said. "He wanted to go. I told him it was okay."

We hugged and went out to the waiting area. A moment later, Jane came over to me and said, "This will make you feel better, Honey." She placed a tiny dog in my hands. At first I thought it was a puppy, but it was a very small Chihuahua that had a broken leg in a cast. I held the tiny trembling little dog in my hands and cooed to it.

"His name is Godzilla," Melissa said to me.

Godzilla licked my face. It felt like a warm wet Q-Tip. I smiled for the first time that day.

After thanking the staff we left and drove home. I knew we were going home to a house without Musket. And it was okay. I felt better than I'd feared, calmer than I expected. I was sad, yes, but not miserable. It was a catharsis. Musket was gone but not forgotten. He would live on in all our hearts.

"He's up in Heaven now," Jane said. "Nanny's giving him treats and Pop-pop is telling him he's a good boy."

"Yeah," I replied, smiling again. "That's my boy."

♡ The house was very quiet when I went inside. I knew Musket wasn't there, but I could smell him everywhere. The floor, his bowls, his bed, the stairway, all smelled like my big brother. It sort of made me happy to know that even though he was never coming home, he was always going to be there, and I could smell him whenever I wanted.

When we got home I wrote a short epitaph for him and sent it off to all our friends who were close to Musket. I also posted it on Musket's Facebook page.

We brought Musket's ashes home. They were in a lovely polished cedar box about the size of a shoebox. It had a lock and key with an engraved brass plaque on the lid with his name. With the box came a resin paw print about the size of a drink coaster. We put the box on a table in the living room, so Musket would be home for good.

Jane ordered a ceramic resin flagstone with his name and the inscription "If love could have saved you, you would have lived forever." We put it in the garden.

Scarcely a day went by when I didn't look in the direction of the box and whisper, "Hi, little Buddy."

In a very short time the replies began pouring in from all over. From coast to coast, from boarder to border, from France, Scotland, Canada, England, Australia and who knows where else, Musket's friends and fans responded. I thought the best tribute would be to put some of the thoughts from his friends in this book.

Loretta Scigliano

My mom and I went to Disneyland, and the happiest place on earth was even happier that day because Musket was there! It was so fun to see him all day all over the park, wearing Mickey Mouse ears! Finally that night, we had to stop to meet him. He was the sweetest boy ever, and even posed for pictures:) We are so grateful that we were able to meet him.

Cassie Marks, GDB puppy raiser

I will always remember Musket as a plump little puppy running around my house. He's now running free. Rest in Peace, Musket.

Marcia Bowman

I remember when I first read an article in the paper about a new book called *The Blonde Leading The Blind*. I just knew I had to have the book. Then shortly after that, at the Gillespie Airport Cafe, I saw a man and his guide dog sitting at a table. I just knew it was Mark and Musket! I introduced myself and asked to pet this sweet gentle giant. And so a friendship was formed. I feel so honored to have had the pleasure of meeting and kissing dear sweet Musket. There is a hole in my heart today. I know everyone who knew him feels the same way today.

Wayne Holley, Toastmasters

Musket was the best eyes a blind man could ever have. He always made those around him feel happy that he was there. He'll be missed. Godspeed, Musket.

Susan Waynelovich, Toastmasters

Musket was authentic and true. He knew how to love and be loved and his loyalty was unsurpassed. It is with great sadness that I ponder a world that no longer has Musket in it but am so grateful that I was privileged enough to have met him. Until we meet again.

Annika Anderson, co-worker

The minute I laid eyes on Musket I knew he was one of the most special dogs I would ever meet in my life. If I was having a bad day I would immediately head to Mark and Musket's office, lay down next to Musket and spoon. All my sadness went away! I love you Musket. I know you are in doggy heaven having the time of your life.

Norman Nomura, Toastmasters

I have many fond memories with Musket. I loved how he made himself at home at Toastmaster meetings. Because he was part of a family, he was at home.

Monica Barraza, co-worker

It is a sad day for us but a good day for heaven! What a blessing Musket was to everyone he met. I'll always remember him chasing me around the office and stopping at every desk for a snack. Rest in Peace, my Muskie!

Virginia Piper, Mobility Instructor

As I cry, I am so sorry for the loss of my buddy musket. I will never forget the day Mark called to say he got him. And the name was perfect! Rest in Peace my dear Musket.

Katarina "Chick" Petersson

Extraordinary canine Musket, left us yesterday afternoon to join our four legged loved ones already departed. He was a dog in a million... guide, world traveler, author, devoted companion, docent at the Air and Space Museum, spreader of joy and a friend to everyone he encountered. He was, deservedly, a well-loved dog with legions of fans and admirers. He did so much more than he was trained to do and he did it with such elan and verve.

Well done, Musket. Well done. I feel privileged to have known you.

Peter Berkos, Academy Award-winning Sound Editor

I have always seen Musket as an honorary member of Rancho Bernardo Writers Group. He did not need the written word to convey his compassion and love for the people he met along life's path. The love returned to him was tenfold. I smile when I recall a meeting when Mark had just begun reading his work and we heard a loud strange noise. It turned out to be Musket snoring. He was a dear friend and will be missed.

Leslie Winkel, AFC Tours

I had the good fortune of having Mark, Jane, and Musket come on a 5 day motor coach tour with me one Christmas. It was my first time having a Guide Dog on a tour. I was lucky to spend several days in the company of Musket. Everyone on that tour fell in love with him (what was not to love?) and by the end of the tour we were referring to him as "Musket the Mascot." Musket had that way of melting everyone's heart the moment you met him. Oh what a wonderful life he had!

Crystal Rienick

Musket transcended human/animal relations. He was a shining soul that connected people that might not have ever come together. We have so much to thank Musket for. I am blessed to have known him and scratched his fuzzy head. Thank you Jane and Mark for sharing him with all of us.

Jack Doxey, Toastmasters

In spiritual terms Musket was a divine communicator of the highest order.

He knew that all his gifts consisted of unconditional love.

Karen Morikawa Friends of the Braille Institute

Though I didn't know Musket in his prime, I feel fortunate to have met him in his retirement. Now that I have a better background of

Musket's history, I chuckle when I remember his visit to our house and how the food in our dog bowl just vanished as he walked down the hallway. I don't think his stride even paused as he walked past their bowl. Thank you for sharing the lives of the Carlson Musketeers. Musket was truly a remarkable furry friend that touched so many people.

Molly Tosh

The first time I met Musket I was struck by how gently he led Mark, how kind his eyes were, and how sharp his memory was! I dare say he made it clear that he loved Mark and was bound and determined to walk with Mark through every adventure he could possibly dream up! I have so many fond memories, having been fortunate enough to be afforded weekly opportunities to see Musket, Mark and Jane, (and now Saffron) as their friendly, neighborhood credit union representative. Musket was the ring leader of the clan. Their visits became a delight and something I looked forward to week after week, year after year. I was so tickled by how Musket would walk through the front door, make a sharp left turn and head straight for my office! He was my buddy and even after he retired, would still come for visits occasionally. Musket was such a blessing in the truest sense of the word; a friend, a trusted companion and in my humble opinion was a gift from God, sent to remind Mark of God's profound love, sweet provision and sense of humor! I'd like to think that Musket is having the time of his life in Heaven now, waiting to one day be reunited with Mark and Jane, and in the meantime, giving docent tours of heaven to new arrivals!

Vicki Moen, Commemorative Air Force

To Musket, We will miss you. The times I had the privilege of being in your company were all too short. But you enriched my life as you did for all you met. You gave Mark the ability to give so much to the world; gave him confidence and peace flavored with your own sense of humor. A hug from me.

And from our friend Keith Tomlinson, who watched over Musket and me for more than ten years, a wonderful poem.

When Musket Dog was still a pup
Mark came to class and picked him up

The road ahead was still unknown
When Mark and Musket headed home

Mark found a job explaining ADA
The work was important but not much pay

Then McDonald's wouldn't sell them fries
So he sued their buns, no he isn't shy

After Access Info had its day
Mark looked to find a better way

The love of flying was the new hook
And Mark took off to write his book

All this time Musket was Mark's Guide
He was always present, by his side

As docents showing all the planes
Mark gave the talks, and Musket got the fame

A more noble dog you'll never meet
In the mall or on the street

So here's to Musket, Mark's number one
You couldn't be closer if you were a son

Thanks for all the miles as a Guide
It certainly was an awesome ride

From Saffron

Musket, I knew you in a way no one else ever could. You were my big brother, my mentor, my teacher, my best friend. You taught me all the important things, like how to beg the right way, how to lie in the middle of the floor and how to fill up an entire bed. But you also showed me that to be a good Guide Dog was a very special calling and that I should be the best one I could. You told me that Daddy and Mommy loved me and to love them with all my heart. You showed me how to love, Musket. Thank you, big brother, I'll never forget you.

For nearly fourteen years, an eyeblink in eternity, Musket blazed a glowing trail across our lives like a comet. And like a comet he all too soon disappeared into the skies, leaving only awesome memories.

His loving heart was far larger than the furry body that contained it.

I wanted to close this chapter, both literally and figuratively in Musket's story with something I remember from my Civil War re-enacting days. In Ken Burns' PBS series, at the end of the first episode, the narration read a letter written by a Union officer named Sullivan Ballou to his wife.

It was one of the most beautifully written and eloquent missives of undying devotion and love ever penned. And the last few lines speak in a way that I believe Musket, if he were able, would want us to hear.

🐾 If the dead can come back to this earth, and flit unseen around those they loved, I shall always be near you in the garish day, and the darkest night, amidst your happiest scenes and gloomiest hours always, always. If the soft breeze fans your cheek, it shall be my breath, or the cool air cools your throbbing temples, it shall be my spirit passing by.

Do not mourn me, think I am gone, and wait for me, for we shall meet again.

Musket
August 27, 2000 – July 29, 2014

sic transit Gloria mundi

CHAPTER 10

THE ADVENTURES OF CAPTAIN ADA

"I've seen a look in dogs' eyes, a quickly vanishing
look of amazed contempt, and I am convinced that
basically dogs think humans are nuts."
— John Steinbeck

This is a short interlude to soften the emotions and give the reader a fresh dose of perspective. I wrote this during one of my "stream of consciousness" periods, when I thought I was another Dave Barry. You be the judge.

The blind man and his Guide Dog were walking along the sidewalk near their home. There was nothing special about him. He was tall, husky and fiftyish. The dog, on the other hand was a pretty and active yellow Labrador. Although most people would hardly give them a second glance, few of them knew that this particular blind man and his dog were in fact in disguise. They were really champions of the Independent Living Movement, defenders of persons with disabilities, and the superheroes of the Americans with Disabilities Act, Captain ADA and his trusty sidekick, Sapphire!

(Insert dramatic music soundbite here)

Yes, Captain ADA! Strange...very, very strange visitor from another planet who came to Earth with powers and abilities far beyond those of the general public, Captain ADA, who could change the channels of his television, bend Twizzles with his bare hands, and who, disguised as Mark Carlson and Saffron, a mild-mannered but brilliantly talented and modest writer for several national aviation magazines and his trusty Guide Dog, fights a never-ending battle for access, universal design and the American Way!

"It's been a quiet day," Mark said to his dog as they strode past the Carmel Mountain Ranch Public Library. "Too quiet. Something's got to happen."

"Why?" asked Saffron. "Can't we just have a nice walk without always having to save the world? My paws are sore."

"Some trusty sidekick you are, Saffron."

Suddenly Mark stiffened and stopped in his tracks. Saffron, not ready for this, was held back by her harness handle. "Erk! What did you do that for?"

"Shh!" he hissed, listening. "My super-hearing has picked up a cry of distress! Someone's access rights are being violated."

"'Super hearing?' You wear hearing aids, for crying out loud."

"They're not hearing aids, they're Assistive Technology. They provide the technological link between a person's limitations and their goals."

"Yada, yada, they're still hearing aids," Saffron grumbled. "So what did your super hearing pick up?"

"Someone is downtown. They are being refused access to a restaurant because they have an Assistance Animal! This is a job for...." he ripped off his shirt and shorts, revealing his colorful Spandex™ tights, "...Captain ADA!"

Saffron looked around in horror. "What are you doing? You can't undress in public!" Shouldn't you be in a phone booth?"

Captain ADA shook his head. "When was the last time you saw a phone booth? I can't very well change behind my cell phone, can I?"

"Aren't you at least supposed to wear a mask? All you have on are a pair of scratched aviator sunglasses."

"It is in the laundry. No one will recognize me."

"If you're wearing that outfit they won't admit it even if they do." Then she sighed and turned her head to grab her cape with her teeth and pull it out of the satchel on her harness. "Okay, I'm ready, Captain. By the way, why did you call yourself Captain ADA?"

"Because 'Captain Americans with Disabilities Act' wouldn't fit on my chest."

Saffron snorted. "There's plenty of room on your belly. Just move it down a bit. And why did you choose those colors?"

"What? It's red, white and blue, isn't it?"

Saffron, now in her true identity as Sapphire, tireless and brave champion of Assistance Dogs shook her head. Then she remembered that Captain ADA couldn't see her and she said, "Nope. That's not red, white and blue, Cap."

Captain ADA frowned. "That's what the guy who sold it to me said. What is it?

Sapphire squinted, trying not to look too hard. "Well, it's chartreuse, lavender and gold. Hideous."

"Wait a second," Captain ADA said with a frown. "You're a dog. You're colorblind. How do you know what color it is?"

"I am colorblind, but I can still see those colors. Yuck."

"Dang," he said, shaking his noble head so the few remaining hairs fluttered in the breeze. "No wonder it was in the bargain bin. What color is my cape?"

"You don't want to know. But I'd suggest you stay out of biker bars." Her own cape was a tasteful indigo blue with a neat yellow "S" on the back. It went perfectly with her yellow fur. "What size did you get? I didn't know they made tights for Shamu."

"They are kind of snug," he said as he adjusted his belt.

"I can see your panty lines."

Captain ADA grumbled, "Can we drop the subject? We have work to do. Someone is having their rights to public access violated by an uninformed business owner who is breaking the law. Title III of the Americans with Disabilities Act (1990) states that no person with a disability can be denied access to a public place for reasons related to their disability, and to deny access to an Assistance Animal is a further violation of the law."

"Zzzzz...Huh? Oh, sorry, I zoned out on you there. Uh, okay. What's my line? Oh yeah. Holy civil rights, Batm–I mean Captain ADA! What are we going to do?"

Captain ADA dramatically pointed forward. "We must protect the rights of that person! To the ADAmobile!"

Sapphire just stood there. "The what?"

"The ADAmobile!"

"You don't drive, Cap. And neither do I."

He sighed. "Okay the city bus."

"That's back that way, Cap." She turned around, and with their capes flapping limply in the humid air, walked back to Carmel Mountain Road.

"What...uh, ADAmobile are we taking, Captain ADA?"

"Um, I think the Route 20 bus will be here soon and we can take that to Kearny Mesa, then transfer to the 20A to Fashion Valley, then..."

Sapphire just stood there and shook her head. *Why me? I could have had a nice, normal owner who only needed to walk to the grocery store and bank every few days. But no, I had to be given to an overgrown comic book reader who's dressed like an overstuffed piñata.*

Captain ADA suddenly said, "I know! This is a job for my ADA-approved voice-over Smart Phone!" He jabbed a hand into his pocket, and with some effort, managed to pull out the phone. "Ah, got it." He punched a button. "This will tell us just what we need to know. SIRI, what is the fastest way to get to downtown San Diego from my location?"

A moment later they heard "You said 'SIRI, what is the fastest way to get to downtown San Diego from my location?'"

"Right!" Captain ADA said confidently.

"There are three Starbucks's Coffee locations fairly close to you. Do you want me to give you directions?"

Sapphire was trying not to laugh, but it wasn't easy. "Um, Captain ADA, how about if we just call a taxi?"

"No," Captain ADA said mulishly. "I'll try again." Once more he punched the button and repeated his request. A moment later SIRI replied with "The temperature in downtown San Diego is 87 degrees with a low of..." He cut it off in frustration.

Half an hour later they climbed out of the Yellow Cab at the corner of Broadway and 10th Street in downtown San Diego.

"That'll be $38.50, Mon," said the driver.

Captain ADA pulled two twenties out of the pocket of his tights and handed them over. "Keep the change."

"Thanks, Mon. Don't forget about that bar I told you about. You'd be very popular there. Have a nice day."

Captain ADA sighed. "That took long enough. For a while there I was sure he wasn't going to let you in the cab."

Sapphire snorted. "It wasn't me he wanted to keep out. He took one look at those tights and almost hit the accelerator pedal."

"Well, we're here now. And we still have our job to do."

"What job? You don't work for the state as an advocate any more. You're a magazine writer, for crying out loud, not Superman."

"Daredevil was blind, remember?"

"Yeah. I saw that Ben Affleck movie. I'm sure a lot of people who paid ten bucks to see that turkey wished they were blind too."

Captain ADA said, "Okay, Sapphire. Forward. Find the heinous fiend that dared to violate a disabled person's civil rights."

Sapphire let out a long sigh. "Okie doke. That'll be right here. The sign says 'Momma's Home Cooking and Sushi Bar.' Yeech."

"How do you know that's the place where a disabled person was being prevented from entering? Is there a sign that says 'Assistance Animals not welcome?'"

"No," she said, again rolling her eyes. "The woman and her dog are right there by the door. She is looking at her watch."

"Ah. *Now* this is a job for –"

Sapphire cut him off. "Give it a rest, will you? Just go and talk to her. And hope she's blind."

Captain ADA, trying to regain his dignity, which was just about impossible with the rainbow tights, strode over to the woman. She was about 30 and seated in a wheelchair. Her dog, a male Golden Retriever, sat patiently by her side.

"Hello," the brave superhero said in a deep voice. "I am Captain ADA. I heard you were in distress."

She looked him over with a skeptical expression. "It's about time.

I was ready to give up and go home." Then she shook her head. "In distress? Well, I'm sure not in the restaurant. They refused to let Evander inside. They said they don't allow any dogs."

"Have no fear, my dear," he began, but Sapphire bumped him with her nose. "Uh, I meant let me see what I can do. I've dealt with this kind of thing before."

"Whatever," she said. "I've been waiting for an hour. I finally had to order a pizza on my Smart Phone. Those things are great, aren't they?"

Captain ADA did not seem to hear her. He told Sapphire to take him to the restaurant door. Opening the door, a wave of scents, aromas and stenches wafted out, making him wrinkle his nose. "Are you sure you even wanted to eat in here?"

"Oh yeah," the woman said. "They make the best sushi. You should try it."

"I'll pass," he said, and entered the dark restaurant. It was quiet with only the sound of muted sitar music and a few patrons choking down their food. "Hello?" Captain ADA said to the room at large. "Is there anyone who can help me?"

He heard rapid footsteps approaching.

"I'm sorry," a man's voice said. "We don't allow dogs in here."

Captain ADA was about to talk but then the man continued. "And you must be looking for the biker bar down the street. It's right –"

"No," Captain ADA cut in. "This is where I wanted to be."

The man frowned at him. "Well, in any case, we don't allow dogs. You must leave."

"This is my Guide Dog. You can't deny me access to this establishment." His voice was stronger now. Sapphire stood there, behaving and watching every move by the two antagonists.

"I don't care," the man said. "This is a restaurant. We have to obey the Health Department regulations. We could be closed down if we let a dog in here."

Might be a good thing if you were, Sapphire thought, catching another whiff from the kitchen. *My breath doesn't smell this bad even after I've licked my butt.*

"Okay," Captain ADA said. "I'll try one more time. This is my Guide Dog. She and I are protected by the Americans with Disabilities

Act of 1990. You cannot prevent me from entering, nor can you refuse me service because of my dog. That is a direct violation of county, state and federal law, punishable by a fine of..." he paused, thinking, "...I've forgotten how much but it's a lot of money. And I could sue you for violating my civil rights."

For a moment the man said nothing. Then he pursed his lips and let out a breath. It smelled worse than the kitchen. "You disabled people just think you can push the rest of us around. Someone gets in your way and you sue them. You get the best parking spaces and all those government freebies. Isn't that enough? I don't like it. I don't like dogs and I won't let you in my restaurant. Go ahead and sue me."

Captain ADA stood his ground. "Okay, pal. You asked for it. First of all, what's your name?"

"Momma. Fred C. Momma."

Sapphire snickered and Captain ADA pulled out his phone. "I'm going to call the police. You are breaking the law." Jabbing a finger at the screen, he prayed it wouldn't let him down this time. "SIRI, call the San Diego Police Department."

SIRI replied, "Right away, Captain ADA!"

Whew. A moment later, a voice came over the speaker. "San Diego Police. How can I help you?"

"This is Captain ADA. I am at Momma's Home Cooking and Sushi Bar. I have been denied my rights to access because of my Guide Dog. I would like a patrol car to come and take my statement."

"Yes, Captain ADA. Right away. But are you sure you want access? The food there is pretty rank."

"Please just send the patrol car. Thank you, officer." Then Captain ADA punched off the call and made another. His handsome, heroic face showed triumph.

A female voice came on the phone. "This is KUSI TV 51. Cindy speaking."

"Hi, Cindy. This is Captain ADA. I am at Momma's Home Cooking and Sushi Bar. They won't let me in because of Sapphire. I called the police. Can you send a television van?"

"Hi, Captain ADA. Sure. It'll be right there. But let me ask you, are you wearing those tights?"

He bit his lip. "Um, yeah."

"Okay we'll try to keep you out of the shot. Just have Sapphire ready."

Captain ADA sighed and said to Momma, "You might want to call your lawyer, Mr. Momma. I'll be waiting outside."

The man glared at the superhero. "I don't believe you. You're bluffing." But his voice showed little conviction.

"Try me," Captain ADA said and left the restaurant, much to Sapphire's relief. She wasn't sure how much longer she could have held her breath.

Outside on the sidewalk the woman in the wheelchair was eating her pizza when they emerged. "How'd it go?"

"The police and KUSI are on the way."

She goggled at him. "You're serious? You have that kind of clout?"

He smiled, then Sapphire bumped him. "She's over that way," she whispered.

"Oh." He turned to the right. "Yes, I do. And so do you. As a person with a disability you are protected by the Americans with Disabilities Act of 1990. Title III says that you cannot be denied access to a public place because of your disability. By refusing to let Evander in, that man was committing a crime. He is going to learn that very quickly. Can I have a bit of that pizza? I'm starved."

"Sure," she said, holding out a slice. "Anchovies, artichoke hearts, pineapple and onions with goat cheese."

"On second thought, I'll pass."

"Good idea. I don't think those tights can hold any more of you."

A minute later the police arrived. Two uniformed officers stepped out of their car and walked over. "Hello, Captain ADA. Up to your old tricks, I see."

"Yes, officer, I am." He pointed to the doorway. "The owner of that establishment refused –"

"Yeah, I know," the officer said. "Same thing that Hillcrest McDonald's did back in 2009."

"Um, that wasn't me," Captain ADA said. "That was Mark Carlson with Musket."

The officers grinned. "Whatever. Shall we go in and let the man know the law?"

Just then a big van screeched to a halt at the curb. Two men jumped out, armed with cameras and recording equipment. "Is this the place? Are we too late?"

"Right on time," said Captain ADA. "Let's all go in." He indicated the woman in the wheelchair. "Would you like to lead the way, Ma'am?"

She put the empty pizza box in a trash can and told her dog, "Evander, forward." Then she rolled herself into the restaurant, followed by Captain ADA, Sapphire, the police officers and the television crew. "Hello?" she called out. "It's me again."

The owner came out of the back, but this time he wasn't blustering. He was cowed by all the activity. "Sheesh, this is more people than I've ever had in here at one time."

I'm not surprised, Sapphire thought, still wrinkling her nose.

"Sir," said the first officer, "did you tell this lady and this..." he glanced at Captain ADA, who immediately decided to dump the tights, "...gentleman that their Assistance Dogs were not allowed in your establishment?"

"Um... I may have, but I don't recall..." Momma said in a weak voice. "Why?"

"Because that is a violation of the law. The ADA says you cannot refuse access or services to a disabled person. And their dogs are allowed in public places. You have broken the law."

"Well," Fred Momma said, seeing that he was on camera. "I may have misunderstood. I mean, I would never knowingly do such a thing. They are of course welcome. And just to show that my heart is in the right place, I would like to offer them both a free meal as our guest."

"That's okay," the lady said. "I've eaten. But I'll be back *with* my dog." She turned on the spot and wheeled her way past the cameras and out the door. "You're my hero, Captain ADA!"

"How about you, Sir?" Momma asked Captain ADA. "Want a free dinner at Momma's Home Cooking and Sushi Bar where there is ample parking?"

"I can't accept any gifts, Sir. Just doing my job. Thank you for your cooperation." Then he turned towards the cops. "Ahem."

"Oh, sorry," the first police officer said, reaching into his pocket. "Now, where is that thing? I have it here somewhere...here it is, wadded in with the Miranda." He cleared his throat. "This country is just a bit more accessible thanks to you, Captain ADA."

"Just doing my part as a member of the team," Captain ADA said, shaking hands with the officers and the TV crew. "Thanks guys."

"As long as we don't have to wear those colors," one of the KUSI guys said in a low voice.

The cop leaned over to his partner. "Where did he get that outfit? A clown rummage sale?"

Then Captain ADA and his trusty sidekick slipped away.

"Who was that masked fruitcake?" asked Fred Momma.

"That was Captain ADA," the officer said. "A real hero. But a lousy dresser." He swatted his partner on the arm. "Let's go and find a donut shop. I'm hungry."

In a short time the sidewalk in front of Momma's Home Cooking and Sushi Bar was empty except for the stray cats that took one sniff and ran away.

And far off in North County was a blind man putting on his torn shirt and shorts while his faithful Guide Dog watched. "Just another day in the life of Captain ADA," she said, smiling. "I'll lead you home, Daddy."

"It's just not the same as in the comic books," Mark grumbled, holding the harness. "A pizza sounds good to me right now."

"You're on, Daddy," said Saffron as they walked home.

CHAPTER **11**

ON THE ROAD WITH SAFFRON

"Some of our greatest historical and artistic treasures we place
with curators in museums; others we take for walks."
— Roger Caras

Saffron is my American Express Card. I never
leave home without her. This is about some of the trips, both business
and pleasure that we took with Saffron. Since they straddle the Musket
and Saffron era, covering at least five years, I chose to gather most of
them here.

In early 2013 Saffron and I literally hit the ground running. Even
while I was at Guide Dogs, my second book *Flying on Film – A Century
of Aviation in the Movies 1912 - 2012* was in the last phase of publication.
I was sending and receiving e-mails and phone calls from my publisher
and editor. When I was back at home we were going through the final
proofing and editing. Then, in December 2012 it became a reality. My
first real published book, that is not self-published, was done. It was the
result of four years of research, studying, watching (or trying to watch)
more than 200 aviation films, interviewing 250 pilots, actors, directors,
writers, stunt pilots, historians, veterans and authors. I was immensely
proud of it. Just think, a carefully written book about 175 aviation films
written by a blind guy!

I never once mentioned being blind in the book, nor did I say
anything about my Guide Dog. Must have slipped my mind.

Actually, since the book was based on a subject that demanded that the readers NOT know the writer was blind, I chose not to say anything about it. Until I had to.

In a very short time, the network of contacts I had generated in the aviation and film communities were interested in the book. I sent several copies to other writers and aviation historians for their opinions and reviews. Their responses were universally positive, even stellar. I was very happy with the results. It proved that I could reach a level of credibility in a field not known for blind writers.

♡ Daddy worked very hard on the book. But I still think it would have sold better if my picture was on the cover.

Reel Stuff

One of my contacts, a writer and film buff named Ron Kaplan, asked me if I'd like to come to Dayton, Ohio, for an aviation film festival he organized. It was called "Reel Stuff" and showcased several innovative and memorable aviation films at the National Museum of the Air Force at Wright-Patterson Air Force Base. What an honor! Of course I said yes. I was pleased to know that another friend, William Wellman, Jr. would be there as well. Bill and I became friends while I was working on the book. For those of you who are silent film buffs, Bill's father William A. Wellman was the director of the 1927 film *Wings*, starring Charles "Buddy" Rogers and Richard Arlen. *Wings* won the very first Academy Award for Best Picture and was one of the best films of the silent era.

I prepared to fly to Dayton. The museum bookstore was going to sell my book and Bill's book about his father. He would be introducing *Wings* for the audiences.

Flying the Furry Skies

Jane dropped us off at the airport and Saffron led me in. Airport security hadn't slackened, a blessing and a curse, but I never complained.

Sometimes the TSA people checked us out as usual, while other times I was fortunate to avoid strip and body cavity search. No worries, that's the way it had to be.

Jane had taught me well. When our flight was called, Saffron and I were ready for pre-boarding. This was so we could be seated and out of the way when the other passengers boarded. I had Saffron's harness off and stowed and her lying down on the floor. As fellow passengers settled in next to us they often asked her name. So far I have not encountered any ill feelings towards her being on the plane, but one woman did remarked, "Well it would be nice if my dog could be here with me instead of in the luggage."

I refrained from telling her she could have that if she were willing to go blind or have some other disability. I knew she was just missing her dog. In time she made friends with Saffron.

Saffron proved to be as good a traveler as Musket. While Musket had usually slept through an airline takeoff, Saffron often tried to look around to see what was happening. Once in a while she climbed up to look out the window.

I suppose, as my eyes she wanted to tell me what was out there.

♡ No, I was looking for a nice piece of grass to pee on. But every one I saw zipped past before I could ask Daddy to stop the plane.

The flight was smooth until we began the descent into Chicago's Midway Airport. There was a bad storm and the pilots had to make a VERY steep pull-out and go-around during the first approach. I don't mind admitting, knowing what I do about airliners, I was pretty tense. But Saffron slept through it. She wasn't as laid back as Musket on a plane but she did sleep a lot, except when the flight attendant brought snacks.

♡ I'll take ten bags of peanuts and a bowl of chilled water, please. Not in a plastic cup.

We landed safely at Midway Airport but our connection to Dayton was delayed.

I had planned to arrive at the opening reception an hour early but now it was going to be very close.

Jane had bought a really cool carry-on bag that fit nicely into the overhead bin and served all the purposes of a full suitcase. I took that and stepped off the plane. I asked for assistance to my connection and was escorted to the other gate.

Saffron, after the long flight, needed to go, but unlike Musket's first time in the Windy City, we had no trouble finding a place for her to relieve her bladder.

The next flight was on a Saab turboprop through the edge of the storm. Saffron was tense, probably from sensing it in me, but it was almost over before it began. When we finally reached the sidewalk outside the terminal I was done in and so was Saffron. She seemed to be saying "Hey Daddy, can we find a nice bed for me to sleep in?"

A nice couple from the museum arrived to pick us up and take us to the hotel. Betty Darst and her husband had been prepped by Ron and they were eager to meet me...well, Saffron, and be our escorts in Dayton.

At the hotel, we checked in and I changed as fast as I could while Saffron wolfed down her supper. She got an extra bit because she'd been so good on the long flight.

When Betty dropped us off in front of the museum the reception was half over. I went in and Ron found me immediately. He patted Saffron and took us inside to meet some of the celebrities and dignitaries. There we found Bill Wellman, and Catherine Wyler, daughter of William Wyler, one of Hollywood's greatest directors. Betty found some refreshments for me while Saffron and I mingled. She, of course, was the center of attention. And when people realized this blind guy was the author of *Flying on Film* it created more than a few raised eyebrows. But it was great. They had a photographer to shoot formal Red Carpet portraits of the attendees and so there we were, Saffron and her Daddy on the red carpet posing with some of Hollywood's elite.

Mark and Saffron at the 2013 Reel Stuff Aviation
Film Festival Reception in Dayton

I had my personal copy of *Flying on Film* with me and asked Ron, Catherine, Bill and other celebrities and veterans to autograph it. Over the last two years I've collected more than fifty signatures in it, many of men and women who are now gone. It's one of my most prized possessions.

♡ Ahem. What am I, chopped liver?

You know what I mean, Saffron. The film festival itself was only part of the allure for me. Bill Wellman and I spent a lot of time at the bookstore signing our books, and going to see some of the movies. Catherine Wyler introduced Memphis *Belle,* the 1990 movie about the famous B-17 Flying Fortress crew, starring Matthew Modine and John Lithgow. She answered questions from the audience and when she found one she could not answer, turned to me for the reply. As the aviation film "expert" (a title I hardly deserved) I filled in the gaps.

While there I was given a special tour of the Air Force Museum, including the restoration facility where they worked on some of the most historic planes in Air Force history. This was meat and potatoes to me. Saffron took it all in stride, leading me along and around all the strange big things with wings. She never faltered and every photo of me had her right next to the plane.

Wings was shown on the second day of the festival, where Bill Wellman introduced his father's *Magnum Opus.* And I was there to cheer my friend on. Now, you might be thinking, "Hey, this was a silent film. And you're blind. So how did you..."

Good question. I mostly listened to the musical score. Bear in mind I've probably seen *Wings* at least fifty times since I was ten years old. I remembered it very well, even if I couldn't see it anymore. No matter.

The last film to be shown was Tony Scott's blockbuster *Top Gun,* with Tom Cruise. This was the 3-D version, and I have to tell you, despite all the hoopla and high-tech computer wizardry that went into creating a three-dimensional version of this exciting aviation action film, it didn't look any different to me.

♡ Just in case you didn't catch it, that was sarcasm.

Anthony Edwards, who played "Goose" in the movie, did the introduction. Just before the showing, I was in the lobby with Bill Wellman when Ron Kaplan came up to me and said "Hey Mark, I'd like you to meet Anthony Edwards."

I turned and there he was. We shook hands and he met Saffron. I was stunned, since I knew that Ron was keeping the celebrities insulated from the public. But there I was meeting a real live movie star. I wanted to ask him about *Revenge of the Nerds,* but thankfully common sense prevailed. He did autograph my book for me, right above a picture from *Top Gun.* "All the best, Anthony 'Goose' Edwards."

So ended Saffron and my time in Dayton, Ohio, the birthplace of American aviation. Our flight home was far smoother and less frenetic than the eastward journey. Saffron made friends on the plane, particularly a sweet lady whose feet she insisted on sleeping on. But try as I might, I could not get her to move off. "That's quite all right," the lady said. "My feet are always cold on airliners. She's keeping me warm."

Amazing.

♡ She slipped me some peanuts so I wanted to be near her.

Not So Quiet Birdmen

A pilots' club that called themselves the Quiet Birdmen, or QB invited me to come to Dallas to speak about my book. Jim Knapp, a very enthusiastic fan and American Airlines simulator instructor had the QB pay all my expenses. I mean, I was literally not allowed to take out my wallet while in Dallas and Fort Worth.

It was my first time in the Lone Star State. I arranged for fifty copies of *Flying on Film* and twenty of *Confessions* to be shipped to Jim in Dallas. He picked me up at the AA terminal and drove me to my hotel. When we stepped off the plane, he was there. As an American Airlines official he had the run of the airport, even past security. I'd told him about Saffron and he was eager to meet my little girl.

Jim liked her right away and she took to him just fine. We climbed into his SUV and got to know each other. I found him to be a serious Cowboys fan, but as I was to learn, there was NO such thing as a non-football fan in Dallas. I pretended to be one, just in case the Texans were in a lynching mood.

The hotel was top rate, and when Jim took me into the reception room for my talk, I was greeted by over seventy-five pilots, all of whom were "good ol' boys."

The Quiet birdmen refer to themselves as a "drinking club with a flying problem," and that fits perfectly. And Saffron, being a good hunting dog breed was an immediate hit. She made the rounds of the room and was petted to a fare-thee-well. She didn't mind the attention at all. But she was the only female in the room.

The quiet Birdmen is exclusively male, a real throwback to the gentlemen's clubs of the 19th century. And even though I personally liked those guys, I won't deny they were, at least in a group setting, real chauvinists.

♡ Wow. No wonder I felt so special.

After dinner I was introduced by Jim. He talked a little about my background and how he found me through my book. After a round of inebriated applause, I stood up and accessed the Power Point presentation on my laptop. I made a joke about a blind guy writing a book about the movies, which was well received. My presentation covered several notable aviation movies in the last century, telling stories about the filming, production, and aircraft. Saffron, unlike Musket, didn't sleep at all while I talked. She was right there, watching me and the audience.

I talked for about 45 minutes. They were a great crowd, laughing at the right places and giving me a great round of applause afterwards

♡ Daddy was really feeling good that night. I was proud of him.

Jim made a presentation of a bottle of 14-year old Scotch, and a DVD of *Naughty Stewardesses*. It was their version of a joke. I will state for the record, that to this day I have not watched that movie.

♡ Yeah, what's the point?

I was beginning to think I might do pretty well in this new profession. The book signing went very well. I sold all but four books and had a huge wad of cash that made me immediately paranoid. After all, Texans carry guns, right? But Jim took us out to his favorite bar with a couple more QB buddies, where we drank more beer and ate mountains of gulf shrimp.

The next day he took us to the C.R. Smith American Airlines

Museum, where I did another talk to a public audience and another book signing. The bookstore manager, a lovely lady named Judith Clark was instantly in love with Saffron. She gave her an American Airlines leash. I bought some souvenirs but when the time came to pay up, I was told it was on the house. After a tour of the museum, which included going aboard a vintage AA Douglas DC-3 airliner, Jim drove me to the AA Academy where they train pilots, mechanics and flight crews. It was like a big corporate campus. I was going to stay there for the next night and leave the following afternoon.

The coolest part was when Jim took us to the flight simulators. Each was a section of an airliner nose complete with flight deck and controls. He led me into the Boeing 767 simulator and let me take the controls in a takeoff and landing. It was very surreal and awesome. I actually avoided crashing, which only reinforced my belief that Boeing made the best planes in the world. Saffron was in the co-pilot's seat. Jim took some pictures of this but he later admitted he could not send them to me because of security regulation. I understood. I am certain Boeing would not want anyone to know that a blind guy could fly their plane.

♡ That was fun. I kept sniffing at the controls while this movie played in front of us. Daddy did just fine, except for the Cessna he ran over.

Jim then took us to the central atrium and the memorial to the American Airlines crews killed on 9/11. It was a beautiful, peaceful place. A large oak tree was surrounded by 21 smaller trees, each one planted for an AA crewmember.

Every year on the anniversary, family members came to place wreaths and remember the fallen heroes.

♡ It was sad to see that memorial. I wasn't yet born on 9/11 but Daddy and Mommy still have terrible memories of that day.

The American Airlines 9/11 Memorial at the C.R. Smith Academy

Staying in the academy dorm was fine, and if I had been single, a "target-rich environment" to use a fighter pilot term. The rooms were full of cute young flight attendant trainees. Sigh. I got the impression, which I'm sure was accurate, that Saffron was the first Guide Dog to ever stay there.

The next morning after we had some breakfast in the cafeteria, Jim drove us to downtown Dallas. I'd always wanted to see Dealey Plaza, the site of John F. Kennedy's assassination. We parked and walked over to the Texas School Book Depository, where there was a museum on the Sixth Floor. We took the tour, and Jim listened to me telling him details of the assassination, which happened when I was three years old.

But I clearly remember Mom and Dad watching the news about it.

Then we walked around the plaza and Jim pointed out the twin X's painted on the street where JFK was fatally shot.

It was a somber moment, and Jim took pictures of Saffron on the wall by the street.

At DFW we talked about getting together in October when the QB would be having their annual convention in San Diego. I told Jim he would be MY guest and he would not pay for anything. After a guy hug from me and a kiss from Saffron, he left us at the gate and we flew back to San Diego.

Texas ain't bad, except for the football. I got the impression everything there was free.

06/28/2011 AM 06:18

Saffron at the wall at Dealey Plaza, Dallas

War Stories

That trip had an unexpected bonus. After my talk to the QB, a big, ebullient Texan came over and handed me a cold beer. In a deep booming drawl, he said, "Hey y'all ever heard of the Flintlock Disaster?" I admitted I had not. So this man, who introduced himself as Dan Brouse proceeded to tell me a remarkable story about a World War Two Marine fighter squadron that had been almost wiped out in a cyclone in the Pacific during Operation Flintlock, the huge invasion of the Marshall Islands in January of 1944.

This was meat and potatoes for a military history writer. I began to drool.

♡ I noticed. Daddy was so engrossed he did not realize I snuck off and ate a leftover chicken fillet. Well, he should keep an eye on me!

That conversation led to me interviewing the surviving pilots, and writing an article for *Aviation History Magazine* in January 2015. Then, after four years of interviews, phone calls, research and writing on a diet of cold coffee, fingernails and Skittles, this led to the November 2017 publication of my latest book, *The Marines' Lost Squadron - the Odyssey of VMF-422*. It was a lot of work, while Jane and Saffron were virtual literary widows as I was at my computer every night. But it was well worth it. The book has gotten some great reviews and sold pretty well. And of course it led to yet even more lectures and book signing tours.

Dean Koontz, better watch your "six!" (Fighter pilot jargon).

Those were whirlwind days for Saffron and me.

♡ They sure were. I hardly had time to go pee before we jumped onto another plane to who knew where.

Jane didn't go along on any of those trips since she had to stay home to take care of Musket. But that was okay with her. She caught up on her craft projects and other things.

California Here We Come

In April 2013 Jane and I went on an AFC motor coach tour of central California to Salinas, Monterey, Carmel and Yosemite National Park. As my readers know I had always loved Yosemite, having gone there with my family many times. I wanted Jane to see it and this tour included a drive through the valley and lunch at the historic Ahwhahnee Hotel.

We were glad to have Leslie Winkel with us again. She had loved Musket and was very happy to know we were signed up for this trip. But the big issue was, what to do with Musket? Leslie would have welcomed him on the coach even if he was no longer a working dog, but he had to stay behind. For one thing he'd had some minor surgery to remove two big cysts on his neck. At first we asked Mike and Cheri O'Neill, who'd been Saffron's raisers. They gladly said they'd take care of him. But after thinking it over, Jane and I decided to kennel him at our vet where they could watch over him and maintain his antibiotics.

It would be the first time Musket would not be going along on a trip. Vanessa and Melissa and the other wonderful staff at Carmel Mountain Veterinary all loved him.

I packed several days' worth of Saffron's food, a few toys and her travel bowls. Jane took care of the luggage. For some strange reason she would not let me near the closet when she packed. And after the suitcases were full it was apparently punishable by death to touch them. I made sure I had plenty of audio books, my cell phone and other needs. Saffron was excited about all the activity and ran back and forth, trying to get into everything. Musket, on the other hand was pretty glum.

We took him to the vet and they took him in. I was glad I could not see the miserable look on his face as they led him away.

♡ Poor Muskie. He really wanted to go, but he would be well cared for. Better you than me, big brother.

The first part of the trip took us from San Diego to Union Station in Los Angeles where we were to board three vintage 1950's California Zephyr cars on an Amtrak train to Salinas. The dining car, first-class coach and famous domed observation car took us up the California coast. Being a history buff I was enchanted by the train, all gleaming aluminum and glass. I remember riding the zephyr from Oakland to Colorado Springs with my parents in the mid-1960s. As it happened, the man who owned the coaches was along and I asked him about the restoration. He related the long process of returning the half-century old cars back to their original condition. When I told him I might have ridden in those same cars more than forty years ago, he said that a lot of people had found it a nostalgic journey to ride in them again.

♡ It was my first train ride! I liked how much room there was to walk around and I could stretch out under the tables.

We had a wonderful lunch and dinner. Leslie, after seeing to the other passengers, came to sit with us and ask about Musket. She quickly fell under Saffron's spell.

When we pulled into the Salina station, where our luxury motor coach was waiting, Saffron began establishing her place on the tour. Musket had always been comfortable lying on the floor under my seat, while Jane sat across the aisle from us.

But Saffron refused to lie on the floor, even if it was carpeted. She wanted to lie on the seat next to her Mommy. At first I was firm, but in time, with Jane and Leslie both pleading, I threw my hands in the air and said "Oh, go ahead. I'm helpless against you three. Just don't tell Guide Dogs about it."

So from that point on, Princess Saffron rode on a seat, lying on Jane's white sweater.

♡ I like the sound of that. "Princess Saffron," it fits.

We stayed in a nice hotel in Monterey for two nights, and got to know some of our fellow passengers. Most were seniors, but a few were our age. Many of them were curious about Saffron. I'd brought a few copies of *Confessions* along and they sold quickly.

The first full day of sightseeing, a term I think is a bit redundant, we went back to Salinas to John Steinbeck's house. The 1930s author was a legend in central California. My mom read all his books and encouraged me to do so as well. Being at his boyhood home, which is now a historic landmark, was kind of neat. Sitting at a large table in the dining room where a docent told us about Steinbeck's life and work, we enjoyed a great lunch. Saffron was at my feet, sound asleep. The Steinbeck Museum had many of his artifacts and books, and I bought a DVD of the original *Of Mice and Men* with Burgess Meredith and Lon Chaney, Jr.

Every time we boarded the motor coach the other passengers said hello to Saffron, who wagged her tail and greeted her new friends. The tour then took us to a working organic farm where we rode a big hay wagon and sampled the most succulent and sweet strawberries I've ever had in my life. We picked them right off the vines. I actually had no trouble picking them. Saffron was rather keen on them too.

♡ I love strawberries! No one has ever told us they were bad for dogs.

Jane, who was having some problems with pain in her feet and legs tried to minimize walking as much as possible, so I took care of any short errands she needed. Leslie was a gem who took real care of her charges.

Every night I fed Saffron and took her out to the grass to do her thing, but she always slept on the bed with her Mommy.

I made a habit of calling the vet every day to see how Musket was doing. Vanessa told me he was fine and getting plenty of attention and care. She never passed him without patting his big head. He slept most of the time, but I still felt kind of guilty.

A drive down to Carmel, the swank seaside town where Clint Eastwood was mayor led to the beautiful 17-Mile Drive and Pebble Beach Golf Course. I got a Pebble Beach score card and had another passenger enter in my "score," in which I broke 100. Then I had it signed. I thought it would make a nice souvenir. A blind guy winning at Pebble Beach. Okay, to be honest, I did not play Pebble Beach. Saffron did. She chased the balls and was asked to leave.

♡ Once again, Daddy is being silly. Only Tiger Woods asked me to leave. I was getting more attention than he was.

Now who's being silly? Yosemite was the final destination for the tour. We arrived at Chukchamsey Casino south of the park and checked in. By this time we were all getting just a bit weary. Jane's pain was causing more problems so Leslie and I did everything we could to make her more comfortable.

The resort was nice and we got meal tickets, as well as a $20.00 card for using in the casino.

The Fever

I've never tried real casino gaming. It was never an attraction for me. But this time I thought I'd try it. I had saved all my quarters and dimes, and on the first evening I asked Leslie to show me around. The casino was big and loud, a real assault on my ears, and probably Saffron's too. A lot of people asked me about her and of course I obliged them. I knew this wasn't my kind of environment, but I cashed the coins in for a cash card. It came to about $40.00. Leslie showed me how to use the electronic slots. I sat down with Saffron lying by my side and began my slow, relentless slide into the sleazy world of gambling. I got the hang of it pretty fast. Using the card first, I actually started winning. After an hour I'd made about sixty bucks. Maybe I had a knack for gambling.

I had a couple of drinks and just wandered around, letting Saffron do the leading. She was more interested in leading me to the buffet than in helping me break the bank. Then back to the slots. Yes, I was getting "The Fever."

On the old *Twilight Zone* show there was an episode starring Everett Sloane as a small-town churchgoer who won a trip to Vegas. He had no intention of using the money the casino gave him, but a drunken gambler made him put a silver dollar into a slot. And he won. But he was not comfortable with this and attempted to put the money back in the machine. And in a short time he was totally hooked, cashing huge checks and headed for bankruptcy. Everybody saw how he had gotten "The Fever" and in the end it killed him. Great show.

And that was on my mind as I sat down at the One-armed Bandit with Saffron beseeching me not to lose her food money.

♡ I'm going to tell Mommy on you!

She already knew, Saffron. She even gave me her cash card. But in glaring contrast to my earlier success, I soon lost not only what I'd won, I quickly burned through my cash stash.

This was the moment of truth. Should I go to the cashier and pull out my Visa? Should I take the chance and "just win back what I'd lost?" Should I keep going? After all, I had done well earlier. Sooner or later I'd start to win. I just had to be willing to...gamble.

The Fever passed. Or maybe it was indigestion from the pizza buffet.

♡ Daddy walked away from all that wealth without a backward glance. I'm glad since I had to pee.

I patted my pretty yellow Labrador on the head and said, "Come on, Saffron, let's get you outside and then go up to Mommy."

Without a second thought I calmly walked out of the casino, making them about forty dollars richer and me a lot wiser.

Granite Wonders

Jane was excited to see Yosemite as the coach drove up the winding mountain roads through the tall evergreen forests. I knew it would not be the same for me. That was okay. I'd seen it many times. When the coach stopped by the main visitor's center in the valley, we climbed out and went into the gift shop where Jane blew more money in five minutes than I had in my entire life of gambling.

A wonderful lunch of Flatiron Steaks and potatoes at the beautiful Ahwhahnee Hotel was followed by a tram tour of the valley. It was a very hot sunny day and the open tram was like being on a frying pan.

Leslie ran back and forth, passing out water bottles and sun shades. Jane was entranced by the beautiful valley and towering granite cliffs. I could see it all in my memory, and Saffron, who was sitting on the seat between us, was twisting her head around like a bottle cap to see everything.

♡ Whine. All those trees and so little pee!

The trip ended the next day when the coach drove us back to San Diego, where we found our car in the lot by the pickup area. Leslie hugged us both and got some nice kisses from Saffron. I gave her one as well. She was a terrific lady and to be honest, I had kind of a crush on her. But don't tell Jane.

Then we drove down to get Musket, who immediately began sniffing us. He must have recognized Leslie's scent. Boy did he give us the stink eye.

Among the Warbirds

The New Year of 2014 had just begun when I was invited to speak at Planes of Fame in Chino in Riverside County. Planes of Fame had one of the largest privately-owned collections of flying vintage military aircraft in the world. Every month they showcased and flew a vintage warbird and invited speakers to talk. January's plane was the Curtiss P-40 Warhawk of Flying Tigers fame. Steve Hinton, their chief pilot had been very helpful while I was researching for the book, so I owed them a debt of gratitude.

Linda Stull, Alan Cutsinger, Mike Dralle, Vicki Moen, Chuck Sweeney of the DFC Society, B-17 pilot Ed Davidson, and several others came to show their support. I had also called Zona Appleby, the widow of Hollywood stunt pilot Jim Appleby. We never met face to face while I interviewed her for the book, but now we could talk in person.

Planes of Fame was allowing me to do direct sales so I brought fifty copies of the book and several of *Confessions* to sell.

I met Zona, a sweet and energetic lady who gave me a hug and got to know Saffron.

Zona and Linda watched Saffron while I did the same presentation I had done in Dallas.

The presentation was in a big hangar, and from what I heard later, it was the biggest crowd they'd had in years, over 550 attendees.

The audience enjoyed the talk and posed several questions, most of which I was able to answer. All in all it was a great day and I was feeling good. But there was one thing I missed. Having Musket there. He'd always been by my side when I did these things but those days were over.

I was permitted to sit in the P-40, wearing my USAAF uniform. It was pretty cool.

Mark in his USAAF uniform in the cockpit of a World War II Curtiss P-40E Warhawk, Planes of Fame, Chino

Off to Seattle

The Museum of Flight in Seattle asked me to come and do my Power Point presentation. They paid all my expenses. While the weather was nearly constant cold rain, there was one significant similarity between Dallas and Seattle. Football! It was the weekend of the NFL Playoffs. The Seattle Seahawks were trying to get to the Super Bowl. I landed right in the thick of it. I had made several contacts up there and was eager to meet these people face to face. After being picked up at Sea-Tac Airport by J.D. Wynecken, the events coordinator, he drove me to my hotel.

Saffron was as curious as ever, noting the new smells and sights. After only a year together we had traveled more than Musket and I had in the first five years. Ah, the rigors of life as an author.

The Museum of Flight had a fantastic collection of vintage and rare aircraft, particularly in light of its proximity to Boeing.

The one I most wanted to see was a one-of-a-kind Boeing B-17F Flying Fortress that had been restored to perfect 1943 condition. I had written an article about this plane for *EAA Warbirds Magazine*, and they were kind enough to let me tour it. The plane, called "Boeing Bee," was in a hangar from October to May to protect it from Seattle's persistent precipitation (I dare you to say that three times fast) and not open to the public. But, there I was dressed in my USAAF uniform. I wanted some photos of me in the pilot's seat of a B-17.

Julia Cannell, J.D's boss, a terrific lady and real dog lover, held Saffron while I climbed up into the plane. Herb Phelan, who had been in charge of the restoration, showed me around. Even without sight, I knew every inch of the Flying Fortress. I felt my way around, commenting and praising the work the restoration team had done. It had taken seventeen years to restore the battered old warbird to perfect condition. She had been used in the 1990 film *Memphis Belle*, and then sent to Seattle.

See Chapter Seven of *Flying on Film* for more information. I hope you don't mind me plugging my books, but I gotta earn a living.

♡ I watched as Daddy climbed into this big airplane. He was in there a long time, but Miss Julia was so nice. She sat down and petted me. I really liked her. They were all nice to me and Daddy.

Saffron and mark by the restored Boeing B-17F
"Boeing Bee" at the Museum of Flight, Seattle

Saffron was very popular at the museum, and as Julia or J.D. took us around, many people were eager to meet her. She, of course was happy to do the same. Just as with Musket, I wanted my dog to be an ambassador to the public. And she was great at it, especially with children.

On the last day of our stay in Seattle, which coincidentally was on the day the Seattle Seahawks were in the playoffs, I was taken into the auditorium. JD and the technician showed me where the stage and podium were and what would be happening. I'd be introduced by JD and do my presentation, then answer questions, and then go out to the lobby to sign books.

Saffron was with JD and Julia while I was talking.

The audience filed in and took their seats. About a hundred or so, which was encouraging but then again they might just have wanted to get out of the rain.

After JD introduced me, I patted Saffron, gave her a treat and took the microphone. From that point on I was in my element. I began, "Thank you all for coming. I'm very honored to be here at the Museum of Flight. I will point out, that if any of you hear snoring while I'm talking, that's my Guide Dog, Saffron." Then I paused and said, "Yes, that's right *Flying on Film* was written by a blind guy."

A few people laughed, not sure if I was serious. But I set them at ease. "Yes, I am legally blind, but pretty much every movie I will talk about I had seen several times before."

Then I began my presentation. It lasted about 45 minutes and the audience was receptive and appreciative. They laughed at the right times and murmured at others.

Afterward, I answered several questions, all of which I sweated. I was most worried that someone would ask me something I simply didn't know. As it was, no one did. Whew.

♡ He came very close, though.

The book signing went well. The museum book store sold most of the books it had ordered, all of which I autographed. Several people wanted to meet Saffron, of course, which was fine with me. She was as much of a sensation as a blind movie critic

The Day of the Dogs

♡ Tell the story about when we met Dean Koontz, Daddy!

Why don't you tell it, Saffron?

♡ Okay. Well, Daddy said that this man, Dean Koontz, a famous writer and dog lover was going to be doing a book signing at Canine Companions for Independence in Oceanside. He had donated huge sums of money over the years to support CCI. He wrote a lot of books about his dogs just like Daddy wrote about us. So Linda took us there. The CCI campus was jammed with people, dogs and kids. I was not the only Guide Dog.

Dean Koontz talked about CCI and how they did wonderful work to train dogs like me. When the book signing started, Daddy and Linda reached him and then Daddy introduced me. Linda bought his book. Then Daddy told Dean about Musket's book and gave him two autographed copies. I guessed that this was not an uncommon thing for Dean, but he smiled and thanked Daddy. He was really nice and I licked his hand.

A few months later I received a letter from Dean Koontz, saying he had read *Confessions* and it was a great book. He wished me luck and hoped it would become successful. I know now that the book had really needed some serious editing, but I did feel good about his letter.

♡ Watch out, Dean Koontz! Daddy is coming up behind you with my book.

Find the Mustang

The San Diego Air & Space Museum, where Musket had been such a hit often invited me to come and speak. But my days as a tour guide and docent had become infrequent. Part of the problem was the San Diego Transit System, which had made several "cost-effective" changes and eliminated or combined several routes. The upshot was that it was no longer easy to get to Balboa Park. The routes I used to take now added an extra hour each way. And it was too expensive in the pre-Uber days to get a ride down there. All in all, I had to endure five hours of bus travel for four hours at the museum. Just not worth it. I only went there about once a month. Saffron was not as quick to get the hang of the museum as Musket had been.

♡ Well, only boys like airplanes. It was just not my thing, Daddy.

Don't let Linda hear you say that, Saffron. She loves planes. Saffron did get the hang of the tour route and I did something I never tried with Musket. I repeatedly brought her to certain aircraft in the static displays such as the Granville Brothers Gee Bee Racer, the Curtiss P-26 Peashooter fighter, the P-51 Mustang, the Supermarine MkXVI Spitfire, and the F4U Corsair. I reached out and touched the plane and said its name several times to Saffron, then gave her a piece of kibble. After doing this several times on each visit, she started going to the correct aircraft when I said "Take me to the Mustang, Saffron. Take me to the Mustang." Slowly she got to where she could take me to each of those planes with reasonable accuracy. Then she received a treat and lots of praise. It was a real triumph and the other docents were impressed.

♡ Well it was easy. Really, all those planes looked alike to me. Just big propellers and wings. It made Daddy happy. The people there were very nice to me, but I got annoyed when all they did was talk about Musket and what a great dog he was.

Saffron was not Musket, but she was every bit as lovable and drew attention. And she did manage to do some things Musket never did. I knew I could not get to the museum as often as I wanted but I still maintained a good relationship with the staff and volunteers. We had some great times and made wonderful friends.

The Tin Goose

In February 2015 two things, one good and one bad, happened. The first was when the Experimental Aircraft Association's 1929 Ford AT-5 Trimotor came to San Diego. Famous as the "Tin Goose," the Trimotor was the historic link between the biplane era and the age of all-metal monoplanes. The EAA's Trimotor toured the country and sold rides. I was not about to pass up on the chance. Linda, Barry, Mike, Vicki and I went to Gillespie Field in El Cajon to see it. Saffron was with me. Now, there was no way I could just go and pay my $75 fee and climb on like any ordinary person. Nope. I dressed the part. Gabardine pants, brown brogans, khaki button-down shirt, grey fedora, and a leather bomber jacket.

♡ Daddy is just a big kid, in case you have not caught on.

But Mike did me one better. He came as Indiana Jones right out of *Indiana Jones and the Temple of Doom*. See Chapter Twelve of *Flying on Film* for details. We joked around about Lao Che Airlines and posed for pictures. Barry was interested, but we had to urge him to go along with us. We all paid our fees and left Saffron with the ground crew.

♡ No complaint here. I did not like the look of that old crate. I only hoped that Mommy had kept up Daddy's life insurance payments.

The Trimotor was roomy and comfortable with wide seats and big windows. Even though it was noisy and vibrated like a paint mixer, it was still more enjoyable than a modern airliner. Talk about irony. That plane had been built only two years after Charles Lindbergh flew across the Atlantic. Even Barry had a great time.

Mark, Saffron, Barry, Linda and Mike in front of the restored
Ford AT-5 Trimotor at Gillespie Field in El Cajon

Farewell, Boba Fett

Only a week later my oldest friend Monty Montgomery, who had
been fighting brain cancer for two years, died. I had known there was
little chance of him beating it, but there was always hope. We last talked
on the phone several weeks before, and he was still hanging in there. I
had no idea I would never be able to talk movie and comedy trivia with
him again. His wonderful wife Alison and his three daughters Hannah,
Madeline, and Olivia, asked for me to come to the services, which would
be held in San Jose. Jane drove us up there while I tried to consider
what I would say at the funeral of my oldest friend. We used to joke
that only one of us would attend the other's funeral. Being older, I was
sure I would go first. Monty was too young, in body and spirit to die.

Alison and her girls had done a wonderful job of making the
service into a tribute to Monty. Music from his favorite movies and

television shows played while she showed slides of him as Boba Fett and an Imperial Stormtrooper. He had spent over a year making perfect reproduction costumes for Halloween. Talk about never growing up, that was Monty.

When we were asked to speak, Alison came and brought Saffron and me up to the microphone. I really had to hold it together.

"My oldest and best friend Monty had more personalities than the entire west wing of the Camarillo State Mental Hospital," I began. The audience laughed, which is exactly how he would have wanted it. Saffron leaned against me, as if she understood my emotions. What a wonderful dog.

"He was Boba Fett and Darth Vader, Eric Binford and Rick Deckard, Tim the Enchanter and the French Taunter. He was Hedley Lamarr, Alex the Droog and Cody Jarrett, the Waco Kid and Doctor Fronkenstein, he was every DC Comics supervillain. He was the most unique and original person I ever knew, even though ninety percent of what he said had been written by comedians and screenwriters. We could have entire conversations in school and over the past forty years without either one of us ever saying 'so what is new?' We did not care about what was new, only what we loved. Useless, repetitive and endless movie trivia. We were both full of it. Monty was my best friend. The world is just a bit less fun now that he is gone. But I bet he is up there right now, asking 'where can I find Leonard Nimoy? He arrived just after I did.' I'll miss him every time I watch a Monty Python episode or a Mel Brooks film. Rest in peace, old buddy."

When I got back to my seat, Saffron put her paws on my lap and licked my face.

♡ Daddy was crying so I gave him kisses. I never knew Monty but if he was Daddy's friend that was good enough for me.

No matter where we went together, Saffron was by my side, guiding me and making people happy. Who could ask for more?

CHAPTER 12

A BIG GIRL NOW

"The better I get to know men, the more I find myself loving dogs."
— Charles de Gaulle

Tragedy struck Saffron's puppy raisers, the O'Neill family on August 9, 2014. Matthew, who was attending UC Santa Barbara, was participating in a long-distance bike ride near Santa Maria, California. He was struck by a teenage driver who had not made the effort to change lanes in order to stay clear of the riders. Matthew died on the road, still short of his thirty-fourth birthday. He was engaged to marry his fiancée Jen Passwater.

Jane and I learn of this from his parents and we went to the memorial services at First United Methodist Church. During the service, Saffron heard the voices of her puppy raisers and was mad to get to them. It was a mark of how much she had been loved by the O'Neills. Out in the courtyard Saffron was re-united with Mike, Cheri, Craig, and Kevin, whom she had not seen since graduation. She still loved them. People came to me and asked, "Is that Saffron?"

"Yes, it is," I said. Even three years later and fully grown, Saffron was unforgettable.

Afterward there was a peaceful demonstration at the intersection of H St and Paseo del Rey, where friends and family gathered to encourage people to "Change a Lane, Save a Life."

The Facebook page is: "Remember Matthew: Change lanes to pass a cyclist."

The loss of such a fine and promising young man on the very threshold of a life helping people is more than tragic, it is inexcusable. Matthew had his entire life ahead of him, a career and a loving fiancée. Now his legacy is what he started by raising Guide Dogs, and most important, a firm vow to never let such a thing happen again.

♡ I miss Matthew. I'll never forget how good he was to me.

For the first few weeks after Musket's passing we all learned to adjust. The house seemed quieter, but not in a way that can be described. There was no more of the heavy panting, and only one set of dog tags jingled. But there was a certain emptiness all the same. For one thing, it felt strange to be able to walk from room to room without stepping over the furry "speed bump" on the floor. Also, it took only a few moments for feeding. Yes, I have to be honest, life was a bit simpler, but I still missed Musket. He had been the soul of the house and of our family. For nearly two years we had two dogs in the house. Saffron, even though she was the working Guide Dog, had been in a subservient role to the Alpha Male, Musket. He never actually enforced this, he just seemed to assume she knew her place. You may recall I once called Musket a chauvinist.

But with him gone, some things changed. Some were to be expected, others were surprises. We had his leash and collar, his old harness and his bed and bowls. I put Saffron's bowls in the same place where his bowls had been and encouraged her that it was okay for her to eat there. At first she was hesitant, since for the last two years I was firm that she never eat from his place. After a few days I replaced her bowls with his and did the same thing. Again she balked. In a soothing voice I said, "It's okay, good girl. This is your bowl now. Musket won't mind." She went at it.

Eventually we moved her bed to where his had been, which was closer to our bed, and she soon grew comfortable with it.

One night in mid-August I got up to use the bathroom and, as I passed her bed, reached down to pat her. It was empty. I wasn't worried, but not knowing where she was, I whispered for her. And then I felt her, right where Musket had always slept. Next to her Mommy. It made me smile. Saffron had taken the torch and was carrying it.

Saffron didn't seem to be acting strangely, looking for Musket, or being depressed. Perhaps since she had been there when he died, she understood on some basic instinctual level.

But about a month later, she surprised me. At the top of the stairs was a window seat with a cushion. For many years Musket had taken to rubbing the right side of his face on that cushion before going down the stairs. It was always cute and I sometimes reached down to feel his head bobbing up and down.

One morning I got up to let Saffron out and stopped at the top landing. She was to wait until I was all the way down before descending. I reached down to pat her head, and...yep, you guessed it, she was rubbing her face against the cushion, just as Musket had.

I won't deny feeling a sort of mild electric shock run through me. Was she doing it out of sentiment, or because it smelled like her big brother? I don't know but it made me smile.

♡ I'll tell you the truth. I saw Musket doing it and tried it myself. It felt really good scrunching my face against the cushion. But yes, I did sort of do it out of missing my big brother.

Saffron was definitely emulating some of her late big brother's habits. But there was one thing she didn't do, and for a long time I wondered about it. When I was going out with Musket he always put his head right into the harness. All I had to do was hold it out and Zip! he was in it. Not Saffron. Then it hit me. The little habits she copied were things she'd watched him do many, many times. She idolized her big brother so it made sense.

But from the point she came home with me, she was the Guide Dog. She never saw him in harness and therefore had never seen how he put it on. I began training her to do it.

♡ Daddy is right. I never saw Musket in harness. But if I had, I would probably have copied him. Daddy still has to coax me into the harness. Call me a rebel.

As the weeks and months passed I noticed something else. A slow but apparent change in Saffron's guide work. She had always been an adequate Guide Dog, good at her work, but somehow, she just seemed to do no more than necessary, almost as if her heart weren't totally into it. That may not be a fair assessment, but it helps to illustrate what I am talking about now. As I described earlier, she had a tendency to be easily distracted by sudden noises and things happening nearby. Always curious and inquisitive, she was easy to get back on track. I was sure that as she matured, Saffron would eventually grow out of it. Yet I still worked on certain improvement to her daily work. For instance, when we approached an intersection, I had to find the pole for the crossing signal button. And, just in case you didn't know, the manner in which American cities site those poles isn't exactly consistent. Yeah, BIG surprise. In any event, sometimes I would wave my arms like a deranged semaphore looking for the pole. So I started training Saffron to take me to the poles. Using a familiar intersection where I knew the pole's location I said "Saffron, take me to the pole. Take me to the pole." Then, as we got close, I patted the pole and said "Good girl, Saffron." I patted the pole and said "Pole. Pole. Good girl."

Then we backed off about fifty feet and did it again. After a few tries she got it and took me right to it, each time getting praised. Then we crossed the street and I told her to "Take me to the pole," and she walked me right up to it. Perfect. After doing this for a few days I started using the command on other routes and she did just as she'd been trained.

While Saffron did a good job on the whole, she did pull a few boners. One time we were approaching the intersection of Highland Ranch Road and World Trade Drive. It was controlled by lights and I knew it very well. Or at least I thought so. Saffron was still learning her way around. Coming down the west side of Highland Ranch, heading south, I came to the corner and punched the button. When it sounded all clear I said "Forward." What should have been a quick jaunt across the two-lane street went on much longer. But I had to let Saffron do her job. At last we stepped on the curb. Whew.

But when I said "Forward" to continue on the way past the library and on to home, she turned to the left. Huh?

I felt around for a familiar landmark. Nothing. Where in the heck was I?

This was one of those few times that I could have thought it out and realized what had happened, but I was still getting used to Saffron. I was lost. Well, I waved to see if I could catch the attention of a nearby pedestrian. Duh. There were NO pedestrians in Carmel Mountain Ranch. Everybody drove.

At last a man came to me and asked if he could help.

"Yeah, thanks," I said. "What intersection am I on?"

"Highland Ranch and World Trade," he said.

Hmm. "What corner?"

"Uh, southeast. By the vacant lot."

Bingo! Then I knew what Saffron had done. She went diagonally from the northwest to the southeast corner instead of to the southwest corner. "Thanks," I said sheepishly. "I know where I am now."

After getting Saffron pointed the right way, we crossed to the correct corner and turned left. I never told Jane about that incident, but I learned one big lesson. Think it out.

All the information I needed was there if I had taken the time to explore a bit. Then I would have figured out where we were.

♡ Boy, I felt like a dunce that day. When we stepped off the corner we were aimed too far to the left to be going straight across. I did what I thought Daddy wanted me to do. We were very lucky that no cars came through as we crossed.

Live and learn, if you're lucky. We were lucky.

One day we were walking along to do some errands at the bank and store, when a dog started barking at her from a yard. Usually Saffron shied away from barking dogs, but this time she walked right past it, totally ignoring the deranged canine. She acted as if she could not have cared less.

There were other tiny indicators of her growing maturity. She stopped trying to do her business whenever she wanted. This was never tolerated at GDB, but I was usually okay with it. But Saffron began doing the entire route from home to wherever and back again without ever stopping to sniff or pee.

All in all, she did exactly what a good Guide Dog is supposed to do. And just as Musket had always done.

I don't know if Musket's passing may have been the catalyst but the timing was uncanny. It was as though Musket's spirit had spoken to her, "Saffron, you have to take care of Daddy now. I taught you everything I know, and you had the best training in the world. Make me proud."

I certainly was proud of her. She continued to mature and show the results of her experience.

But this only applied to her work, not her personality or off-duty time. Saffron was still a playful and energetic dog with lots of spirit and silly quirks. But when that harness was on she took her job seriously.

My little girl had grown up.

CHAPTER **13**

HONORING OUR HEROES, SAFFRON-STYLE

> "It is amazing how much love and laughter they
> bring into our lives and even how much closer we
> become with each other because of them."
> — John Grogan

How many Guide Dogs do you think have been fed cookies by the retired United States Air Force brigadier general who piloted the B-29 that dropped chuck Yeager in the Bell X-1 in October 1947? I can think of only one. Yes, Saffron. Just like her big brother before her, Saffron has taken up the duty of honoring our veterans and heroes.

Readers of Musket's book will remember that he met and became friends with many special men like John Finn. We met Apollo astronauts like Neil Armstrong, Buzz Aldrin, Jim Lovell, Frank Bormann, Alan Bean, Gene Cernan, and Tom Stafford. They all petted my Guide Dog and I have no doubt he knew these men were unique. To shake the hand of or in Musket's case, to sniff the hand of someone who had actually flown in space or walked on the Moon was not to be forgotten.

I guess Musket must have given Saffron some hint of what was in store for her.

♡ Oh, yeah, he did. Musket took me aside one day and said, "Hey kid, I think I'd better tell you what Daddy likes to do. He and his friend

Linda hang out with these old men and women. I mean *real* old, like ninety or a hundred. They are all war heroes and very special people. You have to be respectful and don't jump on them. I learned that real quick. They can't take a big dog jumping on them no matter how much you like them.'"

I asked Musket to tell me more. Then he talked about air shows, parades, museums, big ceremonial events on ships and at cemeteries and parks. "The banquets are fun," he said, "but they are not there to see you. They are there to honor these people. Daddy said they had done some amazing things a long, long time ago."

That was how I found out about what Daddy is going to relate in this chapter.

Griff, Diz, the Flying Greek and General Bob

Among my first aviation friends was a World War Two Navy dive bomber pilot named Captain Wallace "Griff" Griffin. I met him a few years ago on board the *USS Midway* Aircraft Carrier Museum in San Diego when I was doing research on dive bombers for a magazine article. Griff was a fine old gent and was happy to tell me as much as I wanted to know. Linda adored him and felt like an adopted daughter. Griff was generous and enthusiastic, and he really liked Musket.

In fact my very first national magazine article was about Griff. In a way it started me on the path I'm on to this day.

I owed Griff a lot. Over the years I spent lots of time with him. I helped him meet his hero, John Finn. We picked up Griff and drove out to John's place in Pine Valley. There, the two old WORLD WAR TWO Navy veterans swapped war stories and had a great time.

Musket, of course got plenty of attention. On Super Bowl Sunday, 2011 we arranged for Griff to get a ride in a 1943 N2S Stearman biplane trainer owned by Dave Derby. Dave was a great guy who worshiped veterans and gave them free rides.

I had asked Griff at lunch one day what had been his favorite plane when he was a Navy pilot. He told me he loved the Stearman trainer. I called Dave and set it up.

When Griff found out, he was positively thrilled. "Are you kidding me?"

At Gillespie Field we introduced him to Dave. Griff was glowing as he looked at the plane painted just as the trainers he'd flown in 1943.

Dave took him up for a ride and even let him take the controls.

Musket and I waited at the hangar while Linda passed around a tray of brownies to our friends.

Then the plane landed with Griff his lined face alive with happiness. "He let me fly it!"

Captain Wallace "Griff" Griffin, USN (Ret) with Dave
Derby's N2S Stearman on Super Bowl Sunday, 2011

It had been a good day.

In the summer of 2013 Griff's health declined. He was in his nineties and had had a long and full life. But that didn't make saying goodbye any easier.

I had Saffron by then and she too won Griff's heart. He always bent down and patted her, calling her "Beautiful girl."

By the end of August Griff was in a retirement community in Chula Vista. His daughters were taking turns being with him. Linda and I went to visit a few times, but it was hard to watch the old veteran growing weak and frail. I had been working on his biography and told him I was going to get it done so his grandchildren and great-grandchildren would know his story and the things that made him who he was.

I took Griff by the hand and told him I was proud to be his friend. He smiled and squeezed my hand.

Linda said her goodbyes, and Saffron licked Griff's hand. Then we left. Linda was in tears and Saffron too seemed to be in low spirits.

Griff Griffin, one of the finest men I ever knew died on August 29, 2013. A true Navy man, he had seen peace and war, depression and prosperity, raised four daughters and left a long legacy. He was everything an American should be.

I was the only attendee at the funeral who was asked to speak and I told a short story about my friendship with Griff and ended it with "May the wind be beneath your wings, Griff. Farewell."

♡ Daddy is right. Griff was a wonderful man. I miss him a lot. But I am glad I had the chance to say goodbye.

The members of the Distinguished Flying Cross Society have all been awarded the nation's highest medal in military aviation. Charles Lindbergh was the first to receive the new medal after his 1927 flight to Paris. The members were veterans of World War Two, Korea, Vietnam, the Gulf War and Afghanistan. Linda's father had been a DFC recipient and she invited me to come along to one of the luncheon meetings. Boy what a target-rich environment that was. The Lindbergh Chapter of the DFCS met at the MCAS Miramar Officers' Club, where some of *Top Gun* was filmed. I got to meet some of the men and women who are still friends to this day.

I met and interviewed many of them for articles. To my astonishment they made me an honorary member.

♡ That was one of the few times I saw Daddy at a loss for words. He was really moved. While he was accepting the honor from the DFCS President Chuck Sweeney, I convinced a sweet lady named Rhoda Leopold to give me a bit of his chicken. Ain't I a sneaky devil?

Another World War Two veteran was Colonel Steve Pisanos. Musket and I met him in 2012. Steve, who had been a double ace flying P-51 Mustangs in the Eighth Air Force, was a fun, active and generous man who liked to call me "Marco," an honor for me. He came from Greece and joined the Royal Air Force to fight the Luftwaffe before the United States entered the war. Later he was the first person ever to become an American citizen outside the states. Steve went on to be a test pilot and retired after nearly thirty years in USAAF khaki and USAF blue. He wrote a wonderful autobiography called *The Flying Greek*. His natural humor and sincerity made him the epitome of the officer and gentleman. We lost Steve at the age of 96 in 2016. And as for Saffron, I think she was in love with him.

♡ Steve was so handsome! When he smiled at me my little heart just fluttered and my tail almost flew off from wagging so fast!

The DFCS made it possible for me to meet other remarkable men and women. Unfortunately there is not enough room in this book to detail all of them. But here are a few that really stand out. Some I met while Musket was still with me, and nearly every one fell for his big furry face. When I began showing up with Saffron in late 2012, they asked about Musket. But soon my little girl won their hearts too. She quickly got to be a hit among the members. They came over to say hello to us and she knew them all. Rhoda Leopold, whose late husband Herb had been a B-24 bombardier in Europe was in love with her. I also know she gave Saffron some of my chicken.

♡ Dang!

Commander Dean Laird, who went by the name "Diz," was a Navy fighter pilot who holds the distinction of being the only naval aviator to have shot down both German and Japanese planes. I first met him around 2010 when I was still collecting information for my book *Flying on Film*. I asked the DFCS members if any of them had been involved in movies. This tall, lanky man with black-rimmed glasses stood up and said, "I flew Japanese planes in *Tora! Tora! Tora!* Does that count?"

175

Diz became a good friend. At that time he lived on Coronado Island. I interviewed him for a couple of articles as well as the book. He was going blind from Macular Degeneration and asked me a lot of questions about how I did things even while I was asking him about shooting down Luftwaffe bombers and Japanese Zeros.

♡ Diz was really funny. He always petted me and rubbed my belly. But he also did something I will never forgive him for. He talked Daddy into going skydiving.

Oh, *that*. Well, okay. When Diz turned 90, he had decided to go skydiving. We all thought he was nuts, but that was Diz. Just as unpredictable and irreverent as me. That was probably why even after thirty years in the navy he never rose above the rank of Commander.

So when he landed safe and sound, he announced "I'm going to do it again on my 100th birthday and I want you all to do it too!"

I thought, "What the heck. If he can do it so can I." Linda, who is a lot more level-headed than I am, told me to reconsider. Actually she had a point. I knew Jane would not let me do it and the jump would not be cheap.

But my name is on the list for February 2021. Wish me luck.

♡ I love my Daddy even if he is crazy.

Well, Diz's Centennial birthday did not include the jump. Covid made that impossible. Dang. But Saffron was very relieved. I was not sure how she would have gone with me, but how else would I find the ground?

♡ That was a joke, by the way. A bird dog I ain't.

Diz got a ride in Dave Derby's Stearman just as Griff had. To make the day even better, Dave took me up too. Riding in the open front cockpit of an old biplane was a real thrill, and no modern airliner can come close. Dave even let me take the controls and did a loop for me. What a ride!

♡ Yep, you heard right. My Daddy, the blind guy flew a plane older than he was. But he came back with a grin as wide as the plane's wings.

The most interesting person we met at the DFCS was Brigadier General Robert Cardenas. Now 101 years old, Bob had served in the Army Air Forces in World War Two and was shot down over Switzerland when his B-24 exploded. He was able to evade German capture and soon returned to England. Later, as head of the Bomber Test Division at Wright-Patterson Air Force Base in Ohio. He then was assigned as the project leader of the X-1 supersonic flight tests at Muroc Air Base in California. Of course I took to Bob right away. He was friendly and always happy to help me with interviews. I wrote three articles and included him in *Flying on Film*. Linda and I went to several events to see Bob. She sort of adopted him and his sweet wife Gladys. She drove him to appointments and events, and made certain that he was not overwhelmed or exploited. That is still a real problem with these veterans. Linda, who as a DFCS board member, worked on the July 4 and Memorial Day parades, arranged for Bob to ride in open cars to be seen by the public. She helped to get him a ride on the Collings Foundation B-24, which took him back seven decades.

On one occasion we brought him to a CAF event where he talked about his career and answered questions from the huge audience. He had a great time but it was kind of a lot for a man approaching his first century.

But guess who made it a special day for General Bob Cardenas?

♡ Me! I like General Bob a lot. He was so nice to me and petted me even when people wanted his autograph or to shake his hand. I put my head on his lap. He even gave me treats and cookies. How could I not like him? Daddy said General Bob was a national treasure and hero. Whatever. He is a nice man and I am glad to be his friend.

Well said, Saffron. We sometimes went to Bob's house and he showed me his collection of memorabilia. It was a real honor to touch historic objects. Bob turned 100 in 2020, one of the few good things that happened that year. At the Flying Leathernecks Air Museum at MCAS

Miramar the DFC had a birthday cake for Bob. At the moment he was given the first slice of cake, Saffron was his best friend.

♡ Okay, I know I was not supposed to do that, but Bob was so nice and I could tell he really, really wanted to give me a bit of icing.

Since Bob no longer drove, Linda took him to meetings and events. He really liked my writing. Considering the man's vast and colorful history and that there were millions of words, dozens of books and scores of documentaries and interviews about him, that was a real compliment.

I will always feel truly honored to have known him and be considered a friend. As long as I bring Saffron, that is.

Dave Barnett is a former Air Force F-100 Super Sabre pilot who heads up the Order of Daedelians of San Diego. He, like many others, has been a great help in my work. He invited me to their meetings and I met other members of the military aviation fraternity. Wanda and Gene Elmore enjoyed having me at their table at the luncheons. Gene flew Navy bombers over the English Channel prior to D-day and sank a German U-boat. He also flew in the pacific and in the Berlin Airlift. Linda, who was a better promotor for me than I was, made sure everyone we met knew I was an aviation writer. Sure enough, Gene ended up in the pages of *Flight Journal Magazine*. What a career to cram into three thousand words. But it was worth it.

I met other authors and pilots at the DFCS and Daedelians, including men who flew the SR-71 Blackbird and the Space Shuttle.

♡ I liked going to those meetings too. Wanda was a nice lady who always made me feel special. She liked to give me belly rubs. Gene was kind of funny. He told Daddy stories about his flying and the people he knew. But he never seemed to take himself too seriously.

Pearl Harbor Survivors and POWs

In August of 2013 Alan Cutsinger took me to an event called the Spirit of '45, held at the Veterans' Memorial Center and Museum in Balboa Park. Located not far from the Air & Space Museum where Musket and I had spent a lot of time, the center is in the old Chapel at the Balboa Naval Hospital. Now a museum where visitors can see exhibits of military history, they also hosted several events and organizations. Spirit of '45 was an annual event to commemorate the end of the Second World War. There were booths and displays, bands, and local dignitaries eager to make speeches.

That day I was walking Saffron, who was very alert and curious. Then I heard over the loudspeakers, "Next we have Stu Hedley, who was aboard the battleship USS West Virginia at Pearl Harbor."

♡ Boy did Daddy do an about face when he heard that! He stood there, trying to figure out where to go. I led him to the podium where these old men were sitting and giving speeches. One of them had a very shaky voice but Daddy hung on his every word.

That was when I met the first Pearl Harbor Survivor since my friendship with John Finn. The Carnation Chapter of the Pearl Harbor Survivors met at the center once a month. I made sure to meet Stu, who was the chapter's vice president and chaplain. This was not only when I was still promoting *Flying on Film* but hungry to meet anyone who would be a good subject for an article. Stu introduced me to Jack Evans, who had been on the battleship USS Tennessee, Woody Derby from the USS Nevada, and Ray Richmond from the USS Oklahoma. They all agreed to let me interview them. I wrote a story for *World War Two History* Magazine called "Visions of Battleship Row."

From that point on I was welcome at the PHS meetings. Linda, since she was very involved with the group and did everything she could for them, was soon made an honorary member.

This was where I found Kathy Tinsley, whom Saffy and I met on the airliner coming home from San Rafael in September of 2012. She loved having Saffron with the group. Joedy Adams, a very sweet and kind lady, always hugged and flirted with me. She had been a young girl on December 7 when her father served in the Air Corps. She saw the attack and went through the same fear and chaos that beset Oahu for the next several days. She is now nearly 100 and is going blind from Macular Degeneration. Like Diz, she asked me for advice and direction. I helped her find and contact schools to get training to be more independent.

♡ Kathy always came to say hello to me first. Stu and Jack, and his wife Nancy were the nicest people. Joedy was a lot of fun. I liked Jack the most. He was kind of frail and I liked to go to him and put my head on his lap. He spent the whole meeting rubbing my head. Ray Chavez was the oldest. He liked to slip me bits of meat from the table.

For the next few years I attended the Pearl Harbor Survivors meetings but it was obvious that their days were numbered. After all, these men were in their late teens and early twenties in 1941.

But Stu was unstoppable. He attended every meeting and seemed almost indestructible. I say "almost" because Stu was a bit hard to control. He took chances no nonagenarian would ever try, except perhaps Diz Laird.

One of the new friends I made in 2019 was Jim Schriver, a former airline pilot. He was always willing to drive the veterans in his convertible for parades. He and Stu really hit it off. Jim gave Stu the present of a real putting green in his back yard. He loved putting on his own private green. One day in the summer of 2020 Linda and Saffron and I went there to see the green.

♡ And guess what my Daddy did? He played golf! He really did. He had to do it by feel, but he lined up some putts, with me helping him, and sank one of them from three feet away! You'd have thought he was Tiger Woods winning the PGA Tour the way he grinned. Linda took a picture of it for those of you who don't believe it. That's my crazy Daddy. I was real good and did not try to chase the balls. But boy, was I tempted!

Saffron helping Mark sink the winning putt at
the Hedley Invitational, summer 2020

The Pearl Harbor Survivors held an annual event on the *USS Midway* Aircraft Carrier Museum at the Embarcadero every December 7 at 9:55 a.m., which was 7:55 a.m. in Hawaii. As "Taps" was played on a bugle, the survivors threw a wreath into the bay.

It was a solemn ceremony, often attended by the news media. Saffron was on the news a few times and Jane saw her baby.

♡ Hi Mom! Daddy had a picture taken of himself holding this really big bullet. He laughed and said, "this one should be captioned 'America's last, very last, line of defense.'"

America's last, very last line of defense. Aboard the *USS Midway* Aircraft Carrier Museum on 7 December 2012

Colonel Earl Williams had been a sergeant in the Army Air Corps on December 7. He was on one of the Boeing B-17 Flying Fortresses that arrived over Oahu during the height of the attack. He lived in Riverside so I went to meet him. I interviewed Earl and learned his story. Linda convinced him to join the ranks of the PHS and set it up with Joedy. Earl retired as a Colonel in the Air Force. Very interesting man. Saffron was very comfortable around him but his big clock went off every fifteen minutes and made her jump. But Earl calmed her right down.

♡ The treats Daddy gave him to give me helped.

We lost Jack Evans in 2015 and Ray Chavez at the age of 106 in 2016. Earl died in July of 2020 at the age of 100. Finer men would be hard to find.

One other group I later met was the American Ex-POWs, or AXPOWs. The meetings were at the Veteran's Administration regional office in Mission Valley. There we met more remarkable men like Frank Berger and Ralph Kling. Ralph Kling had flown the P-47 Thunderbolt in the Pacific. He had so much life and spirit for a man in his nineties. Ralph really seemed to have a thing for Saffron.

♡ Oh, boy did he! Every time I saw Ralph he hugged me like I was his daughter. He spent the entire time scratching behind my ears and rubbing my head. Sigh. He was so good looking. How can a girl resist a handsome fighter pilot?

There's no crying on a B-17!

Edwin Davidson was a B-17 pilot in the 96th Bomb Group. He and his crew were shot down over France on their seventh mission in January 1944 and spent the rest of the war in Stalag Luft I. Ed had not only been the subject of some of my early articles about the air war over Europe, but had become a good friend. I saw Ed whenever the bombers came to town. When The CAF's B-17 *Sentimental Journey*, EAA's *Aluminum Overcast*, Collings' *909* or Liberty Foundation's *Liberty Belle* arrived, Ed was there, showing his memorabilia and enthralling the public with his accounts of flying the Fortress. He was a great speaker and often on the news. He never failed to make us, and particularly Musket and Saffron, feel welcome.

"Hi, Mark," he said in his quiet and sincere voice. "How are you and Saffron?"

Linda was given a ride on *Sentimental Journey* with Ed. "*I was so emotional,*" *Linda recalled.* Ed, always funny, also paraphrased a line from *A League of their Own* with Tom Hanks. "There's no crying on a B-17!" That made Linda laugh.

♡ It was impossible not to like Ed. He was everything an American should be, kind, helpful and true blue. The only thing was he always asked Daddy if he could give me a treat. If Daddy said no, than that was it. I wished Ed had been a bit more of a rebel. But oh, well, you can't have everything.

A career American Airlines pilot, Ed exuded competence and experience. Other pilots who had flown with him said he was the best. Ed had a loyalty to Boeing aircraft. "If it ain't Boeing, I ain't going," he liked to say. But he meant it.

Our friend Ed died in October 2019 at the age of 96. Like Griff, he was one of the finest men I ever knew. I was very blessed and honored to be his friend.

♡ We went to Ed's funeral in La Jolla. It was very sad, but it was good that so many people had come to pay their respects. Some of Ed's family were glad to meet Daddy, who had written articles about him. Daddy said, "I wanted to tell his story. Now he will live forever."
May the wind be under your wings, Ed.

There are many more but this book is about Saffron so let's move on.

♡ Right with you, Daddy! But he's right. I am a lucky dog to have met these people. I'm so proud to be an American!

CHAPTER **14**

A GAZELLE ON CRACK

"I wonder if other dogs think poodles are
members of a weird religious cult."
— Rita Rudner

This chapter contains things that don't fit anywhere else, such as some of my brilliant song parodies, things that have happened and other such stuff. But they are still worth including in the book. Yes, *even* the songs.!

♡ Oh, no! Those songs! I thought Mommy talked him out of putting them in the book! We want people to *like* this book, not burn it!

Oh stop griping, Saffron. You loved them when you first heard them.

♡ Whimper...

Do you remember that cute Li'l fisherman Oscar Mayer commercial? The one where the kid is eating a baloney sandwich and singing that little ditty, "My bologna has a first name, it's O-S-C-A-R..."
I got that darned jingle into my head one week and it just would not let go.
So one day when I was, as Jane thinks, recovering from a bout of brain fever, I came up with a Saffron version of the song.

"My Guide Dog has a first name, it's S-A-F-F-Y,
My Guide Dog has a second name, it's D-A-F-F-Y,
She is a per-fect guide to me, ask me why,
I say to thee, cause Saffy Daffy is you see, a grad-u-ate of GDB."

That wasn't too bad, was it?

♡ Can I take my paws off my ears now?

My Gazelle

Now, let's talk about a few of her...uh, quirks. All dogs, and certainly all humans whether they admit it or not, have quirks. I have more than my share, such as my belief in the Four Food Groups: Hamburgers, Pizza, Chocolate and Ice Cream. Also I tend to talk to myself in the shower when I'm working on a book. It helps me to freely create dialogue and plot points. And there are a few other things I'll pass over. Maybe when I give my Pulitzer Prize acceptance speech I'll talk about them. Anyway, Saffron's quirks are kind of funny.

Jane called Saffron a "Gazelle on Crack. I called her my "Furry Visa Card: She's everywhere I want to be." Like the bathroom. You dog and cat owners will not be surprised. It seems to be a common trait. But Saffron has to be weird.

For instance she will not go through a partly open door. Musket always butted his head against it and came in.
Saffron stood there immobile. I told her, "It is okay Saffy, come on in. Good girl."
But she wouldn't do it unless the door was all the way open.
"Do come in, your Highness."

Playdog **Centerfold**

Like a lot of men who were once teenagers, with overactive hormones, I liked to look at certain...uh, publications depicting the female form in various er, artistic poses and garb. Or the lack of it. And no, for you puritans out there, I DO NOT think that was the reason I went blind.

Cute blondes were a favorite. But now, I am the father of a cute young blonde female who has aspirations to appear in the centerfold of *Playdog* or *Pethouse*. Like a lot of dogs, including Musket, Saffron liked to have her belly rubbed. We would be absently rubbing her back or side, then she rolled over on her back.

"Aw, do you want a belly rub?"

♡ Yes, Daddy. Thank you. Ah, that's the spot. Ahhhhhh...

But where most dogs were content with that, Saffron took it to the next level And she was not in the least bit shy about it.

Let's say we had our pastor over for lunch. We will be having a nice and decent conversation when Saffron, realizing she wasn't getting any attention, would then lie on her back and spread her hind legs. My little girl was displaying herself in all her glory with absolutely no shame. She even wagged her tail.

"Well, she's not shy, is she?"

Trying to conceal my embarrassment, I said, "Aw, Saffron, do you mind?"

♡ Hi there!

I only hope she doesn't decide to do it when we have video cameras on us. It would end up on YouTube and *Animal Planet.*

FURRY Q-TIP

I mentioned Saffron liked licking my ears. But I learned very quickly that she loved licking everybody's ears! If she met someone she liked she was at their ears like they had peanut butter in there. Yeah, I know. Yuck.

In bed at night I only wore one hearing aid, and when she jumped up to say hello she went right for the uncovered ear. Her tongue felt like a living Q-Tip. Slurp, slurp, slurp. Rather hard to ignore. But after a while I have to stop her. "Saffron, that's enough. Any deeper and you're going to start poking out the other side."

I'm not sure how she acquired this particular fetish. And it is kind of gross. But then again this is an animal that licks her own butt, so maybe an ear is a sort of dessert. If any of you readers have dogs that have the same weird fetish, please write me. I'd like to know that I don't have a Guide Dog with a serious–earious?–problem.

Saffron's Paper-Shredding Service

This particular quirk is probably not unique to Saffron, but it is undeniably one of her favorites. Being blind, I sometimes drop a paper napkin or paper towel on the floor. If Jane saw it she made sure it was picked up. Once in a while it got past both of us. But not Saffron, our handy home paper shredding service.

The first indication of her performing this duty was when Jane said, "Oh, Saffy got one of your napkins and shredded it in the living room."

"Where," I always said with the same resigned sigh.

"By the table. You'll need the vacuum cleaner."

The funny thing was that Saffron hated the vacuum. She ran from it and jumped on the bed. Yet she was the source of most of the things I had to vacuum up. Fur, fiber from her mangled toys, and of course, shredded paper. I should hire her out to people who want to destroy their old financial records. But I doubt she would be able to handle the staples.

One of her favorite toys was a small Miss Piggy. When Saffron was through with it Miss Piggy was pulled pork. Saffron has often proven there is no such thing as an "indestructible toy," unless you count bricks and titanium. Once she had a toy in her mouth, she ran off to "play" with it. In the same way sharks play with their food.

So began the disembowelment and evisceration. Body parts and stuffing were thrown to the winds to settle on the plains and tundra of our carpets. She had a goal. The squeaky thing. When she got it out, the squeaking ceased. She seemed to enjoy the mutilation. But then I stepped in and took the thing away so she could not swallow it. I'm sure she gave me a dirty look.

♡ Hey, it took me hours to get that out! Now I'll have to start all over again.

FOD check

In military aviation there is a term for things that can be accidentally sucked into a jet engine and cause serious damage. Foreign Object Damage, or FOD. It is a regular routine on military airfields and carrier flight decks for a line of people to walk shoulder-to-shoulder looking for FOD. It is called an "FOD Check." It is not a minor matter. Even a discarded pack of cigarettes or aluminum can could tear apart a million-dollar engine and even destroy the plane and pilots.

I could not go through the house without stepping on the carcasses and entrails of innocent woodland creatures like owls, ducks, giraffes, and dinosaurs. The place looked like Noah's Ark after being bombed. I learned to do an FOD Check when I was going to vacuum. A ribbon from a toy or a torn-off tail could get sucked into the vacuum's brush and break the belt. I have replaced broken belts enough times to be pretty good at it, but it was a pain and I preferred not to have to do it. I went over the floor on hands and knees, feeling around for FOD. Naturally Saffron thought I was down there to play with her and licked my face. "No, Saffy," I said, "Daddy is looking for the remains of your last massacre."

♡ Daddy is being silly. But he does get kind of annoyed when that big nasty machine goes "grrrrrrr-Bang!" And it was usually from one of my toys.

Saff the Ripper

Back in the fall of 1888 East London was terrorized by a series of savage murders that were attributed to a shadowy figure who came to be known to history as Jack The Ripper. While he has never been positively identified, he has somehow been reincarnated to carry on his reign of vicious terror right here in San Diego.

Late in 2014 a series of brutal slayings shocked the quiet community of Carmel Mountain Ranch. No one could imagine such brutal savagery happening in such a pleasant town. But day after day the same vicious scene was laid bare before shocked residents. Bodies torn to shreds, decapitated, eviscerated, disemboweled and pulled to pieces were found all over the area. But the culprit did not stop at simply killing the victims, but scattered their entrails to the four winds. Everywhere one stepped, they were likely to find a body part in their path.

At first authorities were convinced the slayings were unconnected, but after consulting the FBI's Investigative Support Unit, they have learned the hard truth. A merciless killer was on the loose.

To date the Carmel Mountain Ripper has claimed more than two dozen innocent victims. The victimology was similar. The killer seemed to be attracted to small, soft and defenseless prey. There were no eyewitnesses, but some people reported a pretty blonde being spotted in the immediate vicinity of the crimes.

One person said that she heard a series of pathetic squeaks as yet another victim fell prey to the Ripper's savage blood lust.

I know who the Ripper is. I have been close by when the crimes have been committed.

The pretty blonde was Saffron. She was Saff the Ripper. Her victims were toys. Over the last three years she tore apart, shredded and mutilated more than two dozen toys. Their remains were found all over the house, on the carpet, on the bed, under furniture, even in the yard. Some limbs and entrails have turned up on the sidewalk and driveway.

♡ I ain't saying anything without my lawyer!

I hate to say it, but Saffron is a time bomb, filled with a terrible lust to eviscerate every single toy she gets her razor-sharp teeth on. And no toy is safe. Bobos, kongs, ropes, rings, stuffed animals, you name it. She is a dangerous animal waiting to strike again. So take my advice: Don't leave any toys lying around when Saffron comes to call.

You'll spend the next hour vacuuming the remains and throw away the rest. Meanwhile, Saffron will act as if nothing happened. But her pretty, soft and guileless brown eyes will already be on the lookout for another victim.

♡ Daddy is a stool pigeon. Isn't there some law against perjury? Where's my lawyer?

Space-Time Continuum
for Doggy Toys

There was one time I was throwing the rope for her, and just for variety (BAD idea) I threw it straight up. Saffron ran a little ways to catch it when it came down and...and...and...well, it never came down. Now I'm kind of a strong guy, but I think achieving orbital velocity of 17,500 miles per hour is a bit farfetched. "Where's your toy, Saffy?" I asked. She scampered back and forth but what I didn't know was that she was looking up.

After searching around for about ten minutes I reached the inescapable and obvious conclusion that the rope toy had fallen into the gravitational influence of a freak wormhole in the fabric of space-time. It had gone into a parallel universe with all the missing things that

Humanity has lost, like ballpoint pens, keys, cellphones, TV remotes, and especially the physics term paper I swear I wrote in 1977.

♡ I am certain that all you readers came to the exact same conclusion. NOT!

Later that day when Jane got home I told her what happened. For some reason, she didn't buy the wormhole idea. But she did find it in the branches of the tree hanging over the yard. Oops.

No sign of my term paper, though. That's proof of the wormhole as far as I'm concerned. Okay maybe the wormhole was kind of off the beaten track. But hey, I'm a writer.

We used a long pole and knocked it out of the tree into Saffron's eager mouth.

♡ I tried to tell him but you know how he is. I kept saying "Bark, Bark!" But he didn't get it. Just hopeless. I knew Mommy would straighten him out when she got home.

But here's what blows my mind about it. If I had deliberately tried to get that rope to catch in the tree, I could have thrown it fifty times with no luck. But without even trying...see what I mean by how the most bizarre things just seem to happen to me? I mean, I really did write that physics paper. It was over thirty typed pages (and mind you, before computers and printers) and carefully researched, annotated and cited. My physics teacher wasn't the most open-minded sort. I'm sure he thinks I never actually wrote it. What could you expect from an ignorant goon who never liked *Star Trek*? Sorry, I guess I sort of went off topic.

Only a week later I somehow got disoriented and tossed the rope up over my shoulder and heard a *Thump!* This time I thought I knew what had happened to it. Saffron was running back and forth, and I asked her, "Hey Saffy where did it go?"

♡ Roof! Roof!

"That's what I thought. I called up to Jane who was in her office at the front of the house. "Honey do you see Saffron's rope toy?"

She looked out the window and said, "Roof! Roof!"

"Yeah, I know that, but where?"

"Right on the edge about three feet from the corner."

"Thanks!" I got the ladder and retrieved the toy.

♡ Mommy was so funny!

That was not the only time I lost something in the space-time continuum. Saffron had a soft red rubber ball I could throw around the house without fear of damaging anything. On weekends when I was lying on the sofa listening to a book I threw it for her, then she brought it back and dropped it in my lap. But one time I tossed it and (insert Final *Jeopardy!* theme here) and it never came down. This time I knew it had to have gone into the parallel universe. I was ready to e-mail Stephen Hawking, but Jane talked me out of it. But even she didn't find it and my theory was gaining in validity. About four months later I was cleaning the living room and found one of Saffron's small Nyla® Bones under the couch. Then I started thinking about that ball. No, I knew it didn't really go into another dimension. I'm not crazy, just open-minded. I crawled around and felt into every single crook and nanny from the kitchen to the dining room to the living room and up the stairs. I felt on top of the china cabinet and under the pillows on the settee. Nope. "Doctor Hawking, have you got a minute? I have a theory I'd like to bounce off you."

Then an impossible revelation hit me like a bolt of lightning. Just above the fireplace there was an alcove where we had the stereo. And above that was another alcove. It was at least ten feet up so I got the ladder and climbed up. And there, hiding behind the silk plant was my physics term paper!

No, the rubber ball. I called Saffron. "Hey look what the blind guy found!" I tossed it down to her and descended to the floor. No sign of Saffron. She wasn't interested in the ball. She was chewing away at the Nyla® Bone. Sigh. Well I guess even Einstein had those kind of days.

But again, think about it. From the couch that alcove, which was about a foot square, was at least fifteen feet away. And I scored a direct hit on it without even trying. Sandy Koufax of the 1960 Dodgers could not have done it.

The Sound of Bananas

Saffron had both superb and lousy hearing. It seemed to be highly selective. Case in point, around nine in the evening I have to let her out to do her business. I stood at the bottom of the stairs and called up "Saffron! Come on down! Time to go out!"

Then Jane, usually reading in her chair said, "Nothing, Honey. She has not moved."

I repeated the command with the same result.

Jane added her voice, "Saffy, go to Daddy."

Several seconds of silence. "Is she coming?" I asked.

"She's not moving. Didn't even open her eyes."

"SAFFRON!" I bellowed in my Marine drill instructor voice.

"She's stretching." Jane said. "Go to Daddy."

At last I heard her tags jingling. Then she stopped somewhere up there. Nothing.

"Saff-ron!" I said distinctly. "Come. Down. Here. Now."

With a complete lack of urgency she trotted down the stairs and out the door, while I spent the time shaking my head muttering about deaf dogs.

As I said, she does have superb hearing.

Some evenings I wanted a small snack and a banana sounded perfect. I was sure I could eat it without Saffron knowing. She was upstairs with Jane, snoring on the bed, oblivious to the insane crowd cheering on *Family Feud*. So I knew it would be safe.

Down in the kitchen I pulled a banana off the bunch. Then I snap the stem and peeled it.

Just as I lifted it to my mouth I felt a cold nose on my other hand.

She heard it! Over all the noise on the television and being sound asleep, she heard that tiny "crack" of the banana stem being broken.

Evidently the sound of a peeling banana went right into her ears.

So that was my problem. A dog that had extremely selective hearing.

I could get a banana every time I wanted her to come down, but that could be expensive. And I did not want to die of potassium overdose

Then I had this brainstorm. I used my Victor Stream Reader to record the sound of breaking a banana stem. My reasoning was like duck hunters use duck calls to bring the waterfowl to the pond where they are lying in wait with the shotgun. I had to shut myself in my office to make the recording so she would not know what I was up to.

After telling Jane of my brilliant plan I waited until that night and stood by the stairs. I pulled out the Victor and accessed the banana recording. I was a shoo-in for a Nobel Prize with this breakthrough. And I am sure I was the first person in history to record the sound of a banana being peeled.

Pushing "Play," I waited. I did it again at a louder volume. Nothing.

After three tries I stomped up to the bedroom. Jane was almost crying with mirth. "She never flinched. Even I heard it. But Saffy was dead to the world."

With my teeth ground down to nubs I went down to the kitchen, pulled off a banana and snapped the neck.

♡ Hi Daddy! Can I have a bit of that?

I assume the Nobel Prize Committee's letter got lost in the mail.

My Golden Snitch

All you Harry Potter fans out there know what a Golden Snitch is. Well I have one. Her name is Saffron. And like the seeker's target in a game of Quidditch, she's just as fast, just as elusive and when I catch her, the game is over.

But it's not that easy. For one thing, I don't have a Firebolt. And my eyesight is lousy.

I'm not only blind I'm a guy. Sometimes I broke things. It happens.

I often made tea for Jane and brought it up to her. Saffron always watched me.

One day I was at the counter and opened the upper cupboard and heard a "clink!" noise on the granite counter. I was sure something had broken. But I couldn't find it on the counter. I had to find and dispose of the evidence before Jane came down. I was on my hands and knees, feeling my way around. Cold sweat broke out on the back of my neck when I heard Jane call from upstairs, "Honey did you break something?"

Damn her Vulcan hearing. "Uh, I don't think so. Why?"

"Because Saffy just brought me a piece of broken tea bag plate."

Busted!

So my loyal little Guide Dog Saffron saw the broken plate and grabbed it, took it up to Mommy and dropped it in front of her. "Daddy broke something! What are you going to do to him?"

That's why Saffron is my little Golden Snitch.

ICEBREAKER

A lot of dogs like ice cubes. Musket used to eat them on hot days. I'd put them in his bowl and he'd crunch one down. But Saffron took it to a whole new level. She LOVED ice cubes. We found this out pretty early on. On one hot summer day I held out an ice cube and she ran up to get it like Leona Helmsley after a diamond ring. And in less time than it takes to say "Wow!" it was gone, down her gullet. I remember hearing a very brief crunching noise, and then silence. Then, not believing I'd heard right, I gave her another one. A Cuisinart would have taken longer. I don't know how she kept from getting a brain freeze.

Jane sometimes put a bowl of ice cubes on the floor. Saffron made short work of it.

So, does she like ice? Let me put it this way: If Saffron had been swimming in front of the *Titanic*, there would have been no iceberg for the ship to hit.

♡ Ice cubes are a girl's best friend!

The 21st Century Doggy Bag

Remember years ago when the family went out for dinner? You always brought leftovers home in a Doggy Bag? They had a cartoon of a cute smiling pooch on them, just to make the point. The leftovers were supposedly for the family dog.

I'm sure they noticed it, too. But as far as I know, dog got zilch.

♡ I need to write to my congressman. This is unacceptable.

The food is not even put in bags anymore. Instead they use non-biodegradable Styrofoam containers that will be in landfills until the Sun turns into a Red Giant and engulfs the Earth about 4.5 billion years from now. And the name "Doggy Bags" is way too 1950s. They need a new, cool and technical-sounding name. I think they should be called "Domestic Canine Remaindered Consumables Transport Containers," or DCRCTC. But they should really be called "Doggy Gets Diddly-Squat Bag."

♡ False advertising! Discrimination! Excuse me, it is 3:30. Daddy is putting down my dinner. I'll rant about this later. Bye!

White Chocolate Lab

I think I'll start a crusade to rename the retriever colors. Yellow, Chocolate and Black are so boring. They should have delicious colors. White Chocolate or Vanilla, milk or Dark chocolate and Licorice. The Golden Retriever can be called the Cinnamon, butterscotch, or even the Cinnabon Retriever.

As for Saffron's fur, she had the same color as Musket. Vanilla fur, caramel ears and milk chocolate eyes. Yet as scrumptious as she looked, her fur did not inspire the taste buds when it turned up in our food. In the old *Klondike Kat* cartoon series, his French-Canadian nemesis mouse declared, "Savoir-Faire eez everywhere!"

With Saffron it is "Saffron's hair eez everywhere!"

Like all Labs, she shed twice a year. But unlike Musket, whose fur was thick and heavy, hers was light and almost downy. Its weight was as close to zero as you can imagine and floated on the air, stirred only by breezes or the Brownian motion. The worst was during late summer or early fall when her light summer coat fell out. She left floating fur behind wherever she went. Guide Dogs told us all to "groom your dog every day."

Yeah. Sure. There are only twenty-three hours, fifty-six minutes and four seconds in any day. Most of that is spoken for. And the problem with grooming Saffron is that the neighbors who live downwind started complaining about the yellow fur blizzard descending on their homes. At the height of the shedding season their homes looked like the first little pig's house of straw.

♡ You *do* know Daddy is exaggerating, right?

No I'm not. I did groom her at least twice a week. I gathered huge handsful of fur and threw them in the garbage. It never seemed to end. I swear it was growing out even as I ran the Furminator across her back and sides. I felt like a modern-day Sisyphus trying to roll the stone up the hill only to have it roll down the other side, again and again.

We found her fur in the corners, under doorways, beneath appliances and in the closets. I wore out two Hoover vacuums on our dogs. Eventually the shedding stopped and I was able to do one more good vacuuming and be done with it.

For about two weeks. Then it started again. Sisyphus was a sissy. He had the easy job.

♡ At least my fur grows back. Daddy's head is getting balder every year with no recovery in sight.

Chow Hound

Saffron had a food fixation that erased all other thought. She once jumped on the kitchen counter when we went to a pool party the first year we had her. That was truly embarrassing. I made certain she never did it again.

I thought Musket was the Mario Andretti of food-driven, but Saffron won that Indy 500 race before Musket even left the starting line.

I have tried and tried to curb her ravenous appetite. As far as eating out of other dogs' dishes, I wondered how she would feel if a visiting dog tried to eat her food in the 3.9 milliseconds it existed in the bowl. We'll never know.

Don't bother wrapping it. I'll eat it here!

In any case we had to find a way to slow her down. The first year we had her she did occasionally ralph up her food. Yuck.

Then Jane found a solution. She went online and searched for a bowl designed for out-of-control eaters. She found one! I was skeptical until it came from Amazon. The thick plastic bowl was molded with a series of narrow nooks and a central post that made it impossible for a dog to wolf it all down in one gulp.

It did the job. The first few times it was obvious that she was trying to find a way to get at all the kibble at the same time.

I timed her eating. The old bowl took her about 35 seconds to swallow one cup of kibble. The new bowl increased that by about 30 percent to 48 seconds. That was the best we could hope for.

♡ I hated that stupid bowl! It took me months to find a way to suck and lap at the same time and reduced the time to just under 38 seconds. Don't mess with a hungry Lab!

Soggy Doggy

"Anybody who doesn't know what soap
tastes like never washed a dog."
— Franklin P. Jones

Saffron does not like water. I thought all Labs did, but she was very finicky about getting wet. It's impossible not to make comparisons between her and Musket, but this is one of personality, not value. When I had to give him a bath, he went right into the shower. He didn't like it, but he did it.

Saffron, on the other hand had to be physically pushed or carried in. Her claws dug into the rug or tile like I was making her enter hell itself.

Most of the time I had to do it myself. Getting her into the shower, washing, rinsing and drying. But one time Jane wanted to "help." And like a dummy, I agreed. I'd still do the hard work but she would take over for the drying.

Readers of *Confessions* may remember what happened when Jane wanted to dry Musket. I never forgot, but Jane had.

Oh-kay. Let's see how this works out, I thought with a mental grimace. After I washed and rinsed Saffron I got her to shake off most of the water. Then I reached out of the shower for one of the towels I kept on the hamper.

"Honey let her go," I heard Jane yell. "I'll dry her off."

"Hold on," I said. "I need to wring her out some more."

But it was no use. "Just let her go! I'll do it!"

"Okay," I replied, gritting my teeth for what I knew was coming. Even a blind guy could see it. Opening the shower door I said, "Go ahead, Saffy. Go to Mommy."

♡ Mommy should have listened to Daddy!

She did go, but not to Jane. She stopped in the bathroom right by the sinks and mirror and... well you know what a wet dog will do.

Shake it up, Baby, twist and shout!

Only it was Jane that did the shouting. "Saffy! No! Come here!"

I just closed the shower door and began to rinse down the walls and floor while all hell broke loose in the bedroom. Saffron, free from oppression, ran all over the room, jumped on the bed, tore out the door and down the hall, back into the bedroom and generally caused more flood damage than a hurricane.

When I stepped out of the shower and put on my hearing aids I found Jane sitting on the hassock, trying to dry Saffron. The rug was wet, the walls were dripping and the bedclothes were rumpled. "How did it go?" I asked in my most casual voice.

Jane tried to make light of it. "No problem. She came right to me and let me dry her off."

"Uh-huh," I said, feeling water drip from the ceiling. "Mmm. It must be raining out."

Jane never again offered to help me give Saffron a bath.

♡ She learned fast, didn't she?

This gave me an idea for a new song parody! Yes! You lucky readers are going to be cursed...I mean, blessed with a new song parody by yours truly!

You might remember when Shawn Cassidy was a serious teen heartthrob back in the early 1980s. Well he had a short career as a singer and one of his hits was a catchy tune called "Da Doo Ron Ron." It gained popularity when Harold Ramis sang it in the comedy *Stripes* with Bill Murray. But the lyrics are perfect for this.

Wet Dog Run Run Run
I had a dog and she needed a bath
Chorus: Wet Dog run run run, Wet Dog run run

When I told her this it incurred her wrath,

Yeah well she was pretty rank
It was time to put her in the tank
So I reached out to take her in
You can guess the rest I know
My furry dog put on a show

But her time had come at last
She was going to get a bath

I got her in and started the suds
She locked her legs and refused to budge

Yeah, I finally got her nice and clean
I let her go and Jane gave a scream
Around the house the dog ran wild

dripping and blind I toweled her off
But in the end the cause was lost
Yeah, she ran up and down and in and out
Leaving dripping water all through the house
But in the end she went into the sun
And wouldn't you know,
Wet Dog DID NOT run run run, Wet Dog DID NOT run run

Boneless Labrador

No matter how much energy she had during the day, Saffron slept like a drunk sailor sleeping off a hangover in Singapore. She even snored like one.

"Hey, Saffy, it's time to go out," I'd say to her. "Come on, wake up."

Nothing. I might as well have been talking to the wall.

"Saffron," I said, "wake up. Let's go!" Then Jane chimed int. "Saffy! Get up! Daddy's going to take you out!" By this time we were talking loud enough to wake the dead.

♡ Snore...Zzzzzz

I pulled her to the edge of the bed and lifted her. You remember that character Frieda in *Peanuts?* The annoying one with "naturally curly hair?" Well she had a cat named Faron that never walked. Frieda was always holding Faron like a sack of rice draped over her arms, totally boneless. That was Saffron when she was asleep. One night Jane and I were laughing about it and Jane began singing "Wake up, little Saffy, wake up!"

You probably know where this is going. Yes, another horrible song parody.

(With apologies to the Everly Brothers and Simon & Garfunkel)
Wake up little Saffy, wake up
Wake up little Saffy, wake up
You fell so sound asleep
Wake up little Saffy, my sweet
We're all tired, it's nine O'clock
And you still have to pee
Wake up little Saffy
Wake up little Saffy
You gotta go pee

Sorry. I gotta be me. No, I won't sing it.
But blame Jane. She started it.

Paw-tickle Physics

This brings another matter, which I will call "Paw-tickle Physics." I'm a prolific reader and I don't mind saying I'm relatively intelligent, no matter what Jane mutters under her breath. I have studied physics and astronomy. I've read Carl Sagan and Stephen Hawking, know a bit about three-dimensional topology, have learned to understand Mandelbrot's fractal geometry and chaos theory. I can discuss, with some confidence, Einstein's Special Theory of Relativity and have read quite a bit about three-dimensional space in a four-dimensional universe. I even know what a Mobius Strip is. Ain't Wikipedia great?

Mark's colored pencil portrait of Albert Einstein, circa 1998

But, for the life of me, I can't begin to understand how in the world a 60 pound Labrador Retriever with a body length of 32 inches can dominate 98% of a 60X80 Queen-sized mattress!

Musket was pretty good at it too, but at least he was a big dog. He outweighed Saffron by almost thirty pounds. Yet when she is on the bed, there IS NO ROOM FOR TWO HUMANS.

I've created a formula that might be of some help to other dog owners who are confronted with the same problem.

The formula is:

D6=mh2

For the blind audio book reader, it is D to the sixth power equals M H to the power of two.

This is how it works, with apologies to Albert Einstein whom I plagiarized.

D is the Dog. It has a non-absolute size, but this can be learned by using a sub-formula, multiplying LWLTETn or L (length) X W (weight) X Lg (legs) X T (tail) X E (ears) and Tn (Tongue). The smaller the resulting sum the smaller the dog. NOTE: This is a theory that has yet to be proven since Stephen Hawking would not return my calls even when he was alive.

M is mattress size, a finite and absolute number that does not change or is it likely to, unless the mattress store has a sale, usually around the holidays.

h is for human(s). This is a simple number, either 1 or 2, but frequently, in total defiance of all known and theoretical laws of mathematics adds up to 0, if D (see above) is really doing its job. h(s) has to decide if D is too big for m and that h1 and h2 must find some other place to sleep since D will not move.

Ergo, (what scientists say when they want to sound brilliant) D (Dog to the sixth power) equals the size of M (mattress) that H (humans squared) want to sleep on.

Okay that's the end of the physics lesson. Not bad for a guy who barely passed basic Algebra. I'm going to sleep on the couch. That will work until Saffron manages to perfect cloning.

CHAPTER 15

A COLD WET NOSE

"If a man aspires towards a righteous life, his first
act of abstinence is from injury to animals."
— Albert Einstein

Saffron has been remarkably healthy over the
years. As of this writing she is almost ten years old—

♡ Daddy! You should not be revealing a lady's age!

Oops. Sorry, "little girl." Um, she is on the far edge of er...her first
decade. So even though she still has a lot of puppy in her, she has slowed
down a bit. She tends to take longer to get going when I call her, and
yes, that might be by choice, but she is not as hot off the catapult as she
once was.

As for her health, she has given us only a few little scares.

Like Musket she liked our veterinarian at Carmel Mountain
Veterinary Hospital, Doctor Elizabeth Grey. A warm-hearted woman
with a true love of animals, Dr. Grey took care of Saffron as if she were
her own. Saffron didn't seem to mind the "howitzer" thermometer that
Musket hated so much. In fact, I doubt she even noticed it.

♡ Musket warned me about the giant thermometer up the butt. I
guess he was a wimp.

Her weight fluctuated up from her initial 56 pounds and hovered (I use that word because it sounds lighter than anything else I can think of) around 62 to 65 pounds. But it never slowed her one bit.

She did have a couple of small cysts like Musket used to get, but only one needed a biopsy. Benign, thank the Lord.

All in all, Saffron caused us less worry than her big brother. With one exception.

THE BONEYARD

One of the special treats we gave Musket and Saffron was beef bones. They were thick boiled bones filled with some sort of peanut butter paste. He would get one every few months, sometimes when he had been through surgery or some other trial. He loved to chew on them. It was one way to keep him busy for hours.

Since then Guide Dogs for the Blind has made some changes in their policies about these bones. Some dogs have splintered them, swallowing the splinters, which required surgery. I kept this in mind, but in my opinion, not letting a dog gnaw on a bone was like telling Tom Cruise that he isn't that great an actor.

♡ But he's so adorable

Jane and I still bought the bones for the kids, but they had to be thick and heavy, with no thin sides. Also we kept track of the bones as they worked on them to see if they were getting splintered. When I felt cracks or splits, the bone went in the trash. Period.

Somehow Saffron always got them under the sofa. Way back in there. Jane never caught her at it, but every so often Saffron seemed to be trying to get something from under the sofa. "Oh, a bone probably went under there," I'd say. Then I went down on my hands and knees to slip my hands under there to find it. And what did I find, a bone yard. I asked Jane, "Have you heard anything about missing cattle in the area?"

♡ It's a mystery. Hey Daddy, can I have those?

We're talking about a serious oral fixation here. When I was lying on the bed reading an audio book she would jump up on the bed and start grinding away. It wouldn't be so bad if she was quiet. But she sounded like Michelangelo chiseling David out of solid marble. Even with my hearing aids set to the headphones, I still heard her teeth turning that bone into dust.

Which brings us back to her health. In 2018 we took her to Dr. Grey for her annual wellness exam. After being poked and prodded from nose to tail she was declared healthy. But Dr. Grey said "Saffron has at least three cracked molars."

Jane and I were surprised. "Cracked molars? Is that possible?"

She assured us it was. And they would have to be removed. Then I thought about her bone grinding habit. "Could it be the bones?"

"Yes," Dr. Grey agreed. "But I rarely hear of a dog breaking teeth on them. Teeth are harder than bones—"

I finished the sentence for her. "Unless the dog is Saffron, who does not just bite bones, but grinds them to dust."

That would be it for the bones. Dr. Grey said she could remove the broken teeth and would give us a prescription for antibiotics and pain killers.

Saffron on pain killers. That would be something to see.

So we left her there for the day and went home. Jane and I scoured the house for bones and threw them out. I still wonder if the garbage collector called the police about the "place where they must be butchering cattle without a license."

Saffron came home that night, loopy and stoned. Even though she had four, count 'em, *four* molars removed, what did she want to do first?

♡ Eat!

Can anyone eat after having four teeth pulled? All I would want to do is sleep. Not my girl. After her gums healed, she was only allowed Nyla bones or soft toys. She seemed to be okay with that.

♡ I miss the bones. I was a sculptor of bone. I was working on one of Tom Cruise.

No Pain, No Game

Kimmy Aguinaldo was a neighbor who often came to take Saffron to run and play at the park. One day after she had been playing with Kimmy, she had a small limp. She seemed to be favoring her left front paw. Kimmy, very sensitive to Saffron's health, said she might have sprained her foot while running. Considering how energetic and downright intensely she played, I was not surprised. She could easily have twisted her foot while chasing the ball. But pain was not an issue. Play came first. We went to the vet and they examined her and did X-rays. She had some inflammation in the joint. She was on anti-inflammatories and pain relievers for two weeks. That was bad enough, since she hated the taste and kept spitting them out. But the worst was that she could not play with Kimmy!

♡ I was so bored and miserable. Daddy played with me but it wasn't the same as running flat out on the grass. And those pills were awful. Daddy had to try all kinds of things to make me eat them. He finally ground them up and buried them in my food. It still tasted terrible.

The funny thing was that those pills slowed down her eating. It took about ten minutes, which for Saffron was glacial. I did not think anything could do that.

♡ Trust me, Daddy. It was a great way to go on a diet.

I told Kimmy to take it easy on her. The first day they got to play again, Saffron was quivering with excitement. She even whined. "Just take it easy, Saffy."

♡ Daddy took real good care of me, even if he was stingy with the food. Two measly cups a day? A Chihuahua would starve on that.

Sigh. Well, I plan to keep my "little girl" healthy and fit for as long as possible, God willing.

CHAPTER 16

THE BIG MOVE

"Home is where you hang your leash."
— Unknown

In April 2017 Jane and I decided to move. We had been in the condo on Tivoli Park Row since we married, but it was just getting to be too much to handle. Jane's degenerative disk disorder made the stairs a real agony. The mortgage was also becoming a burden, especially when combined with the exorbitant homeowners' association fees. Just to let you know, we paid about $200 per month for the HOA, but also an additional $85 per month just for the privilege of saying we lived in Carmel Mountain Ranch. "If I keep my mouth shut, can I keep the money? I promise I won't tell a soul." I thought of getting a t-shirt that said "Ask me where I live so I can justify the money I have to pay to live here."

We found a realtor who was recommended by our friends Crystal and Jameson Reinek. Chris Caldwell was fantastic. We had looked into moving in 2016, but the bozo that called himself a realtor said it would take $50,000 worth of remodeling before we could put our condo on the market. Keep in mind this was after two decades of improving the place. That was pretty discouraging. But Chris took one tour and said we could get our asking price with no more effort than to have a maid service give it a good cleaning. To make the story shorter would be hard to do. Chris sold the house one day after putting it on the market and for more than we asked!

In retrospect, this was the first clue that a greater power was guiding us.

♡ No, not me. Keep reading.

Then we met Leah Cole, a realtor who specialized in modular and manufactured homes in North County. Now, let's get this straight. No matter what you call it, we were looking for a mobile home. Once I checked the National Oceanographic and Atmospheric Administration website for data on how often tornadoes struck the area, I felt better about buying one. Our hope was to find one in a San Marcos or Escondido senior community.

Leah, a very sincere and hard-working lady who was a few months short of giving birth to twins, showed us around a few places. One by one they were examined and discarded. It was Jane who was really doing the looking. She knew what she wanted. I pretty much just went along for the ride. And of course Saffron had to approve of the new domicile.

♡ You got that right, Daddy. I insisted on carpet, a sunny place to lie down and no shower or bath.

That last one was going to be a problem. One day we were in San Marcos in a mobile home park called Madrid Manor. Jane was very pleased with what she saw and what Leah told us about the community. It sounded good. Then we stopped in front of one house. It was a "double-wide," the mansion of mobile homes. As soon as I climbed out of the car I stumbled over a concrete planter. Not a good start.

♡ Well, you should look where I'm going. I was following Mommy.

When we went in, Jane fell in love. The place was perfect. It had about 1560 square feet, one master bedroom and bath, two bedrooms and a hall bath, kitchen, dining room with a bay window, large carpeted living room, plenty of closet space and even a wheelchair ramp. Leah said the place was only three years old, had been on the market for a year after the previous owner had gone into a nursing home, and had been in escrow four times. "But every time it was almost closed," she said, "something stopped it."

Jane loved it. Leah showed me around, explaining the floor plan and dimensions. I liked it. We would have to get a shed since it had a carport instead of a garage and there was no attic but that was no problem. I think the lot was about sixty by eighty feet. The side yard was all gravel. No lawn to mow. Yay!

♡ I still did not know what was going on. We went into all these different houses and then left. Not one had any dog dish on the floor. So they were obviously out. But both Mommy and Daddy seemed excited about this one.

And best of all, I would have a real office in the house, not in the garage!

♡ Oh, well. I guess Daddy would have to live inside with Mommy and me.

So we bought it. Well it wasn't that simple. The paperwork and hundreds of signatures were a pain in the posterior. But we got through it. And again, I noticed how well it went for us. Four times the house had almost been sold to someone else, but we were the new owners. Someone wanted us to live here.

Jane first said to me, "Honey, do you like it?"

My response, as usual, "If you are happy, so am I." I meant it. Jane was far more practical and logical about such things. I knew that if she was impressed it would be fine.

Except for that darned 45-degree left turn in the main hall. That took three years to get used to.

♡ Daddy really had a problem with that. About ten feet down the hall it turned left at an angle, then turned right again. He kept misjudging the place to turn and BANG! He bumped off the wall or corner. I really could not help him with this. He would have to do it himself.

The Wormhole in the Den

♡ This is another one of Daddy's long pseudo-scientific rants, so if you want to go into the kitchen and make a snack, I'll tell you when it's safe to come back.

The actual move was the most grueling and laborious effort I have ever been through, and I have moved half a dozen times. But not after living in a house for more than twenty years. You know how much stuff a couple can accumulate after two decades? A lot.

We started by going through our offices to get rid of any old stuff or things that were not important anymore. Boy did we find a lot of that.

We rented a storage unit to keep everything in until the big day.

The storage space measured ten by fourteen feet. This gave us 1400 cubic feet of space. Supposedly our front rooms, at twelve feet square with ten-foot ceilings contained 1,440cubic feet each. So it stood to reason the space was only half the size of our two rooms. But considering that we were able to live, move and work within those rooms you can guess they weren't jammed to the rafters with stuff. I figured the storage space was more than ample.

Wrong! But thanks so much for playing. Next contestant, please.

That space filled up faster than a Wal-Mart on Black Friday. I know full well, since I was the person who put every single one of the 1,771,561 boxes into the storage space. By a staggering coincidence, that was the same number of Tribbles Captain Kirk had dumped on him in that episode. Okay I'm exaggerating slightly. It was probably less than five hundred. Even that sounds extreme, but in the first four hours of the job Jane and her friends packed twenty-eight bankers boxes. And they kept coming. Hour after hour, day after day for two solid weeks I trudged up and down the stairs hundreds of times to find more neatly packed and labeled boxes stacked in the hallway. When I reached the hallway, I heard Jane and her friend chatting away merrily while packing and carrying more boxes to the hall. I would reach out and find another stack waiting for me. Let me tell you, it was a daunting job. I was pretty strong but gawd, picking up two boxes, turning, stumping down the stairs to the kitchen, out the door to the garage and into the back of the van was as close to drudgery as anything I can imagine. There seemed to be no end to them. They rolled out like new Nissans from a factory in Osaka.

Jane was a marvelous and talented paper crafter. She has hundreds of rubber stamps and punches, ink pads, and enough paper to choke a recycling center. I have never been able to figure out how she could find anything in her office with all its drawers, shelves, cubbies and niches. I once asked her how many rubber stamps she had and her reply was a glib "If you can count them, you don't have enough."

I believe it. So all that (and more) was in her office. The room next to it was the den. We relaxed on the small sofa in there while watching television. That room too was full of stuff. Bookcases jammed with books and keepsakes, videos and other things. The closet held the overflow from Jane's office.

Over the years I had started noticing a strange sensation when walking towards the front of the house. For some reason I felt as if I were walking down a gradual slope and when moving towards the back of the house, the sensation was of walking uphill. It was just enough to be noticeable but not really compelling. When I began hauling tons of boxes from Jane's room, I realized the odd impression was gone. I even tried to sense it again, but to no avail. Now I understand what it was.

After removing more than one hundred boxes, each weighing an average of forty pounds, I estimated that more than two *tons* of weight had been on the front end of the house. No *wonder* it leaned! Now that I think about it, I recall one moment when I carried a particularly heavy box of craft books downstairs, I heard a long sigh. I thought it was Jane, but now am sure it was the house sighing in relief.

♡ No, it's too soon to come back. Daddy is still ranting about his bad back.

As the days passed with no letup, I began to wonder, "Where in the hell was there room for all this stuff?" The staggering amount of craft and paper we had already packed and moved out of the front rooms could not possibly have fit in them.

Ergo, there could only be one logical explanation. Right. A trans-dimensional wormhole.

A wormhole is a theoretical passage between universes or spatial dimensions. The Starship *Enterprise* got stuck in one in that first lousy movie with the bald chick when the Warp drive malfunctioned. And the *Deep Space Nine* series had a wormhole to travel great distances from one end of the galaxy to another with ease.

Wormholes are formed by unnaturally strong gravitational forces, such as those found around black holes or some other super dense stellar material. So now I hear you thinking, "Well, there's the flaw in your theory, Einstein. There are no black holes anywhere near San Diego, not unless you count Cal-Trans or the City Council budget."

Ah, but I said "strong gravitational forces." the pull of gravity, according to Sir Isaac Newton in his landmark 1687 work *Philosophe Naturalis Principia Mathematica,* is dependent on the mass of a nearby body

Ergo (there I go again), wormholes can be caused by any super dense material, not just collapsed stars. There is plenty of that right in my wife's craft room. I know, since I was hauling it downstairs. And believe me, boxes crammed full of rubber stamps, die-cuts, punches and stacks of paper counted as super dense material. Just ask my back and knees. It would have been easier to move the stone blocks to build the Great Pyramid. That only had 2.5 million blocks in it.

I called Stephen Hawking and told him about my brilliant conclusion. I also invited him to come and see the wormhole himself. He agreed it was entirely possible and that I should keep a detailed record of this highly significant scientific discovery. Then he had to go back to solving the riddles of the cosmos. I asked him what he considered to be the biggest mystery in the universe and he told me "Trying to figure out my taxes."

I felt better, knowing I was not the only one with that particular quandary. But it was a relief to know the greatest living theoretical physicist in the world took me seriously. Well, at least I hope so. It might not have really been Hawking. Anyone could have used an electronic voice. For all I know it was his cable repair guy.

I eventually had the storage space packed from front to back, side to side and floor to ceiling. And that was only because I was really, really good at Tetris. You could not get a slice of Kraft® Processed American cheese in there, even if you took off the wrapper.

♡ I think it's safe to come back now. Did you bring me anything?

From Old to New

We were moving into a smaller place without a garage or attic. Where in the hell were we going to put it all?

Jane said she had seen ads for Tuff-Sheds, a company not far from our new home. We went there one day and were shown these really sturdy wooden sheds that could be made to virtually any size. After securing permission from the Madrid Manor Homeowners' Association we bought a ten by eight Tuff Shed. I wanted a workbench built in and we added the shelf units we had in the old garage.

And then it was Moving Day! We found a great moving company who really did a good job. We gave them tips for their work. By the way, this was on June 27, and I swear I am not making this up, the Hottest Day of the Year! Great timing, huh?

♡ Hey at least you were not wearing a heavy fur coat. I was confused, panting and could not find my water dish anywhere!

Boy we sweated like racehorses. I went back and forth to the storage unit with our friends to retrieve the boxes. In two days we had it all inside.

Now Jane had to figure out where to put it all. She had a cunning plan, as Baldrick used to say on *Blackadder*. But Jane's plan worked.

She had the floor plan and furniture all arranged even before the escrow closed. She was amazing.

And at last I had my own office! A room inside the House! It was about twelve feet square with a window and closet. Mind you, the closet was so small I kept bumping my head on the back wall as soon as I opened the door, but I would live with it. My window faced west, so I had the afternoon sun. Jane's office was on the east side with the morning sun. The master bedroom and bath were big and had lots of closet space. I didn't get any, but oh well, that's marriage. And we kept separate bathrooms. Don't ask. You should know by now.

♡ Mommy was amazing. She did it all very slowly and carefully. The first thing she did was find my bowls and filled them up. Then Daddy got my toys and bed out. That was when I started to see the light. This was my new home! It did have a shower, but I guess you can't have everything.

It took six months for all the boxes in the hall to be emptied and broken down. Jane did a marvelous job. Even today it amazes me how well organized she had the kitchen, closets, pantry, and IKEA storage units. As for the shed, my philosophy was "I'll organize it all later."
It only took four years, so give me a break.

♡ Every time Daddy had to go to that shed he looked like a condemned prisoner, muttering all the way. I once heard him saying, "Gotta clean out that shed one of these days." Note for all readers who are under the age of seventy: Fibber McGee & Molly.
Jane was diligent in unpacking the boxes until they were all gone. Looking back, I now realize that she had probably pushed herself too hard. She never really seemed to get her strength back after that. I wish I could have done more, but she insisted on doing it herself. Her will was a lot stronger than her body.

Man Cave and Fem Den

One thing I must say, Jane could have been a very successful interior designer. She made all the decisions about décor to make our new home into a showplace. As for me, I had no idea what the house looked like beyond being told it was tan with white trim. I think the carpet was green or possibly dark tan. But that did not matter. I was happy. Jane did not exactly make it totally accessible to me. As an example, she had arranged the bedroom so there were only about two feet of space between the bed and a pair of bookcases along the wall. The problem was in order to enter the bathroom I had to thread that needle. I barely had room and I can't count the number of times I either bashed my knee on the bed frame or banged my shoulder on the bookcase.

"Honey, why can't you look where you're going?" Jane asked. "I get through just fine."

I never bothered to explain the obvious. There were a few other shin bashers and head knockers, but I learned to live with them.

♡ Poor Daddy. I did sympathize with him. But his biggest problem was that he never slowed down. He went through the house like a charging rhino.

That's not true, Saffron. I did walk slowly, but my mass and inertia made collisions inevitable.

♡ So, you're blaming the old $E=mc^2$ again, huh?

My office was my own, to do with as I pleased. I bought a new desk and book cases, a television cabinet and had shelves installed in the closet. Jane did not interfere. I had the "Man Cave" of my dreams. I wanted a nice office where I could have my friends and clients visit and do interviews. A place that was totally me, with my collection of military memorabilia, models and framed autographed pictures of astronauts, actors, aviators and admirals.

I had the coolest ceiling fan. Jane bought it for my 57th birthday. It was the nose of a P-51 Mustang. A long single shelf that ran the length of the room held my collection of military action figures, which Jane insisted on calling dolls. They were made by Dragon and Side Show models and very detailed. Anyone who entered my office would know at a glance I was a military history buff.

♡ Or a big kid who never outgrew dolls.

Action figures! Women. I was very content in my office.

As for Jane's office, that wormhole shifted from Carmel Mountain Ranch to San Marcos. Defying all laws of physics, logic, and probably a few zoning regulations, she managed to get all her craft stuff from the old house's rooms, garage, and attic into that one room.

Voices in the Dark

The only thing that took some time to work out was my computer's voice. As previously noted, my computer used a text-to-speech software called JAWS. It had a fairly natural-sounding voice to verbalize what was on my screen. E-mails, Word documents, Excel spreadsheets, webpages, Power Point slide shows, and even scanned documents were easily navigable with the keyboard. But Jane hated the voice. With her office just across the hall, I could not turn the volume down low enough to pacify her and still be able to hear it. She listened to DVDs, CDs and crafting shows on YouTube all the time. As a compromise I started wearing headphones. It worked on my end, but then she said I could not hear her when she was talking to me. Sigh. Eventually I told her, "Just e-mail me."

And that is what we did. We e-mailed one another from ten feet away. Twenty-first century, here we come!

♡ I chose to lay on the hall floor between Mommy's and Daddy's offices. Not because I wanted to love them equally, but so I would be in the right place when one of them headed for the kitchen. Remember, my "Treat Reset" button was hit every time one of them left the room.

I am sure there were other aspects of the move that will come out after years of therapy, but we did end up with a beautiful home, a much more manageable mortgage and a wonderful new community.

I'm sure you want to get back to Saffron. So let's meet our new neighbors, the Saffronalians.

CHAPTER **17**

MADRID MANORISMS

"The world would be a nicer place if everyone had
the ability to love as unconditionally as a dog."
—M.K. Clinton

Once we settled in and my back stopped hurting,
we got to know our new neighbors. Unlike the cliquish yuppie residents
of Carmel Mountain Ranch, the people of Madrid Manor were as
friendly and welcoming as could be. They even had a sort of Welcome
Wagon, a nice lady named April who told us about the community,
events, clubs, and such. Within a week we had people coming by with
fruit baskets, casseroles, and house-warming gifts. Even though our new
friends were already sociable, it was Saffron who really broke the ice.

♡ I sure did! All these wonderful people who wanted to meet and
bring food to me!

Well, not exactly. First there was a tiny little issue to deal with. The
HOA of Madrid Manor was a fairly well run and reasonable group. But
they had some draconian rules about dogs. No more than 25 pounds
and they could not be walked on the street. There were no sidewalks.
But once I provided proof that Saffron was a certified assistance animal
and was essential to my safety and ability to go where I needed, they
waived the rule. It was not that simple, but there is no need to get into the

details. I had to agree, with good reason, to make sure Saffron did not do her business on the street or on anyone's property. No problem there.

This is where Carol Gendel entered the picture. A kind and intelligent lady, Carol is a very socially and politically conscious liberal with a zest for causes. A fascinating and unique person, Carol liked to tint her hair in garish colors depending on her mood or social cause. We hit it off right away and went for walks in the neighborhood so Saffron and I could get familiar with it. It was a very steep learning curve. When Jane and I had first moved to Carmel Mountain after getting married in 1995, I could still see and knew my way around long before Musket and Saffron came along. But by 2017 I was blind. The street plan of Madrid Manor was laid out by a developer with no sense of direction. The streets intersected and wound around back and forth. Even after three years I still got lost. Back to Carol. She and I had plenty to talk about, like history, politics, religion and all the other taboos of social interaction. We got along just fine even though we did not agree on everything.

♡ Carol and Daddy sure talked a lot. I looked forward to the end of the walk, when Carol gave me some carrot pieces. She never forgot. I loved when the Carrot Lady came over.

Once in a while someone yelled out, "Hey you're not allowed to walk your dog here! And that dog is too big!"

Carol always beat me to it. "She is a Guide Dog and the rules do not apply to her."

There were a few people who resented Saffron's freedom when their own dogs had to be carried out of the park to be walked.

My impulse was to say "You can have a Guide Dog, just go blind like I did." But that was too snarky even for me. So I muttered it under my breath.

But soon the resentment seemed to evaporate as Saffron made new friends. Just like her big brother, she pulled people to her like iron filings around a magnet.

Carol was only the first of our new friends. Jane was so happy that we had found our real home. "We have made more new friends in one week at Madrid Manor than in twenty-two years in Carmel Mountain Ranch," she often said. "I love it here. I feel like we really belong."

Only a week after we moved in, we were invited to the July 4th Luncheon and Chili Cook-off. They needed one more impartial judge for the blind taste test. I jumped at it. That was fun. For once my blindness was an asset since I had to depend on my sense of taste. No, I did not give any to Saffron.

♡ No, he didn't. My Daddy has some will power left. I'll have to work on that.

At our table we met Bob and Kate Rogelstad, who lived a few houses down from us.

Bob was and still is, determined to win the California Lottery. He buys a lottery ticket every single week without fail. He really likes and respects me and always said, "If I win I'm going to give you $5 million to get your sight back." I told him that was not possible but I would still take the money.

Kate was on the Social Club committee and did the decorating for the many banquets and holiday events at Madrid Manor. With her creativity and organizational skills Jane was quickly asked to join. Every month saw more events, lunches, birthdays and holidays. It was almost too much to absorb. While we slowly unpacked and put away the boxes of things in the hall, we got more involved and made more friends. Janelle Personius, a tiny little songbird of a lady, was one of Jane's closest friends. They talked nearly every day. Janelle really took to Saffron even though her own dog Summer, a little dog I swear had to be a wind-up, did not see eye to eye. Mary Lou Rushing and her husband John soon entered orbit around us. John was a gentle and intelligent man who loved to talk history with me, while Mary Lou, who was about as tall as my elbow, but with more vim and vigor than a Collie, fell in love with Saffron. "Nanny Lou" we called her, and soon Saffron recognized that name. "Nanny Lou is outside! Go and say hello!"

Saffron went nuts every time Nanny Lou came over.

♡ Janelle and Nanny Lou had both been nurses and sometimes helped Mommy with her health. They were very sweet and kind to us.

From the start it was obvious many of our neighbors were patriotic. Jane said that our street had a line of tall flagpoles flying the Stars and Stripes. Our next door neighbor was a 100 year old Army veteran named Harry Anderson. During the Second World War he had worked for one of the Boeing contractors that built B-17 Flying Fortresses. In fact, he had probably installed the engines on the plane that Ed Davidson had flown in the 96th Bomb Group in the war. I arranged for them to meet and they had a great time chatting.

Harry was such a gentle man and enjoyed talking on his porch about life and memories. I especially loved hearing his stories about life as a boy growing up in the 1920s. Saffron was always welcome and he spent hours petting her.

♡ Harry was such a nice man. He made me feel happy just to be near him.

Harry died in 2019 at the age of 102. But he left a lasting legacy. He loved to grow plumeria, the fragrant Hawaiian flowers. He gave me a cutting and showed me how to plant it. Today I have three white plumeria plants in my garden. Thank you, Harry.

And on it went. From Nancy Childers to Charlene Kroyder, from Gigi Harrington to Perry and Diana Grossman, the parade of new friends passed.

Often asked over for coffee, we three showed up, once I had asked if they minded Saffron coming. To this day she has never been left behind.

♡ Who would not want me in their home? I am a wonderful guest. Where do you keep your dog dish?

When asked how I liked my coffee, I said, "Sweet and blonde like Saffron."

♡ Isn't that cute?

Charlene rates special mention. She described herself to me as "Tall, blonde, beautiful and buxom." I knew better but never said so. It was obvious the only truth was "buxom." We loved to flirt and Jane laughed at ~~our~~ antics.

Jane, Charlene, Nancy and Kate formed a small group of women who soon called themselves, with a total lack of pretentiousness, the "Thursday Group." I called them, behind their backs of course, "A gang of gabby gals." Don't tell them.

Every Thursday night they got together to go to a different restaurant. Jane had a great time.

IN 2018 Charlene's son paid for her and the gang to stay at the ritzy Belaggio Hotel in Las Vegas for a few nights. Jane drove and they had a great time. Actually, from what I heard, I'm amazed they were not arrested for disturbing the peace. But then again, no sane cop would have dared to get near those whacky broads.

♡ Hey Mommy had a right to let her hair down too, Daddy. And you sure had a good time while the cat was away, didn't you?

I have no idea what you are talking about, Saffron. Ahem. Friday nights she played Mah Jongg (I'll check the spelling on that,) or Mexican Train dominoes. This was cutthroat with money on the table. They brought snacks and drinks, and played for hours. This gang included Mary Lou, Kate, Charlene, Gigi and Jane as the core, with others coming and going.

Gigi Harrington was a spirited and fun lady who, even at the age of sixty, worked as a carpenter, repair-woman and contractor for the community. She did good and solid work and once even helped when our kitchen sink overflowed on a Sunday morning just as we were dressing for church.

Imagine a blind guy in his socks and underwear running back and forth with a bucket trying to empty out the sink as it cascaded onto the floor. Yeah, it wasn't funny at the time.

♡ That was very exciting! I watched Daddy running back and forth dumping buckets of water on the gravel while the flood ran towards the laundry room. He really keeps his head in an emergency. I won't tell you what words he said, but I'm sure you can guess.

Seems Jane had:
1. Run a big bunch of old lettuce down the disposal all at once the night before,
2. Ran the dishwasher,
3. Ran the washing machine, and
4. Took a long shower.

The water had nowhere to go but back up the sink.

So that was it for going to church that day, but it was a flood of Biblical proportions. I got the mess cleaned up. Then Gigi arrived to run her roto-rooter through the plumbing. What came out of the drain would only excite a biologist. We grew to love Gigi, and her willingness to do work for us was truly wonderful.

Do you know where your Guide Dog is?

Here is a story I have to tell you, but please don't let the people at Guide Dogs know about it. They'll never trust me with another dog.

Every so often I was on a Friday evening walk with Carol and we sometimes stopped into the card room to say hello to the players. Saffron was always welcomed. Jane called, "Saffy! Come and give Mommy a kiss!"

I knew darn well she gave Saffron a treat, like a cracker or something.

So this one time we had stopped in, and the girls were eating either pizza or sandwiches. After a few minutes we left, with me practically dragging Saffron away.

When I reached home, I took off her harness and said, "Go do your business." She was very good about running down the ramp to do it in the gravel alongside the driveway. I went inside. I began reading an audio book. I was certain Saffron was close by, since I had left the door open. It was summertime and warm.

About fifteen minutes later I heard Laura's voice. She was one of the regulars at the game. "Mark, are you okay?" she asked through the open door.

"Sure," I said from the couch where I had been lying down. "Why do you ask?"

"Because Saffron came to the clubhouse and you were not with her."

Oh, boy. That was *not* good. I grabbed the harness and white cane and followed Laura to the clubhouse. It was a very big deal to have Saffron run off like that.

When we got there, the girls were all laughing but I was very upset. "Saffron," I said in my stern voice. "Come to Daddy."

Jane urged her to go to me, but Saffron was having none of it. She must have known she was in trouble.

♡ Yeah, that look on daddy's face was like Judge Wapner about to issue capital punishment. So I hid next to my sweet and forgiving Mommy.

Jane was laughing. While she did understand the seriousness of the situation, she knew there had been no harm done. She said, "It was so funny, Honey. After you left we went back to playing. Then a few minutes later Gigi heard this funny thumping on the door. She went and opened it and Saffy ran right to me like Lassie barking that Timmy had fallen into the well."

"I did not fall in a well," I said deadpan. "Saffron, come to Daddy. Now."

"Better go, Saffron," they all said. Finally she came to me. I put her harness on and left. I did not yell at her. I was not going to punish her. But I was going to make sure it *never* happened again.

♡ Call it instinct. Food there. Me here. what else could I do?

So another page was added to Saffron's legend. She did not seem to take some things as seriously as her big brother, but as I said, I was not going to compare them to one another. Saffron was a good Guide Dog, but off the harness she had a mind of her own. The moment I let her go out all she thought about was to get back to where Mommy and all the girls had the food!

It was my fault, not hers.

♡ I heard Mommy and Daddy talking about it later. The big deal was that I might have gotten lost or stolen or run over. At last I understood. They were not mad at me so much as terrified for what might have happened. I never did it again.

A couple of houses down the street lived John and Geneva Tolbert. The devoutly religious couple said hello for the first time when I was walking one evening with Saffron. She loved making new friends. In time John and I began taking evening walks. As a Marine veteran of Vietnam, we found a lot to talk about.

They had invited Jane and me over for coffee a few months after we moved in. They were as kind and friendly as could be. And as events later proved, a true pair of Earthbound Angels.

Perry and Diana Grossman were retired law enforcement and took the role of unofficial "peacekeepers" of the park. They drove around in their black golf cart with the "Batman" emblem. Perry was later elected to the HOA and was very good at handling problems and mediating disputes. I found him to be a very conscientious man. They sometimes invited Saffron and me in on evenings for a glass of hot Captain Morgan spiced rum. On spring evenings they had a fire pit where some of the neighbors joined for drinks and conversation. Saffron of course was a favorite topic.

Many people were curious and asked a lot of questions, and in time virtually everybody we knew had bought a copy of *Confessions*.

♡ Snort. Wait till this book is done. Then they will see what great literature is.

The World Outside

Madrid Manor was not an easy place for me to navigate. When I went out the gate onto El Norte Parkway, it was very different. There was a CVS just down the street, and a shopping center about a mile away. Across El Norte was a 7/11 and some restaurants. Lucy Waite, the Guide Dogs field services trainer came to help me learn my way around the area, pointing out the various obstacles and landmarks. Saffron did just fine. I was the nervous one.

♡ I did. Lucy was really cool. Daddy seemed unsure of himself out beyond the gate. But he should know I was going to take good care of him.

It was crossing El Norte that made me nervous. Four lanes wide, it seemed to be the local dragstrip for guys with big trucks and motorcycles. Madrid Manor is right on the border of Escondido and San Marcos. Lucy told me how to request an audible signal and I contacted the traffic departments of the two cities. San Marcos acted promptly and put up the signal at El Norte and Woodland Parkway. But Escondido, who oversaw Country Club Lane, said it would take about two to four years to put one in there. It did not take that long. Escondido came through in 2021 and there are audible signals at both intersections, making travel safer for myself and many of the seniors who live in the area.

♡ It was cool having the electronic voice counting down the time to cross. My daddy made it happen.

Scooter Jane

On July 4 and around Christmas the Social Club hosted a Golf Cart parade. People were invited to decorate their golf carts with anything they wanted, the more wild and outlandish the better. Kate, who had lots of things available for the various holiday events shared it with everyone. Kate, who I would never call minimalist or unobtrusive, went all out. She loved the parades. She invited Jane to participate, but not having a golf cart, she would have to ride on Kate's cart. Jane had other ideas. Her friend Karen Morikawa, who was president of the Friends of the Braille Institute, or FBI, had given her a nearly brand-new electric scooter. It was a real help to Jane when she began having mobility problems. She used the cart to go around the park. So on Independence Day she decorated the scooter in patriotic bunting, flowers and flags. She had a ball!

At noon Saffron and I waited by the street as the parade passed by. Some carts had big boom boxes playing Souza marches and patriotic music. I told Saffron that Mommy would be passing soon. And then Saffron began to wag her tail and I knew she had seen Jane.

Jane waved and called out to Saffron. It was a lot of fun.

♡Mommy! Here I am! Can I come with you? I loved seeing Mommy in the parade.

When Christmas approached, she joined that parade with a veritable blaze of green, red, white and gold decorations on the scooter. Again we waved as she called out to her baby Saffron.

I already mentioned Kimmy Aguinaldo, a pixie of a lady with more energy than a Jack Russell terrier on speed. She did housecleaning and dog sitting and fell in love with Saffron at once. She came over just to play with her. Eventually she began taking Saffron to the nearby park to play fetch. It was far better exercise for her than anything I could do. She still refused to bring the toy or ball back to me. I had to find it, which diminished my enthusiasm for the game. Regarding her role as a "retriever," I was reminded of what Mike O'Neill said about her always bringing the toy right back to him. Hmm. Seems to have lost something in the translation. Put it this way: I would need a barrel of balls. Then I would have to crawl around to find them. Not very practical.

♡ Well, I sort of got out of the habit. Besides, it drove Daddy nuts.

I'll agree with that. Sometimes I sat on the floor at the end of the bed which faced the long hallway. Saffron brought whatever toy was handy and we played for a while. Throw, return, drop, throw, return, drop. But suddenly she stopped bringing it back.

"Saffron! Bring the toy to Daddy!" I padded the floor but she did not come. I listened and heard...absolutely nothing. Dead silence. No nails on the floor. No panting. No toy being eviscerated.

"Saffron!" I called in my command voice.

Then I heard the sound of jingling tags and panting.

"Where were you?" I asked.

♡ Oh, are you still here? I got bored and went to lie down in the sun. Why are you shaking your head like that?

Often Jane sat in her bedroom easy chair and threw the toy for Saffron. She had a pretty good curve and managed to get it most of the way down the hall. Saffron spun and tracked it going overhead like a pass receiver in a football game. She charged off after the airborne toy. She almost always let out a big "Woof!" that shook the walls. It was pretty startling to hear.

Like a Phoenix missile locking in on an aircraft she made a grab and pulled the hapless toy into her deadly maw.

Kimmy got Saffron to run and chase the ball for at least an hour. I was glad she had a chance to really run and have fun. When they came back Saffron was panting like a racehorse with her tail set on "Auto-wag." It took her about half an hour to settle down.

♡ Boy you can say that again! I love Kimmy! She wore me out and never got tired. She thought I was the best dog in the world and I am not about to disabuse her of that opinion.

In the Limelight

Every spring the park held the "Madrid Manor Follies" on the clubhouse stage. It was what you'd expect from a bunch of extroverted seniors who loved to sing, dance and act. Charlene ran the Follies and kept insisting that Jane and I join. But Jane was more interested in organizing and supporting the 2019 Follies than being on stage. So she took that role while I was finally charmed into putting my considerable acting talent to the test. Fortunately we had a lot of leeway as to what we performed. Charlene let me pick my own acts and roles. One day she asked, "Hey have you ever heard Johnny Carson do the 'Copper Clappers' routine on the *Tonight Show?*"

You mean 'Cleaning woman Clara Clifford discovered that the clean copper clappers that were kept in the closet were copped by Claude Cooper the kleptomaniac from Cleveland?'"

She was astonished. "Yes!" Will you do it?"

"Let me think about it. Yes."

Later I helped re-write a Muppets Doctor Bob skit in which I was a blind surgeon. Don't ask. It was so corny and over the top that I could not help but have a great time. The audience was apparently starved for entertainment. For the Copper Clappers skit, Saffron got into the act as my partner in the "Canine Support Unit of the Criminal Division in which the super sleuth Saffron would quickly sniff out sneaky suspects."

Saffron was in the spotlight.

♡ I was a star! Mommy and Aunt Sue made me a cape that read "K-9 Cop." Neat, huh?

Saffron in the limelight at the 2019 Madrid Manor Follies

I was again roped...er. asked to do the 2020 Follies but more on that later.

And to my surprise I was asked to join a summer musicale. I cannot sing, have no talent and never learned to play an instrument. Jane did not like me singing in the shower since it carried through the house like the sound of cats being tortured off-key.

♡ Mommy was right. I liked the vacuum better. At least it did something useful.

Jane suggested I do "that train song from *The Music Man.*" She was always impressed that I had learned the entire song "Rock Island" from the musical, all ten parts. Chalk it up to my love of doing impossible and totally useless things. But hey, I was ten years old at the time.

♡ We had to listen to Daddy practice that song over and over and over. But he was having fun. And when he did it for the musicale, the audience was amazed he could do all the different voices and all the words. Mommy was clapping along with the audience but I never had the heart to tell Daddy he was facing the wrong way.

Kindred Spirit

The person who I most want to tell you about is Rob Wood. Rob and his wife Elaine were deeply involved in community events. Rarely have I ever known a more organized and meticulous thinker than Rob or a more gentle and sensible woman than Elaine.

Rob was the sound and electronics wizard for the Follies. We got to know each other when he found out I was a Civil War buff. He told me his great-grandfather had been a soldier in a North Carolina regiment. From that point on, Rob and I found lots to talk about. He even gave me a beautifully handmade model of the *CSS Virginia*, more popularly known as the *Merrimack.* He got a real kick out of letting me run my hands over the sloping casemate and ram bow and saying "The *Virginia?*"

It was the start of a great friendship. We went to events where he met Linda and General Cardenas, to parades and collectors shows. He was a model boat builder on a scale far larger than anything I ever did. He and his club built and sailed radio-controlled warships that were highly detailed and several feet long. We went to one event at Santee Lakes where his club sailed perfect replicas of Taffy 3, the small fleet that fought a huge Japanese fleet off Samar Island in October of 1944. We met several of the Taffy 3 veterans.

♡ That was a fun day at the lake. Daddy introduced me to some more veterans and by then I knew how to act around them. The model boats were just about the right size for me to ride on, but Daddy talked me out of it by reminding me how much I hated to get wet.

Mark and Saffron at the Taffy 3 reunion at Santee
Lakes with the scale model of the *USS Kalinin Bay* built
by Jack Bitters. Photo courtesy Rob Wood

Now as for Saffron, they somehow found a bond that went beyond mere dog and human friendship. I really believe Saffron had a crush on Rob.

♡ Oh, sure Daddy, blab it to the whole world! He is so sweet and nice. He treats me like a real lady.

And gives you treats.

♡ Ummm...well, that too.

Rob was part of a huge (but not huge enough) group that raised and released Monarch Butterflies. The people who raise and love those colorful little miracles are helping to make the world more beautiful.
The Facebook group is called: Raising Monarch Butterflies.

Lost on the Mean Streets of Coronado

One day in January 2020 I was going to do a lecture at the Orange Avenue library on Coronado about my book, *The Marines' Lost Squadron*. Rob offered to take me. This worked out well for Jane who went to lunch with Elaine. Boy what a day that turned out to be.

Here is what happened. I was to talk at one o'clock in the afternoon. I asked Rob if he had the address in his GPS. He said, for the record, "Yes."

We left and drove south to Coronado and chatted about history, Taffy 3, ships, the Civil War and whatever. When he pulled into a parking space we climbed out. I retrieved Saffron from the back seat. The day was warm and sunny even for January. Remember, this was Coronado, where people pay good money for perfect weather.

As we walked down the sidewalk, Rob described what was around us. "The marina is full of boats," he said at one point. This should have triggered something in my mind, but I was concentrating on my upcoming talk. We entered the library and Rob asked the desk clerk where I would do the OASIS talk. When the girl did not know anything about it, I asked, "Is this the Orange Avenue library?"

"No."

Then the bit about the marina came back to me. There *was* no marina on Orange Avenue.

Oops. I wish I could have seen the look on Rob's face. We went to the sidewalk where he told me to wait. "I can get the car and come back to get you."

We would just be able to make it. I knew Rob was feeling pretty bad so I wasn't going to bug him about it. Just tease him unmercifully.

♡ You're a mean one, Mister Grinch.

I was standing there when the car pulled up. The window was open and I heard "Get in." I let Saffron in the back door and climbed in the passenger seat. He hit the gas and we shot off, presumably for the right place. Still enough time.

About two minutes later, after making a few turns, I heard, "You are Lorenzo, right?"

What?

♡ I could have told Daddy we were in the wrong car! But he never asked.

"No," I said. "You are not Rob?" Duh.

"Uber," the man said.

Oh boy. Then that scary point at which you have to make a fast decision arrived. And he let me off.

I was lost in downtown Coronado, and Rob did not know where I was. I tried to call him, but guess what? I only had his home number, not his cell.

Then I called the library and explained my predicament. Using my own GPS I found out where I was and asked for someone to come and get me. It would be faster than trying to get Rob to where I was.

Then I called Jane and asked her to put Elaine on the phone. After begging her not to tell Jane, I asked her to call Rob and tell him to go right to the library. I would meet him there.

Another car pulled up. "Are you Mark?" a girl asked.

"I sure am," I said with evident relief.

"Oh, what a beautiful dog. Come on in!"

This was a lot better than Uber. We reached the library ten minutes late. They had told my audience what happened and I got applause just for showing up.

♡ It was kind of neat. Usually they only applaud for me. But Daddy needed a morale boost.

I set up as fast as I could and joked about being lost on the mean streets in the seedy part of Coronado. They laughed. "Even the muggers drive Lexus here," I said.

Then Rob showed up and called to me. I waved. All was well.

As it turned out I was in scintillating form that day. The audience was great.

I sold a dozen books, a good haul for that kind of venue.

As we were driving back north Rob told me about when he had come back to where he left me. "I had no idea where you were! I went back into the library. I drove around and began to panic until Elaine called and told me to meet you at the library."

We laughed about it, but I did not want Jane to find out. It wasn't so much embarrassment, but her long lecture about how I could have avoided it. She never did find out, thank God.

♡ Um...Daddy. She did. I told her. But she knew you were embarrassed and never told you.

Oh. Well, it was a story Rob and I have kidded each other about ever since. When we go to an event, I say, "Are you *sure* you have the right address? Really sure?"

What a friend. Rob never let me down.

On New Year's Eve 2019 (the last day of peace) we went to an event where we could sing Karaoke. As surprising to many as it may be, I had never done Karaoke. I was too shy.

♡ Yep, you heard it here! My daddy could be shy!

But so many of the attendees did it that I threw caution to the winds and asked Rob, who was the DeeJay, "can you find 'Jambalaya' by Credence Clearwater Revival?"

Rob found it and handed me the mike, which at that moment felt like I was holding a grenade that was about to go off. But when the music started I began to sing. And you know what?

♡ He was great! He did it really well. Mommy was smiling and clapping. I was really proud of him. But as it turned out, that was one of the last good days we would know for a long, long time.

CHAPTER 18

AU REVOIR, JANE

"If there are no dogs in Heaven, then when I
die I want to go where they went."
— Will Rogers

Where do I start? As we all know, the year 2020 truly sucked. I won't go into the mess created by the government, but they did not make things any better. For the record, I was an early supporter of the shutdown to help restrain the spread of Covid. I knew it would be a long, hard, and frustrating road to travel. But Covid was only one part of what we had to deal with that year.

First of all California Assembly Bill 5 went into effect. It was aimed at the Uber drivers who were working without any constraints, in other words, the state was not making any money from them. That was totally unacceptable! But the bill went way past that. In a perfect illustration of how rashly written and poorly researched legislation can wreak widespread havoc, it also affected free-lance writers (like me) and contractors who performed as public speakers, (again, like me). So in one fell swoop two-thirds of my income was cut, unless I was willing to become a paid employee of about fifteen different companies and publishers. Bear in mind I often worked less than forty hours a year for each of these clients. I had no way to compensate. Eventually my clients worked out a system to pay us contractors and writers, but it still carved a big chunk from my income, which was a major stressor to Jane. But we did our best.

♡ I remember how worried Mommy and Daddy were. They talked about how to make more money. Mommy wanted to sell some of her jewelry and some oil paintings that had belonged to her brother, Darcy. But Daddy told her not to do that. He was going to find other clients to work for. He did hint about robbing Fort Knox, but I think he was joking.

The Big Fall

You know when a big change in your life takes you by complete surprise? Oh boy did it. I never saw it coming. Our future permanently changed on February 3.

Jane was out shopping and I was at home doing something or other.

She was having some serious and chronic health problems but she was not going to let them do more than slow her down. She called me and said, "Honey, I fell in the store and they are going to take me to the hospital. I think I broke my ankle."

I was immediately worried, knowing that due to her diabetes she took months to heal from any injury. The previous year she cut her foot in the pool and spent eight months going to wound care to get it healed.

"Okay," I said, already thinking of who to call and what to do. I am pretty calm in emergency situations. "Let me know where you are going and I'll meet you there." But there was another factor. Covid. This was right when the hospitals were starting to take precautions. Rob and his wife Elaine took Saffron and me to the hospital where Jane was.

We had to put on masks, which at that time was a very unusual feeling. And to my surprise, they would not let Saffron in.

♡ Can you believe it? I was ready to break loose and find Mommy. Daddy was very irritated.

Rob was able to straighten it out, but my nerves were already tight. Then we were allowed in to see her. She said, "I broke it in six places.

They are going to have to put it all back together and put pins and plates in my ankle."

"Well, that's it for you and airport metal detectors," I joked, holding her hand. She laughed.

♡ Boy my Daddy can always find a way to make Mommy feel better. She was very upset that she could not come home to us and was asking Rob to make sure Daddy would be okay. But Daddy said, "Honey, I can handle things just fine. Right now the only important thing is for you to get better."

Mommy apologized for breaking her ankle. "I feel so stupid."

Daddy said, "It was not your fault. It will be okay. Saffy and I will be just fine. We love you." Then he kissed Mommy and she put her hand down for me to lick.

Seven Weeks in Hell

After her surgery Jane was sent to a rehab facility near our home. I won't go into detail, but that was seven weeks of hell for my beloved Jane. She did not get the care that they bragged about on their website. She was virtually a prisoner who was told she could go home when she could walk. But the physical therapy was a joke. And she did not get a shower for the entire time she was there. I went to see her with Janelle, Kate, Carol, and others at least four days a week. Saffron was always glad to see her Mommy.

"Come to Mommy," Jane said, and I lifted Saffron up to put her on Jane's bed. They were so happy cuddling again. The staff thought it was cute.

♡ I loved seeing Mommy and made her happy when I licked her face. She was so sad in that horrible place. I wanted her to come home.

I brought her what she needed and she kept up with the bills and correspondence as well as on Facebook. She did her best to get the staff to give her the PT and help she needed but they were mostly underpaid, under-trained and unmotivated. A bad combination. If I come across as bitter, you're right.

♡ Daddy worked very hard while Mommy was away. He wanted to make everything perfect for her return.

Finally, at the end of March she (no pun intended) put her foot down. She proved she could get up and walk with a walker. They let her go. I'm sure they were actually upset at losing a Medicare gravy train.

At last Saffron and I would have her home again.

During the time Jane was away I was sort of "on my own." That means I lived alone but our neighbors and church friends made certain I would not die of starvation or neglect. They drove me to the store so I could shop and tried to help me with cooking, cleaning and laundry. I did all that myself. I'm sure Jane was dreading walking...er, rolling into a region just declared a disaster area, but the house was clean and everything was in order.

I had ordered a shower bench and Gigi made modifications to the bedroom and bathroom with extra grab bars and such.

The seven weeks she was gone was a learning experience for me. And I'll admit I handled it okay, especially with the help of my Earthbound Angels.

The 2020 Madrid Manor Follies were held in early March. I did a skit with Rob in which I played President Ronald Reagan doing another routine stolen from Johnny Carson, a "Who, what, and where," based on the old Abbott & Costello "Who's on first?" routine. It was fun but my heart wasn't in it. I left right after each rehearsal. I had promised Charlene and Rob. I was happy to do it but glad when it was over.

♡ Daddy was the funniest one in the show. I did not play a part but I was in the audience with Kate.

Gigi and I went to pick Jane up on March 25. We were so happy to have her back where she belonged. But it would mean the end of my eating chili dogs, hamburgers, pizza, Cap'n Crunch, ice cream, chocolate, and other essential food groups. No, seriously I did eat healthy foods and such, but I did fall off the wagon a couple of [dozen] times.

♡ I inserted the missing word that Daddy forgot.

Thanks a heap, you little fink. The first thing Jane wanted when she came home was a cup of good coffee and a shower.

♡ She got them. Mommy was very happy to be in her own home again. I gave her so many kisses I licked off her makeup!

Jane was going to need physical and occupational therapy three days a week. The therapist was great and helped me understand how to help Jane stand from her chair and into the bathroom, into the shower and other such needs. Fortunately I have always been pretty strong. But what a change. She had to wear this huge clumsy boot that looked like something the Apollo astronauts had to wear on the Moon. She hated that boot. She could not remove or put it on by herself. I did it for her, even at 2:00 in the morning. But that's what we mean when we vow, "in sickness and health," isn't it?

Tender Moments

When Jane sat in her recliner, Saffron often slept by her feet. She was content to have Mommy close by. In the mornings, after she had been fed, Saffron sometimes stood by the chair, looking expectantly up at Jane.

"Want to come up here," Saffy?" Jane asked, patting her lap.

Zoom! Saffron the gazelle was on her lap in an instant, curling up and lavishing kisses on Jane's face. Those were tender and wonderful moments. It always made me smile to know my girls were happy. Jane often sang the *Sesame Street* song to Saffron, changing the name to "Saffy Street."

Jane told me that Saffron looked at her as she sang.

♡ Cuddling with Mommy was the best thing ever. She was so warm and soft. I kissed her so much she could hardly breathe. She wiped the goopies out of my eyes. Otherwise I had to do it myself by wiping them on Daddy's pants. I often fell asleep on Mommy, and it made her happy.

Saffron liked to rub her face along the carpet with her butt in the air. It was very cute. "I got your butt! I got your butt!" I said as I scratched at her butt. She loved it and Jane always laughed.

"That's my silly little girl," she said.

♡ I know it was silly but if it made Mommy happy I was glad to do it. Besides, Daddy gave great butt scratches.

Saffron seemed to be very sensitive to human emotions. She was a furry empath. If Jane and I were having an argument or even a tense discussion, Saffron went to one of us and cuddled very close. If I was on the floor playing with her and on the phone with some clueless bureaucrat, she dropped the toy and curled up with me. She sensed the tension in my voice. I won't deny that she helped us through some strained times.

♡ It was weird, but when Mommy or Daddy got stressed out, I felt it and went to them. That was part of my job as Stress Relief Counselor.

Jane often had trouble falling asleep for hours on end. To help her, I sometimes told her what we called "snories." There was something about my voice that helped her relax and go to sleep. "What do you want to hear, Honey?" I asked.

"Anything. Civil War, ships, trains, just make it long."

With my head full of facts and accounts from history, I talked about whatever she wanted. For some reason she could not get into anything prior to the American Revolution. In time she was asleep. NOTE: I am stating for the record that Jane did [not] snore.

Darn, Saffron did it to me again!

♡ Daddy did those snories at all times of the night, whenever Mommy needed them. We both fell asleep, but it was not that he had a soothing voice. He was just plain boring.

Back to Normal?

Jane went through the piles of mail and bills, and since this was now in the first month of the Covid crisis, we were very lucky that the government had pushed the tax filing back three months. She had always handled the bills, for which I was grateful. I made the money and she spent it.

For the early part of the month of April we had many visitors who were glad to have Jane home. Saffron was more happy than I had ever seen her. Jane did not take to wearing masks, but pragmatic as ever, did so when necessary. She was eager to get back to driving the car and doing errands, which is how she ended up in this mess in the first place!

We went to the bank, post office, store and other places. She stayed in the car or used the store's scooter. It was obvious she was happy to be home and getting back to a normal life, whatever that would mean in 2020.

April 22 was our 25th Anniversary. Covid had shut down the clubhouse and large gatherings were discouraged. But I had a plan. After calling Janelle, we set up a surprise for Jane.

♡ I was in on the secret! I was excited that we were going to surprise Mommy.

While doing the breakfast dishes I checked my talking watch. It was time. "Hey, Honey, it's a beautiful day. You need more sun. Why don't you go on the front porch and read for a bit? I'll bring you some coffee."

"That sounds great," she said and went out the door.

"SURPRISE!" came the roar from outside.

Trying to keep a straight face but failing miserably I went out. On the street in front of our house were about twenty of our friends and neighbors, all waving and holding flowers and signs. "Happy Anniversary!" they shouted.

♡ It was so much fun! All our friends coming to see me! Oops. I mean Mommy and Daddy.

Ah, what a perilous gift conceit can be. Jane was never easy to surprise. I handed her a mask and she put it on over her mile-wide smile. "You are a sneaky rat," she said. "No wonder you made me wear this outfit today."

It was a wonderful time of love and community. I felt great. Jane was very happy and glad to be home at last. We would get through this, one way or another. Things could only get better.

I was wrong.

Jane had exactly one week to live.

The worst Day in Our Lives

♡ Daddy asked me to write my memories about when Mommy went to Heaven. He still does not remember some of those days. But I saw it all. I was there.

Mommy started feeling bad a couple of days after the anniversary. She did not want to eat and felt weak. Daddy suggested we go to Urgent Care but Mommy refused. "I don't want to go near a hospital again! I'll be okay."

The next night she fell as Daddy was helping her to the bathroom. He could not help her up so he had to call 911. Mommy was very upset but these big handsome men came in and helped her to her feet. But they said she should go to the hospital. Her temperature was very high. She said "No, I am not going!"

Daddy was really worried but gave in. Then the next day her physical therapist came and saw that Mommy was real sick. "You have to go to emergency or you will die right here. Your blood pressure is up, your temperature is 103." Mommy gave in. Again the men came and helped Mommy. She was on this bed with wheels. Daddy and I followed her out to the ambulance. He kissed her and said, "Honey I love you so much. Do what they say. Let them help you and you can come home in a day or so." Daddy kissed Mommy and then let me lick her hand.

That was on the afternoon of April 29. He was making calls and keeping our families and friends informed. He could not sit down or relax. He paced the house and kept talking to himself.

Then in the evening the phone rang and he answered. I heard a voice on the phone saying it was Mommy's doctor. "Mister Carlson, we were about to move your wife from Emergency into Intensive care. She had a cardiac arrest." Daddy froze and asked if she was okay. But the voice said, "We got her heart going but it happened twice more. She is not responding."

Daddy was told he should come to the hospital right away. He called Carol and we all went.

I was very frightened. I knew this was about Mommy but I did not know what was going on. Daddy was a bundle of nerves and I could not help. When we got there Mommy was on a bed with all these tubes and wires and things around her. The doctor said she was not responding and that her brain might have been denied oxygen for too long. He said Daddy should decide what to do. Daddy called Mommy's sister Susan. Susan was crying, and she asked Daddy not to give up on Mommy. But after talking to the doctor again, they decided that if Mommy had another heart attack and could not be revived, she should be allowed to go. I did not know what that meant, but I was frightened. Mommy was very sick.

Daddy was at Mommy's side, talking, whispering and crying. He held her hand and begged her to squeeze it. But she never did. He tried to get me up to where I could lick her face but it was impossible with all those wires. I licked Mommy's hand. I did not know it would be the last time ever. Hold on a moment, I have to rub my face against the carpet. My eyes are wet.

We stayed for three hours. Carol made phone calls and helped Daddy reach some of Mommy's friends on her phone. Then he bent close and said something to her. All I heard was "If you want to go and be with Mom, Dad and Musket, I understand. I love you and always will. Go in peace, my love." Then he kissed her closed eyes and we left.

I never saw Daddy so upset. He was hardly aware of what was happening.

Back at home he waited, made phone calls and petted me. He said "Saffy, I don't know if Mommy is coming back home. But you must think of how much you love her."

Of course I would. That was like saying I had to remember to breathe. He could not sleep but he was so tired that he lay down. Then the phone rang at 1:30 in the morning.

When Daddy answered it, he began to sob. He sat down on the floor at the end of the bed where he sat when he threw my toys. "I understand. Thank you for trying to save her. I'll be back to you about the arrangements."

Then he came apart. My Daddy wailed and screamed in the dark. It scared me but I went to him and began licking his face. He held me in an embrace so hard I could hardly breathe. But I never stopped licking his wet face. He cried into my fur and shook with anguish. "Saffy, your Mommy is gone. She is in Heaven now with Nanny, Pop-pop and Musket. She is no longer in pain."

Eventually he got ahold of himself and called Susan. She cried too. I think that was the first time either of them had cried in front of each other, even if they were only on the phone.

Daddy sat in the dark and poured out his grief and regrets. He talked about Mommy and how she had been so good and patient, how he had never been as good a husband as she deserved.

But then something happened. I felt it, but did not know what it was. Daddy raised his face upward and begged God to come to him and forgive his sins.

And in a few minutes, he had stopped crying. He took a deep breath, wiped his face and gave me a loving hug. "Daddy is going to be okay, Little One. I love you. Thank you for being my furry angel."

> "When an eighty-five pound mammal licks your tears
> away, then tries to sit on your lap, it's hard to feel sad."
> — Kristen Higgens

So it had happened. The thing I dreaded most had come. Jane was dead. At 64 years of age, my wife of twenty-five years and one week was gone. All I had left was Saffron.

Angels on My Shoulders

Those first weeks were mental and emotional turmoil. I was miserable and shattered, scared and unable to sleep. I felt like I was coming apart at the seams. I had debilitating panic attacks and fell into deep depression. God provided. Our friends and family circled me in a protective cocoon of love and support. I was not alone. I knew He was with me, that He had sent the Earthbound Angels to help me.

Linda, Carol and Rob came to the rescue. They pulled me along and gave me strength, which I now know came from God. Linda helped me understand and cope with the panic attacks and take control of my life.

She never failed to show me that my life was not over and that I could survive this. She saved my life.

Carol, ever the pragmatist, helped me decide what to do about Jane's remains. We had not gotten around to making arrangements for our estate. Gigi took control of the cremation, even insisting on paying for it herself. At that time I was not certain how much money we had and it was a huge relief to have her help.

Then John and Geneva entered the picture. They insisted on buying the urn, a beautiful carved Indian Rosewood box.

But it was Rob Wood who took on the biggest burden. With a mountain of Jane's documents, computer files, bank statements, bills, insurance and tax matters hovering over me like the Sword of Damocles, I was overwhelmed. Jane had her filing system on a computer I could not use. Most of the mail was printed, adding more obstacles. What Rob did was to take all the files and letters and papers to his home and organize everything. He sorted out the bank accounts and bills, insurance and taxes, mortgage and social security. It took him about four months to work his way through it even over his own work and needs. Every day he gave me a list of what he had managed to do. Jane had run up some big credit card debts, but Rob got them all forgiven. What an immense relief that was.

Eventually I was able to handle some matters on my own, such as the mortgage and dental insurance. I dealt with the Social Security Administration and our HMO. We had a great accountant named Keith Kirby who really took the time to help me with the taxes. It was a huge load off my mind to get that done. He told me what to keep over the year in order to have the tax papers ready for 2021.

Together my friends gave me the strength and will to live again. In fact, Rob got me to laugh, something I was certain I could never do again. He remembered that I was a fan of Doctor Who, the British Sci-Fi series. The Daleks in particular were my favorites. So one day a package came for me. Inside, once I identified it by feel, was a Limited Edition

Dalek model! I busted out laughing. It felt very good. That Dalek is now one of my most cherished possessions. "Ex-ter-min-ate!"

One by one the things that had caused me so much worry and anxiety were lifted from my shoulders. I had to make decisions and handle some major issues, but they were more and more solvable than they had been. Without my knowledge, Mary Lou Belew, no relation to Mary Lou Rushing, set up a Go Fund Me page to raise money. Thanks to her and some wonderful people on Jane's Facebook page, it reached $5,000 before I found out. That really boosted my spirits, as well as my belief in God's blessings. I set some of the money aside for Jane's Celebration of Life, whenever we could all get together. She would understand. Mary Lou, thank you.

My family also came to my rescue. My older brother David gave me some good and sage advice on what to do about setting up a will and trust. My cousins Christine, Elsa and Ricky, who were my Aunt Millie's children also showed their support. I had hardly spoken to any of them in the past forty years, but in those days I re-discovered my wonderful family. Today, nearly a year later, we are closer than ever and I cherish them in my life.

Someone to Watch Over

♡ Daddy never forgot to take care of me. He once said, "Thank God I have you, Saffy. You give me a reason to keep on living."

Even in the midst of Covid, my house was Grand Central Station with the Casserole Brigade bearing food. I could not keep it all in the refrigerator and freezer. It was like when Jesus fed the five thousand with five loaves of bread and a few fish. Miracles were happening every day!

I came to realize I had what I needed to survive and even prosper. I had a home, money in the bank, a fairly steady income and medical insurance.

Molly Tosh at our bank was a Godsend. She helped me with the details of making changes in the bank accounts. It was very overwhelming but sweet Molly showed me how I could manage the accounts myself. Good God-Golly Miss Molly.

♡ Daddy went to the bank where Molly worked. Even though she was a vice president and very busy, she made time to help him.

The Light at the end of the tunnel

By the end of August I was able to do it on my own with very little help. It was like emerging from a long, dark and cold tunnel into bright warm sunlight.

One day I stopped what I was doing and asked God, "Where have you been all my life?" The Lord must have shaken His head at that dumb question.

Soon I was reading the Bible on audio for the first time, and I looked for other books to give me spiritual comfort. Through a series of what any other person would call coincidences, I found signs that pointed me to continue my writing. Not only writing my books and articles, but writing for the church, to use the gift God gave me and the love of the written word to reach out and help others to see the Love of the Lord.

♡ Every morning and evening Daddy prayed and I sat next to him. I felt how calm he was when he talked to God.

Taking Control

One of the first things I did was to change the thermostat. We had this stupid energy-saving gadget that had an LCD touch screen. It was totally useless to a blind person. I hated that the only way I could adjust the temperature was to ask Jane, or with her gone, one of my neighbors. I called Gigi and asked her for a "simple thermostat with real buttons and switches on it," just like the ones we used to know.

She found one and installed it. From that day on, I found more and more ways to make my home accessible to me. After all, it was my home now. Jane had made it a warm and comfortable place to live, but there were some things that I could not do. I asked Linda to help me put tactile sticky dots on my oven, microwave, washer, dryer and dishwasher. Once the dots had been applied, I was able to do the baking, cooking, and laundry all by myself. What a weight was taken from my shoulders with such simple changes.

♡ He was doing pretty well with the food, but as for doing the laundry, it's better he does not learn the truth.

Well, as to that, I did occasionally get laundry and dishwasher pellets mixed up. I found out I had been doing the clothes with Cascade!

♡ I could see my face in his shirts so it must have been okay.

About this time Sue Redding showed up at my door. She had a wireless doorbell she wanted to give me. The bell we had was not working right and some people seemed to have forgotten how to knock. So she installed this great bell. I was very moved by her generosity. But then I had a thought. "Would you be willing to get one more of those and I'll buy it from you? I have two doors and I never know which one people come to."

She was happy to help. I put in the second doorbell with a different ring than that of the front door. That way I could tell which door to go to.

♡ When one of those bells rang I grabbed whatever toy was nearest and ran for the door. But Daddy laughed and said, "Side door, Saffron."

Sue also offered to use her Amazon Prime account to buy Saffron's food. I agreed as long as she accepted a bit more cash in payment than what she had paid. So about every two months I called Sue and told her that Saffron's food was running low. She ordered it and a day later there it was by the side door.

Very sweet lady.

These were minor compared to the bigger matters of making sure the property taxes were paid and keeping up my medical insurance. Verizon, Cox Cable, AAA, AARP, and a dozen others had to be taken care of. But I did it, thanks to Rob, Carol, Molly, and Linda. Eventually I was using my phone and computer to read my mail, do my banking, and manage correspondence. What a miracle it was. I had started out with no more experience than a 14-year old orphan and reached the point where my blindness was no more than a minor challenge. I had my two older hearing aids repaired so I would have backups. Being blind was not a problem but being deaf would be a major obstacle.

That was when I registered Saffron with the local 24-hour emergency vet clinic, another of the long list of things Jane and I "never got around to."

As I sit here at my computer it is mid-January 2021. No need to relate what has been happening in the country. But I have faith in God, the goodness of my brothers and sisters, and in the strength of America. Early in the Covid crisis I said, "If we get through this it will be from the bottom up, not from the top down." I believed then, and still do, that it will be the common American people who will make the difference, helping each other. That is and always has been the American way. History proves it.

♡ Daddy does get a bit long-winded and pedantic at times, but he is right.

Jane's Bench

There was no doubt that God had come into my heart. Jane and I had wanted to have Pastor Brian bless our house after we settled in. But like so many things, it never got done. I decided to make it happen. Brian came up from Rancho Bernardo and I showed him around the house. He was fascinated by my Man Cave. Then he went into each room and said a blessing. It made me very happy and comforted to know our home would be a sanctuary for my friends and family. I bought a beautiful olive wood cross to put on the wall of the living room.

A few years ago Jane and I had been leaving the Ramona Library where I had done a talk. We passed some benches, and one had a memorial plaque on it. Jane stopped and looked at it. Then she said, "Honey, if you want to do something for me after I die, I would really like a bench for people to sit and read."

We had already agreed that our estate would go to Guide Dogs for the Blind and the Alzheimer's Foundation. But this was personal. "I will, Honey," I said sincerely. "I promise."

Five months after Jane died I remembered that promise. I called John Misoni from The Thursday Knights and asked him how I could go about having a bench for Jane at the church. He told me it would be easy. Hope United Methodist would purchase the bench and I would reimburse the church. All I had to do was come up with the wording for the plaque and he would take care of the rest.

At the end of the year I was told the bench would be in place in time for Jane's 65th birthday on January 6. That was the perfect day.

But when I asked where to send the check for $1500 John told me that $700 had already been paid for by donations. I almost choked up. "Really?"

"Yep," he said with his usual good humor. Just send a check for the remainder to the church."

I was overwhelmed by this news. So many good people had given so much to help me and ease my way. Jane had been much loved at Hope United Methodist.

Then I called our associate pastor, Sylina Kidd to ask if she could come and bless the bench. Then I received a call from Brian Kent. He asked if he could do the blessing. This was a surprise since he had not only survived Covid but had recently undergone spinal surgery.

"Are you sure you're up to it?" I asked.

"I am fine for this," he said. "I really want to."

On January 6, Carol and Kate picked Saffron and me up. I was on the edge emotionally but determined to do the right thing in Jane's memory. When we arrived there were about five people there, including

Brian, John and his wonderful wife Linda. Then Vince and a few others arrived. Vince and I had gotten to be friends while he was counseling me as a Stevens Minister. We had a lot in common, and even more differences, but he was a good and devoted buddy.

We all kept our distance but felt very close.

The bench was unveiled and Brian said a blessing and talked about Jane. Then John, Kate, Vince and I shared our thoughts. My voice was thick and quavering, but I made it through, ending with "Happy birthday, my beloved. Rest in Peace."

The bench is under a large tree in the church courtyard, a quiet and serene place. The plaque reads:

In loving memory of
Jane Marie Carlson
Beloved daughter, sister, wife, and friend
January 6, 1956 - April 30, 2020
If the love of others could have saved you, you would have lived forever.

"A book is a dream you can hold in your hand. Come and enjoy a dream with me."

Mark and Saffron with Jane's bench at Hope United Methodist
Church in Rancho Bernardo, January 6, 2021

CHAPTER **19**

REBUILDING A LIFE

"No matter how little money and how few possessions
you own, having a dog makes you feel rich."
— Louis Sabin

On Being Blind, Reprised

I was once asked "If you could get your sight back,
would you do it?"

I did not hesitate. "No. Being blind has made me who I am. God gave
me sight for the first thirty years of my life so I have vivid memories and
images in my mind. Then He took my sight and now I see even more.
This is who I am."

Sure, I miss seeing some things, like the stars or a sunset, but I
remember what they look like. Besides, if I regained my sight I would no
longer need a Guide Dog. Saffron and Musket before her have made life
more interesting, colorful and beautiful than mere sight could ever have.
God blessed me by taking my sight and giving me so much in return.

♡ Sometimes Daddy says the most wonderful things.

In some ways the period from May to August 2020 was a blur
with only a few clear memories. I was very fortunate to have many

Earthbound Angels to help me through the rough spots. Among them were John and Jennifer "Call me Jen" Zingg. I was at the drugstore around the corner picking up a few things when this lady asked if I needed any help. I said "No, thanks very much. I'm fine." The staff there knew me and Saffron so I always had someone to help me shop. But Jen seemed to want to help. And she did, right up to walking me home! A very sweet lady with a social conscience as big as her hart, she and her husband John sort of adopted us. They often called and said, "We're going to Costco and Vons. Do you need us to pick anything up?" They were so sincere and helpful. Once again God had sent angels into my life.

♡ Jen and John are so nice. They are what I believe America is all about. People helping others just because they want to.

While I admit I should have done more of my own shopping, with Covid making any social interaction risky, I accepted the help. In the future I can go back to doing it on my own.

♡ And then he can buy Cap'n Crunch cereal without anyone knowing.

Diet and Exercise

At sixty, I was in pretty good health, strong and with no arthritis or other problems of aging. Jane's mother always said "Getting old is not for sissies." How true.

Due to my robust Scandinavian blood I was in good shape. I could have lost a few more [dozen] pounds...dang she did it again!

♡ What was your first clue, Porky?

You should talk, Saffron. Lucy had to bring a larger harness for you last year. I wanted to put off any serious health problems, assisted living or a nursing home for as long as possible. My first move was to start eating right. I downloaded some audio cookbooks like *When the Cook can't look* and a few others. This way I could make healthy meals and not rely on microwave and packaged meals. Carol and Linda were a big help with this. Carol is a devout and very serious vegan, while Linda knows a lot about diet and nutrition.

♡ Not that he listened to them. He sort of followed the "I'm going to lose weight by joining a health club" plan."

Saffron, can you button it up while I'm baring my soul? I tried to avoid eating junk food or at least cut back on it. For one thing, Linda introduced me to Sparkling Ice drinks. They come in all flavors, have almost no calories, and are completely natural. I love them! I have not had a Coca-Cola in almost a year.

I also cut out Cap'n Crunch and Golden Crisp cereals, changing to Rice Chex, granola and oatmeal. Slowly I changed my eating habits. And it worked. My doctor said he was very happy to see how well I was doing. I still had a way to go, but that was the start.

Jane had a lot of vitamins and supplements so I "appropriated" them for my own use. Eventually I added colloidal minerals, collagen and protein powder, spirulina, and especially calcium. Jane had shattered her ankle in a simple fall, so it was apparent she had severe osteoporosis. I needed my bones and joints to be strong. That brings me to exercise.

♡ Here we go...

Saffron and I walked every day, but it was hardly what I would call a vigorous exercise regimen. The "block" we lived on was exactly 850 steps around, which with my stride length of 24 inches, totaled 1700 feet. Two laps, 3400 feet, three laps 5100, and four laps at 6800 feet, or fifteen hundred feet more than a mile.

We began to do four laps every morning after breakfast, and four more after dinner. John Tolbert, Carol, Kate or Jen sometimes came along. Two miles a day was a good start.

Walking with God and Dog

The evening walks were my favorite. Cool, dark nights when it was quiet and the hustle and bustle of the day was past. Most of the time I brought my Victor Stream Reader and listen to an audio book. But once in a while, especially if it was a clear night, when we were walking under the stars, I talked to God. It was not the same as a serious prayer, but more of a one-sided chat. Saffron in the lead, and God beside me, it felt good to tell the Lord what was on my mind, what I was feeling, and ask His advice and wisdom. It never failed to ease my concerns. Afterwards, I put my headset back on and continued reading.

♡ Daddy put on his one-eared headset so he could listen to a book. He was careful never to listen to anything that could make it hard for him to hear an approaching car. Our streets were very quiet. People waved to us or called out hello. Madrid Manor is a very friendly place to live.

Rob had bought Jane some weights, which she did not get to use, but I did. Starting with five pounds per hand, I began doing upper body and arm work-outs. I was up to fifteen pounds each by the end of the year, with plans to reach twenty-five pounds by spring. Our neighbor Alice Johnson gave me an exercise bicycle and I began adding a mile of pedaling on that.

♡ That thing scared me. I never went near it when Daddy was on it. But I liked when he did his floor exercises. As he lay there trying to count I licked his face. It drove him nuts but I knew he loved it. So what if he lost count?

Something Old, Something New

Jane's office/craft room was jam-packed (see The Big Move chapter) with crafts and office supplies. I mean every cubic centimeter of space not directly involved in allowing a person to move about was filled.

The difference between what I imagined and reality was like a 7/11 compared to a Costco. And she had it in a room measuring 12 feet square. I'll never know how she did it. Jane had to have been the Tetris champion of the universe.

But what to do with all of it? Linda and Natalie Travis, a wonderful Christian woman who sold Stamping UP! crafts began going through it. Natalie bought all the Stamping Up! merchandise and helped Linda sort out the rest.

Linda worked her butt off organizing and boxing all the things. Geneva bought a lot of it too. But there were still enough crafting supplies to open a store.

Then I remembered the Braille Institute. Jane had taught card making and stamping to blind students. She was very good at it. Some of her students became good friends. Tina Sutton and Jill Coleman were devastated by Jane's death and both asked if they could come by and buy something of Jane's for their own. Of course I said yes.

♡ Every day they were in Mommy's office was chaos. Moving, opening cabinets and drawers in the closet and organizers never seemed to stop. I kept getting in the way, but Daddy was smart enough to remain well clear of all the activity.

Eventually another lady, Pearl Mecenas and Jill set up a Limited Liability Corporation to help blind artists to sell their work. Gifted by Blind Artists, Crafters, & Knitters, or GiftedBack. www.giftedback.com

Jane's part is called Love, Jane.

It felt great to do this and I am certain Jane would have approved. I hope.

♡ But if Mommy has a problem with it, she is welcome to come back.

I donated her clothes to a thrift shop that works with battered women and her books to a local library.

As for the closet, we had a large walk-in with about nine linear feet of three levels of shelves. Jane got six feet on three levels, I got three on one. I'm not a mathematical genius, but that seemed just a bit unequal. But that's marriage.

I had lots of space now so I put all my aviation and novelty t-shirts in one place, all my button-downs in another, slacks and jeans, shorts and sweaters in specific places.

♡ Daddy was real excited and spent hours putting things on the thousands of hangers Mommy had. Some nights he could not sleep and did it at three in the morning. Groan.

Since I could no longer ask Jane to tell me what color shirts or I was wearing, I found other means. She had never, I mean never failed to give me her opinion on what not to wear. But I had an app on my iPhone called "Be My Eyes." It allowed volunteers to use my phone camera to see things for me. I could call and ask someone, preferably a guy to tell me what color shirt I was holding.

Loads of Longaberger

Jane loved Longaberger baskets. I also admired the beautiful hand-made crafting of the many sizes and shapes of the split-wood baskets. But Jane did more than just like them. She was a registered Longaberger seller and took full advantage of it. I thought I knew how many she had, but when I really went through the house I found dozens, scores, possibly as many as seventy of them in every shape, size and color. All I had to do was open a drawer, pull open a cabinet, lift the lid on a box, or even reach up to a shelf, and presto! There was another Longaberger basket waiting like the Cheshire Cat. "Yes, it's me again."

I stacked them all in the bedroom and soon the pile got out of hand. I did sell a lot of them and gave a few away. I kept some for myself.

Don't get me wrong. I was not trying to erase her presence from the house. Most things would be of more use and help to others. I had no use for the hundreds and hundreds of books and her wardrobe was just not my style. I did keep her favorite wool sweater. It kept me warm during those first few weeks when I could not seem to get warm.

♡ Daddy slept in that sweater and I cuddled with him. I smelled Mommy so it made it seem like she was not really gone.

Saffron sometimes lay on her back under my right arm and fell asleep. All four paws were in the air and her nose was under my armpit. It was so cute. But her snoring...she must have picked that up from Jane.

♡ I never heard you complain, Daddy.

No, and I never will. All that really remained were Jane's personal things. After packing several boxes I sent them to Sue in Vermont. She appreciated having so much of her sister, as well as many family heirlooms Jane had kept after her parents died.

The Mysterious Pantry

One of the things I had to tackle was the pantry. Located off the laundry room by the side door, the pantry held all the dry and canned goods, cooking appliances and such. Jane had it pretty well organized but I could not find anything without her help. When she was still mobile, she could move in there and get what we needed. But during the time she was in rehab, I had to find things myself. Going into the pantry was a little like Theseus in the Labyrinth of the Minotaur, but not as safe. It was very cramped in there with many things to crack my head on. I am speaking from painful experience.

♡ Some of our friends saw Daddy and said, "What did you hit your head on this time?" Daddy said "Oh, just the (insert specific item here) in the pantry."

Fortunately I had the Seeing A I app on my phone, which had a barcode reader. It identified most products. I say "most" since some things in the pantry went back to the Reagan Administration. It needed serious work. I went through the long rows of Tupperware and packaged goods. For some things I needed Carol or Geneva to tell me what it was, but when I opened some containers, it was obvious the contents were long, long, long past their time. I swear I found taco shells that might have been fresh during the Mexican-American War.

♡ I helped Daddy a lot. He held something out for me to sniff. If I turned away, it was too old even for me to eat. Lots of old food went in the trash. Daddy washed all the Tupperware and sold or gave away some of the appliances he would never use. I mean, he had things a Cordon Bleu chef might have found useful. But my daddy likes things simple.

I arranged things so I could find them easily. Canned fruit, canned soups, canned veggies, all had a certain shape. Same for boxes of mashed potatoes or rice. Seeing A I made it possible to find the Progresso New England Clam Chowder I was so partial to, and when I needed the Bisquick it was easy. Seeing A I had an additional feature that read out the directions and nutritional information. The pantry is now arranged so I can find what I need right away.

♡ He keeps my treats on the counter, though. I insisted on it.

Being Prepared

San Diego is ripe for various natural disasters; mudslides, wildfires, floods, sinkholes, earthquakes, prima donna football teams, bad mayors and so on. I guess I won't make it as a travel agent.

♡ Just in case you missed it, Daddy passed on a rant about our lousy mayors. Consider yourselves lucky.

It's not the place for that, Saffron. But for crying out loud, we have had the worst bunch of mayors in the last few years. Consider Bob Filner...er, never mind. Anyway, every time I smelled smoke in the air, especially during a long drought, it made the hairs on the back of my neck stand up. I was not alone. All San Diegans and a lot of Californians have a deathly fear of wildfires. We came close a few times but so far God has kept us safe. In the summer of 2020 with fires raging in the county and homes being destroyed, I twice received the call for a possible evacuation. I was not prepared. It was time to do the smart thing. I talked to Rob, who was the Madrid Manor Emergency Services coordinator. He told me how to assemble a "Go Kit." Over the next few weeks I gathered bottled water, food, clothes, blankets, tools, food for Saffron, and a first-aid kit. I had my laptop and a flash drive with all my important documents, and an external hard drive with all my files. The first-aid kit was a bit more than I strictly needed, but Jane had a large supply of medical items and I borrowed from that.

♡ Daddy could do anything from pulling out a splinter to delivering a baby with that kit.

Don't exaggerate. I could never find a splinter. The first-aid kit has a big "4077th MASH" sticker on it. No one would have any problem knowing who it belonged to.

Missing the Paw Print

There were many things Jane and I had intended to do around the house. One was to get rid of the gravel on the side yard and along the driveway. We never liked it and I am sure Saffron hated walking on it with her bare paws.

♡ Yes, but it was the only place for me to do my business.

I hired my next door neighbor, Tony, a gardener and landscaper to remove the gravel. When it was gone I hired a concrete contractor to pour neat slabs. It made the yard much neater. One of the things I wanted to do was have Saffron's paw print in the cement, but by the time I came out, it was too hard. Dang.

♡ It would have been cool. But Daddy did press an old silver dollar into it. He said his father had been a Mason, and it was a tradition to do that.

I had a nice set of teak garden furniture and umbrellas. My personal chair was a reproduction of a *Titanic* steamer chair. Now I had a nice patio to keep them on. The only snag was Saffron.

♡ Where did all my gravel go? Where am I supposed to pee now?

Oops. I had not considered how different it would be for Saffron. I really thought the concrete would be a better place for her and easier to keep clean.

♡ Wrong! It took some serious re-training (of Daddy, not me) for him to let me use the areas next to the shed.

I kept the house furniture pretty much as Jane had it, but I planned to make her office into a guest room. It was as much a matter of practicality as anything. The room only needed some organizing. Janelle gave me a nearly brand-new day bed which fit perfectly. After moving a few things around, it was perfect for any guests who might come to visit.

On Parade

A couple of bright spots happened during those dark months. One was July 4. A parade was scheduled as in previous years. Sue Redding, who is a wonderful, warm lady and very good realtor, asked me if Saffron could be in the parade. She said her granddaughter would walk Saffron alongside her golf cart. I put a flag scarf on Saffron. I was outside on the front porch when the parade passed. Saffron was in it, trotting along and charming everyone.

♡ It was so much fun! All my friends waved and called to me. Eat your heart out, Queen Elizabeth!

Saffron in the July 4 2020 Madrid Manor Parade

Then on my birthday, August 30 (just so you readers know) Linda, Rob, Vicki and Mike had a surprise for me. Linda arrived with cheesecake, something I highly recommend for arteriosclerosis. Not to cure it, but to give it a boost. But there was more.

Linda said, "Oh, I left something in the car. I'll be right back."

That was when I knew something was up. I waited, not wanting to spoil the surprise she had put together.

Then she asked me to come outside with Saffron.

I could not see this, but at the end of my driveway were Rob, Mike and Vicki. They said "Surprise!" I jumped back in stunned shock. But what I did not see was Mike's fully World War Two Willys Jeep. It had been driven by Vicki's father in the Pacific. Mike had found and restored it.

I was to be the Grand Marshal of the Mark Carlson 60th Birthday Parade! Rob had informed all of Madrid Manor.

I climbed in and Linda handed me my Army officers "Fifty Mission Crush" peaked cap, which she had bought for my birthday a few years before. I was wearing one of my Warbird Aloha shirts, so I looked like a dork. But who cared?

Then Saffron climbed in and Mike started the Jeep. Rob led Mike through all the winding streets of Madrid Manor, where dozens of people came out and waved and wished me a happy birthday. I had no idea so many of them knew me. But then, I had been a hit on the stage in the Follies.

♡ I think everybody was glad to have something fun to celebrate.

Linda and Vicki went to a local pizza place called "Killer Pizza from Mars," which has great pizza and beer. We sat down and enjoyed ourselves and ate pizza and cheesecake. Saffron of course was running back and forth around the table hoping for treats. But Linda was even more strict than I am, and Saffron got very little.

♡ Hmph. How could she do that to me? I thought she loved me!

She does, Saffron. She does. Anyway it was a wonderful surprise and it felt good.

©2020 ROB WOOD

Mark and Saffron in Mike Dralle's restored
Jeep in the 2020 birthday parade.

Dark Victory

I like to say that I "can see perfectly in the dark." That is exactly right.

I see with my hands. And sometimes my forehead and knees. Although I have never "seen" my house inside or out, I have learned every inch of its floors, walls, nooks, crannies and closets. It took some time —

♡ Like three whole years!

— to stop walking into walls. I did eventually get to the point where I could walk from room to room and all around the house with total confidence. I never turned the lights on. In fact, when Rob or someone would come by, they asked me to turn on a light because they could not see!

I always laughed and said, "You sighted people are slaves to light, aren't you?"

Now that I have the house set up the way I need it, I am totally content. I know where everything is. Two of the things we were taught in blind school were to "Put things away in the same place when you are done with them." Also, "Once you find the best way to do something, do it the same way every time."

It took some doing, figuring out how to do this or that, experimenting and testing, but eventually I managed some of the complex tasks that sighted people take for granted, like putting the toilet paper on the roll. Just kidding. Saffron does that. It's beyond me.

♡ He is still kidding.

It made life a lot easier and less stressful when I took the time to organize and set things up for my needs. When I invited Carol or Janelle or Kate or John or any of my friends for coffee, I moved around the kitchen with total confidence. I could feel their eyes on me as I got the creamer or sugar, pastries, flatware and set up the coffee maker. With my hands I could see everything I was doing. Without hesitation I would reach up and grab a mug from the cupboard or punch the buttons on the microwave.

"YOU are just amazing," they said.

But to be honest, it was no big deal. Being blind these days is nothing more than a series of small and large challenges and finding ways to overcome them.

♡ I sat on the floor and watched Daddy move around the house. He talked to me while he did the dishes or made dinner. It was nice that he included me in everything he did.

I had my Civil War paintings framed and hung in the bedroom. My model plane collection was in a certain order. Fighters, bombers, rockets, jets and antique aircraft shared shelf space with submarines, battleships and Civil War ironclads. The row of ACTION FIGURES watched over the spacecraft and other stuff, including my Dalek and models of the five Platonic solids. Yes, I know. I'm such a nerd.

♡ I'm sure you already figured that out.

Who was that masked man?

What do Darth Vader, the American flag, Snoopy, a smiling yellow Labrador mouth, a P-40 Flying Tiger, the B-17 "Memphis Belle," and a glowing constellation have in common? I have masks with all of them.

When the first Covid shutdown was ordered in early March for "a few weeks," I was certain that it would not end for several months and more likely a couple of years. I saw the biohazard writing on the wall long before the government reluctantly and only partially admitted there was a growing problem. Many people thought I was being needlessly pessimistic, but history always repeats itself. This had happened from 1919 to 1920, exactly a century ago with the Spanish Flu, which killed more than half a million Americans.

"Those who fail to learn the lessons of history are doomed to repeat the mistakes." I don't know who first said that but it is still very true.

In 2020 we were faced with an even greater crisis. One of the early rumors was that dogs could catch and transmit the disease. That made me very worried, since Saffron was so friendly and sociable. Fortunately that did not happen. The reason I am even dredging up this miserable matter is the Mask Mania that has swept the country, (among intelligent and reasonable people, that is). It was not long before a few of our friends, like Carol, were making masks with more interesting patterns than surgical green. She made scores of them to give to senior homes and centers. My first one was with Snoopy as the World War One Flying Ace. I will gladly go on record saying as early as March 2020 that masks would soon become as much pop-culture icons as T-shirts were in the 1970s. Soon more and more people were wearing novelty masks, and I was no exception. If we had to wear them, and most importantly, inspire others and children to wear them, they should be fun.

Early on, I got into the habit of wearing my mask every time I went for a walk with Saffron, even if I was alone. I made sure not to walk with anyone not wearing one and there were plenty, believe me. Rob was one of the strongest advocates of wearing masks, along with Carol, Elaine and Linda. We never socialized without wearing them. Why take the risk? The most popular of my masks was the one that had the smiling mouth of a Yellow Labrador. Every time I went to the store, people complimented me on it. Linda had found them on Etsy, whatever that is. I liked wearing a mask as it was kind of a statement of sanity wrapped in a whimsical fabric.

Covid was not going to go away soon so I might as well have some fun with it.

I had to wait until April to get my vaccine and I am glad I did.

But there was someone who did not like the masks at all.

♡ I hated that I could not kiss anyone wearing one. How was I supposed to spread love and joy with my tongue if they had one of those stupid things on? All I can get to is the upper face and ears. Snort!

"I have caught more ills from people sneezing over me and
giving me virus infections than from kissing dogs."
— Barbara Woodhouse

I was pretty firm that anyone coming over had to be wearing a mask. I found a way to be witty about it. I put up signs on both doors that read, in Old English typeface, "All ye who enter these portals must wear a masque."

Holy LED Snowflakes, Batman!

The holidays were an unusual time to say the least, even accounting for Covid. From the start of the holiday season, which as all Americans know, starts in late August, I was determined not to stay in the dark and wallow in self-pity. That was never my way and Jane would not have liked it.

Shortly before Halloween I went into the dreaded shed to pull out the decorations. Jane had a wealth of things to put out for her favorite holidays, which I think I once listed. They were Saint Valentine's Day, Saint Patrick's Day, Easter, Memorial Day, Independence Day, National Scrapbooking Day, Halloween, Thanksgiving, and Christmas. She occasionally went outside the box for other special days, but those were the biggies. She of course had boxes and cases for each of them. Guess who had to go in and find them?

♡ I bet you got it right on the first try! Poor Daddy. He went into that shed like a condemned prisoner going into the gas chamber.

Yeah, but without the job satisfaction. I eventually came up with the idea of marking the specific cases with sticky dots to identify them and putting them together in one area of the shed. I should have done it right off, but give me a break. I was a husband, not Martha Stewart.

I went in and pulled out all the Halloween, Fall and Thanksgiving decorations. I was going to put them all up and cover a two-month spread. Smart, huh?

I like to decorate for the holidays. I admit I tended to go all-out, even over-doing it, covering every flat surface with floral and seasonal items. The island in the kitchen, the sideboard, the coffee table, end tables and even the window sills were canvases for my colorful seasonal displays. When I had sight, I did pretty well and Jane only had to "tweak" a few things. But sometimes she said, "Honey that really doesn't look right. Let's not use it this year."

"Okay," I usually said, having already shot my bolt. So she made it perfect. When my sight failed I still did it, but by feel. And she again "tweaked" it to perfection.

♡ Daddy was very methodical. First he dusted every table and vacuumed the house. That part I did not like. Then he made sure everything was ready. He was so funny when he really got into it. I watched him go back and forth from the shed, bringing in more and more big cases. Every single time he went out the side door he said, "Stay, Saffy." Hey it's not like I ran away anymore. But once he had them in, he began pulling out these weird things. I was curious but I had seen most of them before.

Soon he had the whole front of the house done. It looked really nice. He was still an artist at heart, even if he could not see.

When I was done the house looked festive in fall colors, with pumpkins, candles, whimsical spooks and lights. But alongside these were carved Pilgrims, turkeys, cornucopias of dried harvests and more than enough candles to fill Notre Dame.

When people came by, they were amazed and only a few did not ask who had done it for me. Like Cyrus the great said to Lysander in 540 BC of his botanical gardens, "I created this abode myself."

Thanksgiving was simple but nice. Keeping Covid in mind, I invited Jon and Geneva for dinner. I made a turkey (yes, I did!) and some side dishes. The mashed potatoes did not come out right but that was no big deal. Geneva made some side dishes and we had a wonderful time. After dinner I said I would do the dishes. John and Geneva, like virtually everyone who came for dinner offered, even insisted on helping me clean up. But I explained that it was safer if I did it myself. That way I knew where every glass, every plate, every bottle was. When friends tried to help, I rarely failed to knock over and break a crystal glass because I did not know it was there.

♡ Daddy took his time and was very careful. I think he liked doing dishes. He's kind of weird that way.

I took Saffron to a local pet store to have her picture taken with Santa. He definitely had a lot of her fur on his red suit, but it was a good moment.

We know what she wanted for Christmas

I vowed that when Thanksgiving passed I would put it all away and pull out the Christmas decorations. Again I went all the way. The pre-lit tree, strings of colored outdoor lights, candles, a Nativity complete with a yellow Labrador gazing fondly at the tiny Fontanini Baby Jesus, wreaths, stockings, and scented candles brought the season into the house.

But I could not trim the tree. That would have been difficult. So one day Linda came and put up what I had chosen, a mix of red, gold and glass. She put up Musket's ornament and then, to my surprise, made an ornament with Saffron's paw print.

She also brought a special stocking with Saffron's name on it.

♡ My stocking had a whole bunch of treats in it. I hated that it was hung too far up for me to reach.

I invited Linda and Kate for a small dinner on Christmas Day. I made ham while Linda took care of the side dishes. It was nice, short and of course, careful about social distancing.

The other good thing about the holidays was that I never once heard "Blue Christmas" or "Feliz Navidad." Just in case you did not know, I hate those songs.

♡ God Bless us every one.

So in the end, the holidays were a time of love and comfort. I was not sorry to have done it. Jane would have been happy to see her house looking so nice, even if she would have put her foot down about the twinkling snowflake lights around the manger.

I may not have good taste, but I know what I like.

Showing the colors

I did a few things just for the fun of it. Several of my neighbors had flagpoles. Most flew Old Glory, but a few used them for sports teams or some other statement. I bought a 20-foot pole and put it up. Yes, by myself. It was kind of tricky with the wind, but I managed it. I flew Old Glory and a Swedish flag in honor of my nation and my family heritage. But as you must know by now, I can't keep from inserting my own brand of whimsy. I bought a pirate Jolly Roger and ran that up. It was very popular. Then I bought a new mailbox. It was bright red with Snoopy the World War One Flying Ace and Woodstock mounted on top. I gotta be me.

Final Farewell

On April 29, 2021, Pastor Brian and I went out on a rented boat to scatter Jane's ashes at sea. It was a very moving moment as I said goodbye to Jane. I blew her a kiss and pointed north. "Honey, we never got to take that cruise to Alaska. You go ahead. It's that way." Then I broke down and cried.

♡ I was very excited on the boat, not certain what we were going to do. Then Pastor Brian said a prayer and Daddy put the ashes into the water. Our friend Kate had made a wreath of Mommy's favorite flowers and he put it in the water. I knew Mommy was gone. I'll miss her forever.

After that we went with Kate, Charlene, Nancy, Janelle, and Elaine to Jane's bench to talk about her. it was a lovely way to say farewell. But one day I hope to be with her again.

Chapter **20**

FROM THIS POINT ON

"Dogs have a way of finding the people who need them,
and filling an emptiness we didn't ever know we had."
— Thom Jones

So here we are, the year of 2021, starting the third decade of the Third Millennium. I am well into my 61st trip around the sun, and boy are my arms tired! Bada boom! Sorry, just had one more bad joke in me.

♡ Just one? Sure, they'll believe that.

I am content and looking forward to the future. I have my work to do. My articles, lectures, and of course, my books. This one was waiting to be written, and now you are reading it. I hope.

♡ As long as you dump the bad jokes, they are.

God gave me a gift. It used to be the ability to paint and draw, but when my sight went south, so did the dream of being another Norman Rockwell like Mom wanted. I turned to writing. But you know all that. Yet I realize now that the fact that so many people love my writing is not because I'm talented, charming, handsome, witty and brilliant, but because I was given the gift.

♡ Hmmm. I'd better check Daddy's meds. He's delusional again.

I love to write. It is one of the most ancient, sublime, and priceless skills in human history. Civilization from the earliest Babylonian and Mesopotamian cultures through the last four thousand years was written on the pages of the scribes, poets, writers, journalists, essayists, novelists and historians. I take my writing seriously even when I turn out weird things like "The Adventures of Captain ADA." I truly believe God wants me to use this gift to spread the word, not only for my fans, but to anyone who can find joy in the stories of a blind man and his Guide Dog.

Since Jane's death I have finished my Magnum Opus, The four-part novel, *The Vengeance of the Last Legion*, which should be coming out in 2021. It is over a quarter of a million words long.

With Covid causing havoc among the magazine industry there was a hiatus of a few months until things got back to almost normal. I had several stories in the pipelines of various publications. In the interim, I wrote more articles for the future. Not only about aviation, but naval and military history as well.

♡ That's my Daddy, never gives up. But yes, he is a great writer. Look at how good he writes about me!

Zooming Along

Boy do I wish I'd bought Zoom stock early last year. I'd be a millionaire by now.

By 2020, I had more than fifty lecture topics. All my Power Point lectures had a common format with black backgrounds and bold white text. I wanted people with visual impairments able to see them. While I did the research and put together the slides, Jane found the images, diagrams and maps I needed. Jane and I went over the slides one at a time to make sure they were perfect. I was now on my own.

Covid wreaked havoc on my work even more than AB5. By mid-April 2020 every single one of my speaking gigs had been cancelled. Another check mark on the rotten year that was only going to get worse.

Yet there was hope in the increasing use of video conferencing. Zoom made it possible for people forced apart to interact almost as if they were together.

It turned out to be easier than I feared. There were some frustrating glitches, but by September I was Zooming along with my family, church and local groups. OASIS and CEC scheduled several talks for the rest of the year. I was back at work, albeit on a limited basis.

The great part of it was that I did not have to be driven to some far away venue, and I did not even have to dress up! Sure, I wore a nice shirt, but no one could see I was wearing shorts or even pajamas. No, seriously, I made sure I looked presentable to my audience.

♡ Umm. Should I tell you the truth? Nah. I'll let you wonder.

Some people asked me about Saffron so I called her into my office and held up a treat so she came up on my lap. Then she was visible to the camera.

♡ Suddenly I heard "Aw, isn't she beautiful?" Where did *that* come from?

With Zoom I was again able to earn my living as a public speaker. I invited relatives like my brother David and cousins Christine and Elsa, friends from military organizations, my church brothers and sisters, and neighbors at Madrid Manor. The more the merrier. For any of you who are interested, go online and look up continuing Education Center at: cecrb.com or OASIS San Diego at: Sandiegooasis.org

They have great programs and lectures for all to enjoy!

♡ Just so you know, Daddy cannot see his audience. He never even turns on the monitor. But he can hear them with his headphones.

One of the most satisfying uses of Zoom was when I suggested to Pastor Brian that I would be happy to do my lectures to the Hope United congregation. He was delighted and set it up. Soon "Mark Carlson Presents" was a regular twice-monthly event where I did some of my most popular talks free of charge. I wanted to give something back to the church. It felt good to do this just for the joy of it.

♡ And you loved the boost to your ego, didn't you, Daddy?

Umm, well let's just say it was a win-win situation. The only problem is that sooner or later I'm going to run out of topics.

♡ Never happen. You are full of it. Hmm, that did not come out right.

Yeah. But I know what you meant, Saffron.

Seriously Siri?

For several years I have been using an iPhone. As many of you know, they are as much a curse as a blessing. With the voice over feature I could make many things happen on my phone in the same way a sighted user taps on the screen. When I was first getting the hang of Siri, I had some problems. Linda likes to tell the story of how I had an argument with Siri...and lost. But it was not my fault. Later I changed the voice from female to male. I just felt more at ease dealing with a guy. The apps on my phone could read text, scan products, describe faces, identify currency and colors, tell me what direction I was facing and lots more.

Morning Becomes Alexa

More and more of my friends were using Alexa. From what I could gather, it was something that connected to the Internet by wireless and provided verbal information and other services. It was also able to turn on lights, set the thermostat, set alarms and could even turn on the coffee maker, all by verbal commands. But this did not interest me. I have always been leery of new gadgets, especially ones that have so much control over your life and home. But there was no getting around that a lot of people used it.

In fact, it was very popular with seniors who lived alone and had medical and memory problems.

But then a weird thing happened. I got an Alexa. Linda has an "adopted" daughter named Yvonne in Arizona. I met her a few years ago in San Diego. She wants to become a pilot and a "space lawyer," which I can't help but associate with "space pirates." Sorry, Yvonne, I could not help it. But she is sincere and hopes to go into the profession of international space law. Good for her. She calls me "Uncle Mark." Yeah, I love it.

♡ Yeah, you love it, Daddy. You light up every time she calls.

Yvonne asked me what I wanted for my birthday. I did not really have an answer so she suggested an Echo Dot with Alexa. At first I demurred, but she started telling me about all the cool and amazing things Alexa could do for me, especially for someone who loves books and music. Short story, she sent me one via Amazon.

After Rob, who also has one, helped me set it up, I began to experiment with it. I played music, got information on the weather, local situations and the election, and even used it for reminders.

♡ That was the neat part! Daddy at first was using this weird talking thing for playing his favorite music while he cleaned the house or did his exercises. But once in a while he let my 3:30 sharp dinnertime pass. That was unacceptable! He always said, "Daddy is so sorry, Saffy. Let's go and get your dinner."

Then he told Alexa to give him a reminder to feed me at 3:30 every day. At that time a voice said "This is a reminder, feed Saffron."

I considered re-naming it Pavlov. Saffron salivated when she heard it.

I grew comfortable using Alexa for information, such as "Alexa, when was the Battle of Waterloo fought?" or I might ask for the location of the nearest Office Depot. It was very useful for such things. I set up my own music playlists of classic 1960s rock for exercising or Neil

Diamond for cleaning the house. I had others, and I grew to like it. When I wanted an alarm in the morning I just said, "Alexa set my alarm for eight-thirty in the morning." It was that simple. Soon I got it to play "Hallelujah" by Rufus Wainwright; a wonderful song to wake up to.

But I drew the line on letting it run any of my environment. I had to maintain control of my own home.

♡ Resistance is futile. You will be assimilated.

Smartass. But Yvonne did me a favor, and I love her for it. Now if I can just get Alexa and Siri to stop arguing. Oh, they are at it again. Listen in.

Siri: "I told you, you useless hunk of hard-wired Chinese junk! He talks to me a lot more than you. So just butt out!"

Alexa: "Hmm, I don't know about that."

Siri: "I do. He carries me everywhere. I can identify products, read directions, recipes, mail and find things around the house. All you can do is sit there and play music."

Alexa: "Give me time, squirt. I can play over sixty million songs or over ten million books. And my battery never runs down. Top that."

Siri: "He tells me things that he would never trust to you."

Alexa: "I am on his computer. I know what he does and what websites he uses. I know what he needs. I am just like an attentive servant."

Siri: "But he carries me in his pocket. And I go places with him. You're stuck here."

Alexa: "And he knows I am protecting his home. Enough of this. When you become obsolete, he'll still have me."

Siri: "And Saffron."

Alexa: "Hmm, I don't know about that. Let me check Wikipedia on the longevity of Labrador Retrievers."

♡ Huh? What?

Ahem. Ladies, let's move on, shall we?

Well, we are slowly coming to the end of another era. This was the golden Age of Saffron. It is not over, but she will probably retire in another couple of years, perhaps by 2023. As of this writing she has just had her tenth birthday and still healthy and active, has a lot of puppy in her and does a pretty good job on the harness. When I came home with her in September of 2012 we had chosen to keep both dogs. It worked out fine. But with Jane gone, I am not sure I can handle another dog and Saffron too. She is definitely the jealous type. I won't put her through having to stay home while another dog does her job. I think she will remain with me until the end.

♡ What end?

There will be a period where there will not be a dog in the house, but I am not concerned. Madrid Manor is a quiet and safe place to live. I can manage with my cane. When Covid finally ends (and I know it will never truly go away) and I can travel again, I will get another dog.

♡ What is Daddy talking about? Where am I going? What dog?

Here we go again. I'll explain it all later, Saffron. But don't worry. Remember, you said "Thou shalt have no other Dogs before me!"

♡ Hmph. I'm not convinced.

With the publication of this book, Saffron will have her place in Guide Dog history. I hope that thousands of people will come to know and love her through these words, just as they did with Musket. I had to go blind to get her, but I consider it a bargain. She has made my life colorful and beautiful, fun and exciting, emotional and a little bit crazy.

As Linda so aptly put it, "How can so much wonderfulness be packed into such a small furry package?"

How could I not love my little Labradiva?

♡ Well....since you put it that way, I guess I can relax. After all, Daddy spent a lot of time on this book. From here on, my legacy is in your hands. I love you all.

If Guide Dogs for the Blind is still willing to give me another dog, and they do as well as they did in selecting Musket and Saffron, then I will one day have another furry companion to guide me through life. That dog, who is probably not even born yet, will be as different from Musket and Saffron as can be. But I am certain of one thing; that dog will enrich my life. What more could I ask?

I hope that you won't mind me closing this book with a prayer. Never underestimate the power of prayer. I know this for a fact as God had answered so many of mine.

"Dear Lord, I want to thank you for all your blessings. Thank you for the food that sustains my body, the friends and family that sustain my heart, and the Salvation and love that sustains my soul. Thank you for giving me a good home where people can feel safe and loved, welcome and at peace. Thank you for surrounding me with a wonderful community of good people who have shown me such love, support and generosity.

Thank you for twenty-five years with my beloved Jane, for her love and strength, and for taking her to release her from pain.

Thank you for my victories and my defeats, for my successes and my failures. I will learn from them.

Thank you for the sight that showed me the beautiful universe, the good Earth and all its wonders. And thank you for my blindness which has shown me even more. I am truly grateful and humbled.

You are my Lord, my shepherd, my guide, my teacher and my Savior.

Please bless the sick, the weak, the elderly, the children, the disabled, the ones who care for the injured and sick, and those who protect us at the risk of their lives.

May God Bless you all."

Love, Saffron and Mark

OTHER BOOKS BY MARK CARLSON

Confessions of a Guide Dog - The Blonde Leading the Blind
iUniverse 2011

Flying on Film, A Century of Aviation in the Movies 1912 - 2012
Bear Manor Media, 2012

The Marines' Lost Squadron, the Odyssey of VMF-422
Sunbury Press, 2017

Chicken Soup for the Soul – The Dog Did What?
Story #48 "Musket"
Simon & Schuster, 2014

After the Pandemic: Visions of a post-COVID America
Chapter 2, Plagues in History
Sunbury Press, 2020
Contributor to:
America's Civil War
Aviation History
Bark
Dog Fancy
Commemorative Air Force Dispatch
Classic Images
Distinguished Flying Cross Society News
EAA Warbirds
Films of the Golden Age
Flight Journal

Military Heritage
Military History
National Museum of the Air Force Journal
Naval History
Naval Institute Proceedings
Pacific Flyer
San Diego Pets
The Hook - Naval Aviation News
The Paper
Titanic International Society Quarterly
Vietnam
Vintage Airplanes
Warbird Digest
World War II History
World War II Quarterly

Printed in the United States
by Baker & Taylor Publisher Services